PAN STUDY AIDS

COMMERCE

R. P. Jones and Ian Hobday

A Pan Original
Pan Books London and Sydney

First published 1987 by Pan Books Ltd,
Cavaye Place, London SW10 9PG

9 8 7 6 5 4 3 2 1

ISBN 0 330 29986 7

Text design by Peter Ward
Text illustration by M L Design
Photoset by Parker Typesetting Service, Leicester
Printed and bound in Spain by
Mateu Cromo SA, Madrid

CONTENTS

INTRODUCTION TO GCSE

From 1988, there will be a single system of examining at 16 plus in England and Wales and Northern Ireland. The General Certificate of Secondary Education (GCSE) will replace the General Certificate of Education (GCE) and the Certificate of Secondary Education (CSE) In Scotland candidates will be entering for the O grade and Standard Grade examinations leading to the award of the Scottish Certificate of Education (SCE).

The Pan Study Aids GCSE series has been specially written by practising teachers and examiners to enable you to prepare successfully for this new examination.

GCSE introduces several important changes in the way in which you are tested. First, the examinations will be structured so that you can show *what* you know rather than what you do *not* know. Of critical importance here is the work you produce during the course of the examination year, which will be given much greater emphasis than before. Second, courses are set and marked by six examining groups instead of the previous twenty GCE/CSE boards. The groups are:

Northern Examining Association (NEA)
Midland Examining Group(MEG)
London and East Anglian Group (LEAG)
Southern Examining Group (SEG)
Welsh Joint Examinations Council (WJEC)
Northern Ireland Schools Examination Council (NISEC)

One of the most useful changes introduced by GCSE is the single award system of grades A–G. This should permit you and future employers more accurately to assess your qualifications.

GCSE	GCE O Level	CSE
A	A	–
B	B	–
C	C	1
D	D	2
E	E	3
F	F	4
G		5

Remember that, whatever examinations you take, the grades you are awarded will be based on how well you have done.

Pan Study Aids are geared for use throughout the duration of your courses. The text layout has been carefully designed to provide all the information and skills you need for GCSE and SCE examinations – please feel free to use the margins for additional notes.

N.B. Where questions are drawn from former O level examination papers, the following abbreviations are used to identify the boards:

UCLES (University of Cambridge Local Examinations Syndicate)
AEB (Associated Examining Board)
ULSEB (University of London Schools Examination Board)
SUJB (Southern Universities Joint Board)
O&C (Oxford & Cambridge)
SCE (Scottish Certificate of Education Examination Board)
JMB (Joint Matriculation Board)
SEB (Scottish Examining Board)
ODLE (Oxford Delegacy of Local Examinations)
WJEC (Welsh Joint Examinations Council)

PREFACE

This edition has been written for the new General Certificate of Secondary Education (GCSE) examinations covering the Boards listed on page 7. The authors are indebted to Her Majesty's Stationery Office for permission to quote from official statistics and to the various examining boards for their co-operation in providing material necessary for the successful application of relevant skills and techniques appropriate to the understanding of this subject.

The last decade has been one of the most eventful in history, in terms of the pace of events and need to adapt. New techniques have been introduced, fresh ideas displacing old-established methods and new products invented at a seemingly ever-increasing rate. No wonder therefore Commerce itself has needed to adapt in order to cope with and cater for modern standards.

It is one of the aims of this book, as part of the Pan Study Aids series, to assess the cause and effect of these changes on industry, business and the service occupations. Material has been carefully presented within each chapter in a readable manner to assist students with their studies. By such a straightforward approach it is hoped that they will learn, understand and critically examine the commercial aspects of local, national and international trade. In addition, it should also enable them to pass examinations in Commerce and the Structure of Business and interpret the complexities of modern society more readily.

Multiple choice question papers are common in Commerce examinations. Practice is given in the text – each question is preceded by the intials MC, e.g. MC11. *Answers* to these questions are given at the end of each chapter.

I.L.H.
R.P.J.

GCSE COMMERCE

1 COMMERCE SYLLABUS CONTENT

The content of the examining groups is essentially the same. However, you should be aware that there are differences between the boards in approach and differences in content detail. Students will need to study syllabuses and specimen papers to gauge these differences between the groups.

The following is an outline of various syllabuses and can be used by you as a guide to syllabus content.

London and East Anglia

PAPER 1 (1 hour)
Section A: 25 objective test type questions (10% of marks)
Section B: Compulsory short answer questions (20% of marks)

PAPER 2 (1 hr 40 mins)
Section A: 1 compulsory data response question (15% of marks)
Section B: 3 structured essay-type questions (15% of marks) Answer 1.
Section C: 3 essay type questions (20% of marks). Answer 1

Coursework The Examining Group will prescribe 6 assignments. Candidates select 2. (20% of marks).

Northern Examining Association

Examination paper
(2 hrs 30 mins)
Between 4 and 7 compulsory structured or essay-type questions (70% of marks)

Coursework Candidates will submit 1, 2 or 3 assignments (30% of marks)

Southern Examining Group

PAPER 1 (1 hour)
40 objective test questions (30% of marks)

PAPER 2 (2 hours)
Section A: 3 compulsory data response questions (30% of marks)
Section B: 5 structured essay questions. Choose 2. (20% of marks)

Coursework 2 items of between 750–1000 words (20% of total marks)

Welsh Joint Education Committee

PAPER 1 (1 hour)
Compulsory short answer type questions and compulsory data response type questions (25% of marks).

Either

PAPER 2 (2 hours)
Compulsory structured questions of various types (45% of marks).

or

PAPER 3 (2 hours)
Compulsory structured questions of various types (45% of marks).
Candidates take paper 2 or paper 3 according to their ability. Paper 2 for grade ranges C–G. Paper 3 for grade ranges A–C.

Coursework A maximum of 3 assignments (30% of marks).

Midland Examining Group

PAPER 1 (¾ hour)
40 multiple choice questions (20% of marks).

PAPER 2 (2¼ hours)
5 structured questions without any choice (60% of marks).

Coursework A written assignment of about 2500 words or a number of shorter assignments (20% of marks).

Northern Ireland Schools Examination Council

PAPER 1 (1½ hours)
Section A: 10 compulsory short answer questions – 30 minutes.
Section B: 3 compulsory structured questions – 1 hour (40% of marks).

*PAPER 2 (1½ hours) a number of compulsory questions (40% of marks).

PAPER 3 (1½ hours) 3 compulsory structured questions (40% of marks).

**Coursework* 3 assignments each selected from a different area of the syllabus (20% of marks).

*Paper 2 and Coursework are common components to be taken by all candidates. Paper 1 (but not Paper 3) will also be taken by candidates for awards limited in the grade range C–G. Paper 3 (but not Paper 1) will also be taken by candidates for awards in the grade range A–E. Paper 3 will be more difficult than Papers 1 and 2.

London and East Anglia

1 Production: factors of production, specialisation, industry, commerce and direct services
2 Trade: retail trade and wholesale trade
3 International trade
4 Markets and commodity markets
5 Advertising and consumer protection
6 Money and banking
7 Insurance
8 Transport and communications
9 Organisation of business units: private sector and public sector
10 The stock exchange

Northern Examining Association

1 The individual, production and commerce
2 The chain of distribution: wholesalers and retailers
3 Foreign trade
4 Aids to trade: finance and banking, insurance, communications, transport, advertising and sales promotion
5 Business units: private and public enterprise
6 The stock exchange; turnover and capital
7 Consumer protection
8 Government and commercial activity; sources of revenue and expenditure, central and local government

Southern Examining Group

1 The economic environment: production, division of labour and exchange
2 The chain of distribution: retailing and wholesaling, commodity markets
3 Buying and selling, market research, business documents, advertising, consumer protection
4 Business organisation: private and public sector
5 Business finance, balance sheets
6 Personal finance, personal budgeting, saving and borrowing
7 Commercial aids: banking, insurance, communications, transport, warehousing
8 International trade
9 The role of the State: taxation, economic policy, influence on business location, local government.

Welsh Joint Education Committee

1 Production
2 Trade: retail and wholesale trade, documents, consumer protection, international trade
3 Money and banking
4 Insurance
5 Transport and communications
6 Advertising
7 Warehousing
8 Business organisation: public and private enterprise, finance of the business unit, the stock exchange

Midland Examining Group

1 The individual and the economy: industry, commerce and direct services. Specialisation
2 The consumer and the chain of distribution
3 Business ownership; public and private enterprise capital and profit
4 Private savings
5 The role of the State; central and local government, revenue and expenditure
6 Aids to trade: banking, insurance, communications, transport, marketing, warehousing
7 Overseas trade

Northern Ireland Schools Examination Council

Business Studies syllabus (Commerce not offered)
1 External environment of the business: Government and business, the economic framework; the banking system, markets insurance; population, trade, specialisation and division of labour.
2 Business structure and organisation; types of business organisation, aims, objectives and policies of firms in private and public sector, organisational structure, current trends in business, the need and sources of finance, the stock exchange.
3 Business behaviour. Production and marketing, advertising, retailing and wholesaling, transport, revenues and costs, location of industry, economies of scale, business accounts.
4 People in business; recruitment and training, motivation, communication, employee/employer relationship
5 Controlling business activities, financial aid, advice and information from central government and non-government sources. Consumer protection. Public expenditure and taxes. Pressure groups.

2 ASSESSMENT TECHNIQUE

All the examining groups use one or more of these four main assessment techniques.

(a) Short answer questions (perhaps data based). These may be of the multiple-choice type or open response short answer question (i.e. one or two sentences in response).

(b) Data response questions. Questions are set on a prose passage, table of statistics, pie diagrams or photographs.

(c) Extended writing questions. These may be essay type or extended structured (perhaps data based).

(d) Coursework. This will be internally set and may be essay based.

Each group differs in the weighting it gives to each of the four main types of assessment techniques and the time allocated to each. The following is a guide to the assessement techniques employed by the different groups. Students need to refer to a copy of a commerce specimen paper of the group for which they are sitting the examination.

3 ASSESSMENT OBJECTIVES

In the four main assessment techniques the examining groups are attempting to satisfy broadly five assessment objectives. These are that candidates will be expected to:

- demonstrate recall of knowledge in relation to a specified syllabus;
- demonstrate an ability to use this knowledge in verbal, numerical, diagrammatic, pictorial and graphical form;
- demonstrate an ability to explain and apply appropriate terminology, concepts and elementary theories;
- select, analyse, interpret and apply data;
- distinguish between evidence and opinion, make reasoned judgements and communicate them in an accurate and logical manner.

THE STRUCTURE OF INDUSTRY AND COMMERCE

CONTENTS

An understanding of the terms 'production', 'division of labour', 'commerce' and 'direct services' is essential to any study of commerce. This chapter explains these terms, and shows the way in which they are interrelated, through the following sections:

1 The satisfaction of wants the meaning of wants, how these wants are satisfied, the factors of production (land, labour, capital and enterprise).

2 Types of economy market economy, planned economy and mixed economy.

3 The division of labour meaning, advantages and disadvantages, division of labour requires exchange and is limited by the size of market, mass production.

4 The meaning of 'production'.

5 Production: primary, secondary and tertiary production the meaning of each category, the increasing proportion of the tertiary sector.

6 Production: industry, commerce and direct services the meaning of each category, the divisions of commerce – trade, transport, warehousing, banking, insurance and advertising.

The following diagram shows how production is divided between industry, commerce and direct services, and the subdivisions within each sector.

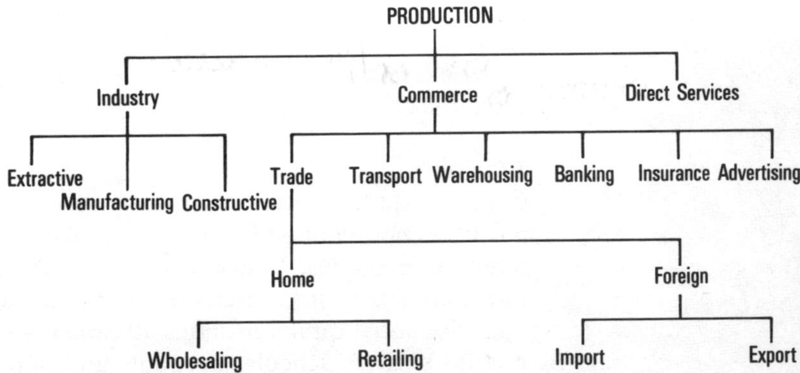

Before discussing this division of production, it is necessary to understand why production takes place, and this requires a discussion of the satisfaction of wants.

THE SATISFACTION OF WANTS

THE MEANING OF WANTS

Wants are defined as the goods and services or commodities which a person wishes to possess; that is, the visible items such as clothes, food and radios, and such 'invisible' items as education and health services. The three basic human wants are for food, clothing and shelter, upon which survival on earth depends.

THE SATISFACTION OF WANTS

Human wants are unlimited in the sense that as soon as some are satisfied new ones emerge to take their place. For example, people first want shelter but may then want more comfortable surroundings; man not only wants food but wants more variety and certain kinds of food. It is the aim of production to satisfy as many of these wants as possible. However, people will never have all their wants provided for because there are not enough resources or factors of production (land, labour, capital and enterprise) to produce all the commodities required. There is a problem of scarcity of factors of production.

THE FACTORS OF PRODUCTION

The quality and quantity of production depends on the quality and quantity of resources available. By resources is meant the factors of production: land, labour, capital and enterprise.

1 Labour

Labour is the mental and physical human effort involved in the production process. It is regarded with special concern because it involves human beings. Labour therefore earns an income, or reward, called wages.

2 Land

Land has a wide definition. It includes all kinds of natural resources such as farm land, raw material deposits, climate, forests and fishing grounds. Owners of land earn a reward or income called rent.

3 Capital

Capital is not the same as money. Capital comprises of all those resources not required for their own sakes since it is used to produce other commodities. It would include factory premises, machinery, raw materials in stock, transport vehicles and partly finished goods. Likewise social capital includes all capital which belongs to the community such as schools, hospitals and libraries. Owners of capital earn a reward or income called interest.

4 Enterprise

Enterprise is the factor of production which brings together the other three factors. The **entrepreneur** is the organiser who decides what is to be produced, where it is to be produced and how it is to be produced. Without the entrepreneur the other resources have no economic importance – they need to be brought together and organised for production. The functions of the entrepreneur includes management control and risk-bearing (uncertainty).

This distinguishes enterprise from labour because the entrepreneur carries the risks of production. If the entrepreneur makes successful decisions then a **profit** is the reward or income received. Of course, bad decisions can result in losses. However, the entrepreneur need not be an individual – it could be the government in the public sector (see Chapter 6).

Consider the following question.

1 ▶ 'The reason wants are not satisfied is because there is a lack of resources called factors of production.'

(a) Briefly describe what is meant by the term 'factors of production'.

(*b*) What is the problem concerning scarcity of resources?

(*c*) What is the most important factor of production?

Explain your answers.

TYPES OF ECONOMY

It is not possible to produce the quantity of goods and services needed to satisfy our unlimited wants since the supply of the factors of production are limited. In response to this problem three different types of economy have developed each attempting to provide a solution. These are:

1 The market or price economy.
2 The planned or command economy.
3 The mixed economy.

THE MARKET OR PRICE ECONOMY

The market economy is based on the workings of the market and the two forces of supply and demand. Scarce resources are allocated by private entrepreneurs (or businesspersons) whose main objective is to make profits. If the price of a commodity is high then entrepreneurs believe profits will be greater and they will increase supply. The opposite will happen if prices are low.

Price is determined by the interaction of supply and demand in the market situation. It is the 'signal' to the entrepreneur whether to produce or not to produce. The nearest example of a pure market economy is the United States of America compared with a command economy as found in numerous Eastern bloc countries.

Advantages of the price economy

1 Many small firms will produce a variety of commodities for consumers.
2 The profit motive acts as an incentive to entrepreneurs and workers.
3 There is freedom to choose what to consume and produce.

Disadvantages of the price economy

1 Wealthy consumers exist who will ensure that luxury commodities are produced which only they can afford.
2 Essential commodities which may not be profitable to manufacture may not be produced.
3 Some small firms may develop into large firms and dominate the industry (monopolies). Ultimately they may charge higher prices.

THE PLANNED ECONOMY

Here the government decides what commodities to produce. It does not allow the forces of demand and supply to influence prices and what will be produced; it will itself fix prices. Private businessmen are not encouraged as they are in the West since the government plans the economy for years ahead. The best example of a planned economy is the Union of Soviet Socialist Republics (USSR or Russia).

Advantages of a planned economy

1 There is more equality of income and wealth distribution.
2 The government will ensure that unprofitable but essential goods and services will be produced.
3 The government can plan and direct the economy.

Disadvantages of a planned economy

1 The planners make mistakes that may be costly to the nation as a whole.
2 There is no profit motive to ensure workers work with effort.
3 People have less choice and freedom.

THE MIXED ECONOMY

The mixed economy is a combination of both the market economy and the planned economy. As such it has many of the advantages and disadvantages of the other two types. In a sense all economies are mixed, having elements of both the market and planned varieties. The United Kingdom is a good example of this.

Consider the following question.

2 ▶ (*a*) What are the main differences between a market economy and a planned economy?
(*b*) What are the main functions of the price mechanism in a private enterprise economy?
(*c*) What criticisms are often made about a planned economy?

MC1. A mixed economy is defined as having
A primary and secondary industries
B private and public enterprise
C primary and tertiary industries
D internal and external trade
E producers and consumers

THE DIVISION OF LABOUR

You should know what is meant by **specialisation** or **division of labour** and be able to discuss its advantages and disadvantages – examination questions are often set on this topic.

If a person working alone undertakes the entire production of some commodity then there is no division of labour, for example if a person rears sheep, clips the wool, cleans and combs it, and spins it into yarn. Division of labour occurs where one person undertakes only a small part of the work and each individual specialises in a single process. As a result output is increased and costs per unit of output are decreased.

ADVANTAGES OF SPECIALISATION

1 Leads to greater skill amongst workers.
2 Saves time in training, etc.
3 Enables specialists to be employed.
4 Is economic in the use of tools.
5 Allows the use of specialist machinery.

Disadvantages of specialisation

1 Boredom and monotony soon occur, leading to sickness and absenteeism.
2 Leads to a decline in craftsmanship and alienation of workers.
3 All the products are much the same or standardised.
4 A greater risk of unemployment through increased use of robots, computers, etc.
5 A greater risk of occupational disease.

These advantages have led certain firms to break away from traditional division of labour techniques; for instance the Volvo Motor Company (in Sweden) allows its workers to change jobs or work in groups to produce the finished product.

Division of labour requires exchange

There must be exchange if division of labour is to be successful. The baker must exchange bread for clothes, etc., whilst a good monetary and transport system is also needed to help the process of exchange.

Division of labour is limited by the size of the market

Division of labour increases output. However, it would be unwise to increase the output of a product if there was only a small demand for it. Thus division is limited by the market – the **demand** must exist for increased production to be possible.

Since Adam Smith (a well-known economist, 1723–1790) first argued in favour of division of labour it has been extended and developed. In America Henry Ford when making Model-T Ford motor cars introduced the technique of **mass production**. This involves setting up an assembly line where the work flows endlessly through the factory with operators performing their tasks as each unit passes by. It leads to **standardisation** of goods (i.e. they are virtually identical), and because the same task is being repeated operators are able to work very quickly – there is high output. Modern industry, as well as introducing division of labour and mass production techniques, also aims to take advantage of the **economies of scale** (see page 101).

MC2. The employment of most workers in specialist occupations is called

A subsistence economy
B mobility of labour
C skilled labour
D division of labour
E automation

MC3. Which of the following is not true in connection with the division of labour?

A widens the choice to consumers
B application is limited by the extent of the market
C increases the risk of unemployment
D increases output per person
E improves craftsmanship

MC4. As division of labour increases in an economy

A greater percentage of the working population is employed in primary industries
B interdependence between people and firms diminishes
C the standard of living of workers falls
D the proportion of specialists in the labour force declines
E the proportion of workers employed in tertiary production rises

3 ▶ 'It is the satisfaction of wants that has led to the need for man increasingly to specialise.' Explain

(*a*) the term satisfaction of wants and
(*b*) how specialisation has affected
(i) the individual, and
(ii) the community.
(*c*) Are there any reasons why a firm may not introduce division of labour?

In order to answer (*a*), discuss the fact that human wants are unlimited. Consumer wants include food – and better choice; shelter – and better surroundings; clothes – and finer quality, etc. The aim of production is to satisfy as many of these wants as possible. However, resources (factors of production – land, labour, capital and enterprise) are limited and consequently there is a scarcity. Not all of the consumer wants will (or can be) satisfied and consumers have to make a choice as to which wants need to be satisfied.

To answer (*b*) discuss the meaning of specialisation (division of labour) – the advantages and disadvantages as far as the individual is concerned, e.g. less job satisfaction but greater output, decline in craftsmanship but a saving in time, lower costs but standard products, etc. Also discuss the advantages and disadvantages from the point of view of the community: more goods, etc. at a lower price but less variety; a better standard of living at the cost of uniformity.

To answer (*c*) you need to discuss why some firms are either unwilling or unable to introduce specialisation. A firm may be unwilling because there may not be the high level of demand for its product. A firm may be unable to introduce specialisation because there is no adequate system of transport or exchange. Also not all production processes can be easily divided up.

4 ▶ (*a*) Using modern examples explain the meaning of division of labour.
(*b*) What is meant by the statement 'specialisation is limited by the extent of the market'?
(*c*) What are the advantages and disadvantages of division of labour?
(*d*) Explain the meaning of mass production.

THE MEANING OF PRODUCTION

THE DEFINITION OF PRODUCTION

You **must** understand the meaning of production since it is important and included as part of many examination questions.

Any commodity which gives satisfaction to consumers (people who buy commodities) is said to have **utility** – it satisfies human wants. Production may therefore be defined as the satisfaction of human wants by creating new utilities.

There are two types of wants or needs which must be satisfied: **material** and **immaterial**.

1 Material wants These are wants for visible goods.
(*a*) **consumer goods** – those which give the consumer direct satisfaction from their use, e.g. food, clothes, etc. Also consumer durable goods are consumer items which have a comparatively long life, e.g. televisions, radios, washing machines, cars;
(*b*) **capital or producer goods** – which are not bought for their

own sakes but because they produce other goods (either other capital or consumer goods), e.g. lathes, machinery, tractors.

2 Immaterial wants This term covers people's wants for the social services such as education or health or leisure acitivities such as sport, discos, etc. They are satisfied by personal services; for instance, doctors satisfy people's wants for medical help, teachers satisfy our needs for education whilst the local authority or council often provides facilities for our recreation.

PRODUCTION: PRIMARY, SECONDARY AND TERTIARY PRODUCTIONS

Production is subdivided into three main categories of production:

- Primary production
- Secondary production
- Tertiary production

Primary production

This is the first (primary) stage in the production process. These industries obtain raw materials and the products of nature, e.g. coal mining, iron ore mining, oil extraction, dairying and wheat farming. They provide the raw materials which are made into finished commodities by manufacturing industries.

Secondary production

These industries manufacture the finished or partly finished commodities (secondary production) which satisfy human wants, e.g. bakeries, steel production, plastics. Closely allied to these industries are the **constructive industries** which take the finished commodities of the manufacturing industries and organise them into the whole, e.g. car manufacturers take the finished goods of many other industries to produce one final product: they require tyres, steel plate, glass, plastics, carpets, etc.

Tertiary Production

Commerce and direct services are both part of **tertiary production** and you should be able to distinguish clearly between them. This is a popular topic with examiners.

Commerce is that part of production concerned with the provision of **commercial** services, e.g. wholesaling, retailing and banking. **Direct services** are concerned with **personal or social** services and include doctors, dentists and teachers. Both commerce and direct services are essential for the well-being and efficiency of the economy.

The importance of tertiary production in the modern economy

Prior to the Industrial Revolution in Britain, tertiary production was not an important sector in the economy. This is true of many developing economies today, where most of the working population is involved in primary industries, particularly agriculture. However, as an economy becomes more industrialised the percentage of workers in secondary industries increases. When the economy is advanced and heavily industrialised, as in Britain today, secondary industries need more services and thus tertiary production becomes extremely important. In most advanced economies at the present time tertiary production is of increasing importance particularly with increased use of machinery and microtechnology in the industrial sector.

% Shares of UK's total domestic output

	% share 1974	% share in 1979	% share 1986
Primary	7.2	10.2	13.5
Secondary	37.9	34.7	29.9
Tertiary	54.9	55.1	56.6

Primary production employs fewer people today because of improved methods of processing coupled with new capital investment in labour-saving machinery which has taken over much of the work previously done by 'unskilled' labour. Since 1970, however, primary production accounts for a larger proportion of UK total output because of the discovery of North Sea oil.

Secondary production in recent years has also reduced its share of employment despite an increased demand for manufactured goods. A larger proportion of products previously made in Britian is now being imported from countries such as Japan, etc. In addition, at home, improved production processes and use of resources has led to the shedding of much surplus labour, causing unemployment – often of a severe nature. This is particularly the case in areas of the country where the old established 'heavy' industries such as steel, and shipbuilding were situated. In the 'newer' industries such as electronics, bio-technics, etc, a smaller and more highly qualified workforce is often required.

Tertiary production is now the largest section in the UK economy and has become so because:

1 The primary and secondary industries, having increased volume and value of output, need further advertising, banking, transport, insurance and other facilities (commercial services); and
2 The living standard of most of the population has improved and people spend money on holidays and leisure pursuits, etc., (personal services).
3 The government has also become increasingly involved in the economy to extend and improve the provision of education and health

services – more doctors, nurses, teachers and civil servants are required (direct services).

5 ▶ (*a*) Distinguish between primary and secondary production.
(*b*) Explain the meaning of tertiary production, giving appropriate examples.
(*c*) Why may this branch of production be considered as essential as the primary and secondary industries?

To answer (*a*) you need to state that primary production is the first stage in the production process and is concerned with the extraction of raw materials, growing of food, fishing and forestry, etc. Secondary production uses the products of the primary producer to manufacture the finished product. For instance the baker uses the farmer's wheat to make bread.

To answer (*b*) you should explain that tertiary production is concerned with the production of services – it does not produce raw materials or finished goods. It consists of two parts: the commercial service sector and the direct (or personal) services. You should clearly distinguish between these two and give examples.

To answer (*c*) explain that the tertiary sector is as essential as primary production and secondary production. Explain what you mean by these terms. Commercial services are necessary so as to ensure that commodities reach the consumer at the right time, place, condition, quantity, quality and price. Discuss, using examples, the importance of each of the six branches of commercial activity (see pages 26–8). Direct services are likewise essential since in order for all the above to take place a country needs a well-educated, healthy labour force having the opportunity to take part and enjoy the available leisure services.

6 ▶ (*a*) Distinguish between tertiary, secondary and primary production.
(*b*) As an economy develops what changes usually occur in the relative importance of these forms of production?
(*c*) Explain the recent relative increase of primary production in the UK.
(*d*) Why is tertiary production now the largest sector in the UK economy?

MC5. In which class of occupation would you place a dentist?

A extractive industry
B manufacturing industry
C commerce
D direct services
E primary industry

In order to answer MC6 and MC7 one or more of the options may be correct.

A if (i) and (ii) only
B if (i) and (v) only
C if (ii) and (v) only
D if (iii) and (iv) only
E all of them

MC6. Which of the occupations listed below (in **MC7**) are engaged in the primary stage of production?

MC7. Which are engaged in the tertiary stage of production?
(i) manufacturing
(ii) mining and quarrying
(iii) administration
(iv) distribution
(v) agriculture, forestry and fishing

In order to answer MC6 and MC7 one or more of the options may be correct.

MC8. Which of the following is a primary producer?
A schoolteacher
B copper miner
C docker
D lathe operator
E steel worker

MC9. Which of the following is an example of tertiary production?
A a diary farmer supplying a local cheese to the manufacturer
B a nationalised steel producer
C a car producer who exports to European distributors
D a machine tool producer who supplies car manufacturers
E a travel agent providing details of, and arranging holidays at home and abroad

MC10. Tertiary industries are responsible for the production of:
A goods for export
B goods for domestic consumption
C services such as banking and insurance
D goods and services
E a country's basic needs

PRODUCTION: INDUSTRY, COMMERCE AND DIRECT SERVICES

THE BRANCHES OF PRODUCTION

The term production includes those occupations which aim to satisfy all human wants. The **production cycle** is not complete until the commodity is in the hands of the consumer.

As we read on page 22 production is often sub-divided into

primary, secondary and tertiary sectors. There is an alternative categorisation of production into:

(*a*) industry
(*b*) commerce
(*c*) direct services

Industry That branch of production engaged in obtaining the raw materials or manufacturing them into finished (or partly finished) commodities, or constructing the final commodities. Industry can be subdivided into **primary** and **secondary** production.

Commerce The sector engaged in the distribution processes including the necessary facilities for transporting the commodities, paying for them, selling and insurance. Commerce is part of **tertiary** production, and a very important process which links the producer and the consumer.

Direct services These are services not rendered to material goods, as in commerce, but to persons from, for example, doctors and teachers. These are also very important to the production process because they increase its efficiency – e.g. through a healthy and educated work force. Direct services (or personal services) are also part of **tertiary** production.

THE DIVISIONS OF COMMERCE

The term commerce covers that large variety of occupations all engaged in the movement of commodities so that they reach the final consumer in the *right place*, in the *right condition*, at the *right time*, in the *right quantity* and at the *right price*.

The different branches of commerce need to be known in detail as examination questions are regularly set on them. There are six divisions which in summary form are as follows:

1 Trade

This is an essential part of commerce. Regions and countries are able to specialise in the production of commodities in which they have special advantages. The function of trade is to distribute the surplus to other regions and countries where supplies are lacking. Trade may be divided into:

Home trade This is the *internal* commerce of a country and includes the buying and selling of commodities between the inhabitants themselves. It consists of two branches:

(*a*) **Wholesale trade** – purchases raw material or finished manufactures in large quantities sells them in smaller quantities to the retailer (or direct to the consumer).

(*b*) **Retail trade** – buys commodities from the wholesaler and sells them in smaller quantities to the consumer. Retailers include small corner shops, department stores, supermarkets, hypermarkets and superstores.

The wholesale trade and retail trade are often collectively referred to as the **distribution process** and form an important part of the national economy.

Foreign trade This is the *external* trade of the country and refers to the exchange of commodities between different countries. Foreign trade may be divided into:

(*a*) **Import trade** – all those activities engaged in bringing commodities to a country such as food, raw materials and manufactured goods.

(*b*) **Export trade** – includes activities engaged in sending commodities from a country to other countries. Britian sells mainly finished manufactures and '**invisibles**' such as banking, insurance and tourism (see page 161).

2 Transport

This involves those occupations engaged in the movement of commodities from place to place. The development of road, rail, air and sea transport facilities allows countries to move commodities all over the world more cheaply, quickly and safely.

It is important to note however in the study of commerce, as in real life, there are no 'water-tight' compartments. Transport for example can be either a commercial or a direct service. A lorry taking commodities from one place to another is clearly part of commerce, whereas a public transport bus taking passengers into town is a direct service.

3 Warehousing

Storage of commodities is vital in order to maintain regular supplies, so large warehouses may be found at most ports and cities to store goods until required on the home and exports markets. Raw materials and finished manufactures are stored so that demand can be met at all times. It enables production to take place ahead of demand and avoids changes in prices which may result from shortages or gluts.

Privately owned specialist warehouses under the control of the Customs and Excise authorities known as **bonded warehouses** are places where dutiable commodities are stored until import duties have been paid. These warehouses are found at Britain's principal sea and air ports storing commodities such as tea, wines, tobacco, spirits, etc.

4 Banking

Banking helps distribution and exchange of commodities because it eases and simplifies payments which have to be made between buyer and seller. Cheques, bankers' drafts, documentary credits, bills of exchange and giro credits have been developed to allow trade, wage and salary payments, etc., to take place smoothly.

5 Insurance

This division of commerce overcomes some of the risks of trade which will always be present. There are four groups: fire, life, accident and marine. Small amounts of money called premiums are collected on a regular basis from many sources so that people and traders suffering losses are able to claim on the large fund thus created.

6 Advertising

This allows the producer, wholesaler or retailer to bring his or her commodities to the attention of the consumer. There are many different methods of advertising, including television, radio, local and national press and bill-boards. There are numerous specialist agencies whose services are employed to advertise commodities, and services.

MC11. That part of production which is concerned with trade (home and foreign) and the aids to trade (finance, insurance, transport, advertising and warehousing) is known as
A commerce
B industry
C manufacturing
D distribution
E specialisation

MC12. Which of the following occupations is commercial?
A miner
B bank clerk
C bricklayer
D doctor
E teacher

7 ▶ Production is said to cover all activities which contribute to the satisfaction of the consumers' demand for goods and services.
(*a*) Using a diagram show the part played by industry and commerce in that process.
(*b*) Compare and contrast direct service occupations with commercial occupations. Give examples.
(*c*) Why are commercial services essential in a developed economy based on division of labour?

8 ▶ (*a*) Besides the trader who actually buys and sells goods what other main occupations would you include under the heading commerce?
(*b*) 'Commercial activities change the ownership and location of goods.'
Explain the meaning of this statement.
(*c*) Which of the following people are engaged in commercial occupations and in which division of commerce would you place them?

(i) lawyer
(ii) lorry driver
(iii) miner
(iv) plumber
(v) postman
(vi) trawler fisherman
(vii) underwriter?

Indicate your reasons.

DATA RESPONSE QUESTION

1 Study the various illustrations which are labelled A to F.

A

B

C

D

E

F

(*a*) Distinguish between:
(i) a good and a service – give one example of each from the illustrations.
(ii) a capital good and a consumer good – give one example of each from the illustrations.

(*b*) Classify into primary production, secondary production and tertiary production the people working in
(i) illustration B
(ii) illustration D
(iii) illustration F

2 Study the pie charts below then answer questions(*c*) to (*e*).

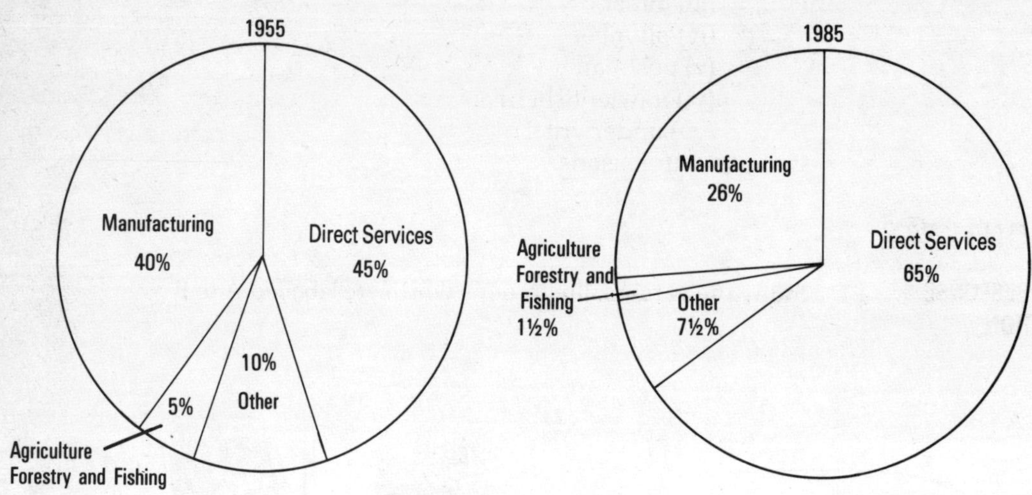

Distribution of employment in the UK

(*c*) Describe the changes which have taken place in the distribution of employment in the UK between 1955 and 1985.
(*d*) Give reasons for these changes.
(*e*) Examine the likely economic effects to the country as a whole.

Answers to multiple choice questions

MC1	B	MC7	D
MC2	D	MC8	B
MC3	A	MC9	E
MC4	E	MC10	C
MC5	D	MC11	A
MC6	C	MC12	B

THE RETAIL TRADE

CONTENTS

This chapter on retail trade covers the following areas:

1 The channels of distribution – the 'normal' channel of distribution; the manufacturer dealing directly with the retailer, and the manufacturer dealing directly with the consumer-branded goods.

2 The functions of the retailer – a study of the services provided by the retailer for consumers, manufacturers and wholesalers.

3 The advantages and disadvantages of large and small-scale retailing.

4 Types of retail selling – independent shops, multiple chain stores, supermarkets, department stores, retail co-operative stores, mail order selling, vending machines, mobile shops, direct selling, party selling and discount warehouses.

5 Franchising.

CHANNELS OF DISTRIBUTION

Manufacturer → wholesaler → retailer → consumer

The most common channel of distribution is for products to be transferred from the manufacturer to the wholesaler, then to the retailer and, finally, the consumer.

Wholesalers traditionally act as 'middlemen' between producers and retailers. A wholesaler buys in very large quantities from the producer and sells to the retailer in smaller quantities. The traditional chain of distribution has been:

Producer → wholesaler → retailer → consumer

However, the traditional wholesaler has been heavily criticised and the functions often taken over by the producer or indeed the retailer. The manufacturer may deal directly with either the retailer or the consumer, thus completely bypassing the wholesaler.

The functions of wholesalers and how they have fought back by forming voluntary chains and self-service operations is discussed on page 56.

Manufacturer to retailer to consumer

The manufacturer may deal directly with the retailer when:

1 turnover (sales) of the product is slow, e.g. furniture, cars;
2 the product is very expensive or a luxury article, e.g. jewellery, grand piano;
3 the product has a regular demand and has perhaps been made popular by advertising (see section on branded goods).

When dealing directly with the retailer the manufacturer will usually establish a selling department and take on the work of the wholesaler. Any additional profits made through bypassing the wholesaler are either absorbed by the manufacturer or passed on to the retailer and consumer in the form of lower prices.

Large retail groups (multiple chains such as Marks and Spencer, Tesco, Littlewoods, Sainsbury's) can afford to buy from the manufacturer. Thus the functions of the wholesaler are taken over by the retailer.

Manufacturer to consumer

The manufacturer may sometimes deal directly with the consumer, cutting out both the wholesaler and retailer. He or she will either retain the profits for his or her own use or future expansion or pass them on to the consumer in the form of lower prices.

TYPES OF DIRECT SELLING

Direct orders This could occur when a specialised product is required by the consumer, e.g. spare parts for machinery. In addition, products which are either very expensive or only in occasional demand would probably be sold directly to the consumer. Another example – especially with the increase in ownership of food freezers – is farmers selling directly to the public. Likewise a manufacturer may employ salespersons and use direct selling techniques.

Mail order This is dealt with on pages 44–5. However, manufacturers may sell by mail order dealing with direct orders from consumers. Much money is spent on postage, advertising and catalogues but it is a popular form of selling especially for members of the family who have limited time for shopping. Manufacturers may also advertise through the local or national press.

Retail shops When demand is regular the manufacturer may open a retail outlet. Shoe manufacturers have for example opened their own shops in many parts of the country under well-known names, thus guaranteeing a steady sale of products produced in their own factories. Shops have been opened by farmers at the farm to sell directly to the consumer, whilst public houses are often owned by brewers.

Advantages of direct selling from manufacturer to consumer

1 Manufacturer's profits are increased – these can either be retained or be passed on to consumers.
2 Perishable goods are quickly distributed.
3 Personal contact is made between consumer and producer.
4 Changes in consumer demand are quickly identified.
5 Products which carry a great deal of technical information are better sold directly to the consumer.

Branded goods

The selling of products by the manufacturer directly to the retailer or consumer has been made more successful by the development of branded products. These are products which are usually widely advertised and easily recognised by consumers – Heinz products for example. They have distinctive trade-marks or containers and demand is usually high. Branded goods have the following advantages:

1 The *trade-mark* is exclusive to the manufacturer.
2 Recommended prices are proposed by the manufacturer.
3 The quality of the goods is known and maintained.
4 The manufacturer, to maintain its good name, will replace faulty products without question.
5 Successful advertising and market research enables the economies of scale to be enjoyed (see page 101).

Trade-marks An important aspect of selling is customer confidence in the product. This can be achieved by the use of well-known trade-marks registered at the Patent Office. Examples include Heinz Beans, Persil, Fairy Snow, etc., which may not be legally used by any other organisation. These products and many others have long enjoyed a high reputation as to both quality and customer satisfaction.

Service marks In 1986 Parliament introduced the registration of service marks at the Patent Office covering identifiable logos relating to 'service' industries. This covers a fixed area including Advertising, Education, Transport, etc. Well-known examples frequently displayed include British Rail, National Westminster Bank etc., and relate only to those organisations.

1 ▶ (*a*) Describe three different methods of direct selling to consumers used by producers.
(*b*) Why are these methods preferred by manufacturers to selling through intermediaries?
(*c*) What has been the effect of the branding of goods
(i) on a manufacturer
(ii) on a retail organisation
(iii) on a consumer?

THE FUNCTIONS OF THE RETAILER

You need to know the functions of the retailer and these are as follows:

Buys from the wholesaler or manufacturer The retailer buys in quite large quantities and sells to the consumer in smaller lots. Consumers very rarely require bulk products so the retailer breaks these up into smaller more manageable amounts.

Keeps stock of a variety of products The retailer must have the correct type, quality and quantity of a product available to meet consumer demands. These may be seasonal or according to regional likes and dislikes and it is the retailer's job to know what customers require.

Provides a convenient source of supply Consumers do not wish to travel miles to purchase products which they may need urgently. Consequently retailers are situated in places convenient for consumers, either in the local neighbourhood or town centre.

Distribution of sales – by day of week

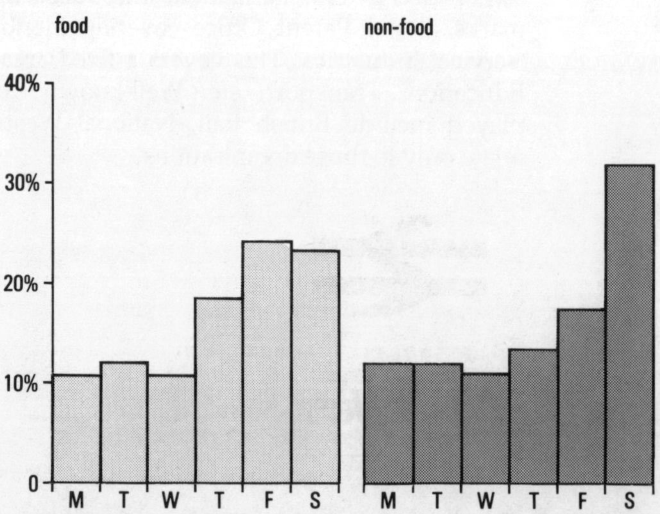

Provides a personal service for consumers For example:

1 When the product is not available the retailer will order it from the supplier.
2 When technical advice or information is required the retailer will give this to the consumer.
3 When the consumer requires credit facilities these may be made available possibly through the hire purchase or credit sales system.
4 Certain products may be prepared for resale. Consumers normally require small quantities of foodstuffs such as meat and cheese. These have to be cut, weighed and wrapped.
5 An after-sales service may be provided. When consumer durables such as for example televisions, refrigerators, washing machines are purchased, the retailer may guarantee to correct any faults occurring within a certain time free of charge.

The linkman The retailer is often the link between the consumer and the wholesaler and manufacturer. He or she can provide the wholesaler or manufacturer with information gained from consumers – whether the product could be improved in any respect. On the other hand consumers can be informed, through the retailer, about the correct ways to use certain products in order to maintain them in good condition, prevent breakdown, etc.

LARGE- AND SMALL-SCALE RETAILING

In recent years the trend in retailing has led to the growth of large retailers known as superstores, hypermarkets and multiple chains. They have the following advantages:

1 They achieve the economies of scale in retailing: bulk buying, advertising, modern purpose-built equipment and centralised buying.
2 The opportunity to introduce self-service. For the consumers this has the advantages of time-saving, convenience, well-displayed products and individually priced goods. For the retailer the advantages are labour saving, quicker turnover and more effective displays.
3 There is a greater division of labour and specialisation.
4 A convenience for working people since all the products are close at hand in one shop, a speedy service allowing the consumer to purchase bulk supplies.

There are certain disadvantages however and these include:

1 a lack of personal service and staff incentive;
2 too much red-tape and bureaucracy, slow decision making, control from Head Office;
3 the risks of substantial shop-lifting and pilfering which add to costs.

Despite the trend towards large-scale retailing however, small-scale retailers are still the most numerous type of retail outlet. In terms of volume however their share of trade has declined from about 54 per cent in 1966 to 30 per cent in 1986. The advantages and disadvantages for small-scale retailers are dealt with in the section dealing with independent retailers.

2 ▶ (*a*) Why are both wholesalers and retailers often necessary in the distribution process of goods from producers to consumers?
(*b*) How do you account for the growth of large-scale retailing?
(*c*) To what extent is it true to say that large retailers are similar to wholesalers?
(*d*) How would you account for the continued existence of small retailers?

3 ▶ (*a*) What are the differences between consumer goods and capital goods?
(*b*) Outline the channels (not forms of transport) used in the distribution of manufactured goods from the producer to the final consumer.
(*c*) Describe the role of the retailer and wholesaler in this distribution.

In order to answer

(*a*) Consumer goods are visible and tangible products which give satisfaction to consumers, e.g. food, clothes, televisions, etc. Consumer durables are consumer goods which have a fairly long life, e.g. videos, cars, freezers. Capital goods are also termed producer goods they are used to produce other products (either producer or consumer goods). Examples includes tractors, machines, etc.
(*b*) There needs to be a discussion of the normal distribution channel of manufacturer to wholesaler to retailer to consumer. The answer also needs a discussion of the manufacturer selling to retailers and then to consumer. Also the manufacturer selling directly to consumer.
(*c*) The role of retailers and wholesalers needs to be fully explained.
(*d*) Discuss local needs, personal service, family businesses, etc.

TYPES OF RETAIL OUTLET

Retail outlets in Britain

Food retailers	82630
Drink, confectionery, tobacco	40860
Clothing, footwear, leather	28920
Household goods	39110
Non-food retailers	33760
Mixed retail business	5205
Hire-purchase business	2460
Total	232945

This is an extremely important part of this chapter. You can expect essay questions to be set on the different types of retail outlet and you should be able to compare them.

Retailing can be classified into the following types of outlet:

INDEPENDENT RETAILERS

These are often referred to as 'unit retailers' or 'corner shops'. They are the most numerous type of retail outlet and account for approximately one third (in terms of value) of retail sales. In recent years independent retailers have been in decline owing to the competition from multiple chain stores (especially hypermarkets and superstores) and mail order selling. Independent retailers are however able to overcome this to a certain extent by forming voluntary chain stores with wholesalers (see page 56).

Advantages of independence

1. Provides a friendly personal service knowing customer needs.
2. A convenient and local source of supply (hence 'corner shop').
3. Sells in very small quantities if required.
4. Some of these shops are open for long and irregular hours.
5. Certain types of product are best sold by small independent shops, especially those requiring a personal service.
6. Enjoys the economies of small scale production.

Disadvantages of independence

1. Can be slow and inconvenient in service.
2. Cannot keep a great amount of stock or a large variety of products.
3. Usually do not have limited liability (see page 92) and therefore are not able to compete with firms that have.
4. Cannot enjoy the economies of scale such as bulk buying, advertising and receiving large loans at preferential rates of interest.
5. Costs and prices tend to be higher.
6. Often short of capital, which hinders progress.
7. May be unwilling to offer self-service.

MULTIPLE CHAIN STORES

Multiple chain stores can be defined as a chain of ten or more branches under a single ownership e.g. Marks and Spencer. They tend to be large limited liability organisations with the branches run from a central or regional head office. They have one common feature – centralised buying, large orders being distributed amongst many manufacturers. These chain stores have easily recognisable and standardised shop fronts with branches spread all over the country. Thus they become well known to the public as a whole and able to offer a standard of service that is often of a high quality throughout.

Single trade shops These deal with a narrow range of goods and rely on a quick turnover. Examples include: WH Smith & Son – stationery and books; Dixons – electrical goods; Halfords – car accessories.

Variety chain shops These sell a wider range of goods under one roof, e.g. Woolworths, Littlewoods. These stores and shops have been most successful forms of retail outlet and account for a high proportion of total retail turnover. Their objective has been to achieve large sales using small numbers of staff.

Advantages of multiple chain stores

1 Centralised buying enables the multiple to buy in bulk at favourable terms.
2 Limited liability and large capital investment.
3 Standardised and easily recognised shop fronts.
4 Quick turnover of products.
5 Transport improvements have meant easy distribution of products to branches, often by own transport.
6 Are able to achieve the economies of large-scale retailing.
7 Low unit costs and prices.
8 Often perform their own wholesaling functions.

Disadvantages of multiple chain stores

1 Narrow range of goods (except variety chains).
2 Personal service is less important.
3 Not so convenient as independent shops; do not enjoy advantages of independents.
4 Aggressive product promotion campaigns may tempt consumer to purchase what he or she cannot afford.

SUPERMARKETS

Supermarkets are a type of self-service multiple chain store. They must have a minimum sales area of over two hundred square metres and have at least three checkout points. They sell mainly foodstuffs but some are now branching out into clothes and household wares. Supermarket selling is based on price cutting, no credit, careful selection and presentation of goods together with self-selling service. Examples include Tesco, Sainsbury's, Asda and Kwik-Save. They have been a very successful form of retail outlet and have developed at the expense of the independent shop as shown by the following table:

Supermarket Annual Sales in £bn

Sainsbury 4.1	Asda 3.3
Tesco 3.7	Kwik-Save 2.1

Advantages of supermarkets

1 Self-service selling is quick and convenient.
2 New selling methods can be used, such as music to promote a relaxed atmosphere, loss leaders (selling at below cost price to bring customers into the shop), selling certain products off cheaply near to closing time.

Disadvantages of supermarkets

1 Disadvantages of self-service retailing (see below).
2 Loss of personal service.
3 Customers not always able to calculate cost of purchase at checkout because of other pressures.

Supermarkets are now an important type of retail outlet. More recently very large supermarkets known as hypermarkets and superstores have developed selling a larger variety and wider selection of products. They achieve the economies of scale and their major attraction to the consumer is greatly reduced prices. Examples include Carrefours near Southampton and Tesco in Cwmbran.

Self-service retailing is essentially an attempt to increase the productivity of retail sales staff. The aim is principally to increase sales and at the same time reduce the need for labour.

Effects on the consumer

1 The consumer performs many of the tasks traditionally performed by sales staff. Customers serve themselves while staff keep the shelves full and collect money at the checkouts.
2 Consumers are able to manage because many of the goods are well advertised, include branded products which are instantly recognisable and clearly priced. This method saves customers' time.
3 Consumers are confronted with 'loss leaders'. These serve to attract customers into the shop where it is hoped they will make other purchases.

Effects on the retailer

1 Retailers have to maintain a high rate of stock turn. Stocks have always to be sufficient to support a quick turnover.
2 Prices have to be competitive.
3 Products of a perishable nature have to be monitored closely in case they are in stock, or left on the shelves, for a long time.
4 Problems of pilfering from the shelves may arise and store detectives have to be employed.

HYPERMARKETS/ SUPERSTORES

These are in reality very large supermarkets and it is sometimes difficult to distinguish between superstores and true hypermarkets. A hypermarket has a minimum sales area of 450 square metres whilst a superstore is a very large supermarket often with subsidiary retail outlets within the store. In both instances they are usually free-standing, single-storeyed stores having provision for the car-borne shopper.

They offer a wider range of goods than supermarkets, their principal attraction being the wide range of products at comparatively low prices. They are usually situated on the outskirts of the large cities and towns thus avoiding the high rent and rates of city centres which is again reflected in product prices. However they are often criticised for being large and ugly buildings causing traffic disruption and pollution problems in previously peaceful country surroundings. They have benefited from two major factors:

1 increased car ownership and changed shopping habits has allowed greater freedom of choice to the shoppers;
2 increased ownership of freezers has allowed the consumer to purchase in bulk.

Evidence suggests that despite the hypermarkets and supermarkets, etc, the independent retailer can co-exist because of the special advantages available to that method of retailing – convenience and personal service.

DEPARTMENT STORES

Department stores are those types of retail outlet which sell a wide range of goods under one roof. They tend to be situated in the centre of towns and examples include Harrods and Selfridges (London), Debenhams and John Lewis (Leeds), and Jenners (Edinburgh). They have developed for two reasons:

1 transport improvements enables consumers to travel into the city centre;
2 standardised products can be bought directly from the manufacturer and bought in bulk.

Advantages of department stores

1 They offer luxurious conditions such as carpets, uniformed sales staff, restaurants.
2 Staff are well trained and possess a good deal of product knowledge.
3 Consumers are attracted from a large area.
4 They can maintain a mail order and delivery service.
5 A wide range of goods is available.
6 Credit accounts can be opened.
7 They achieve many of the economies of large-scale retailing.

Disadvantages of department stores

1 Situated in town centres, they may be inconvenient to travel to because of overcrowding, lack of car parking, expense, etc.
2 They tend to be a little more expensive than other retail outlets because of the facilities they provide.

3 They may be impersonal compared with the sole trader.
4 They may be part of a larger group owned by multiples.

Consider the following:

4 ▶ (*a*) Branded goods have facilitated self-service, and self-service is essential to the operation of the supermarket. Explain this statement.

(*b*) Hypermarkets may sell the same products as department stores but their prices may be lower. Explain why this is so.

(*c*) In spite of competition from large scale retailers, why do many small shops continue to survive?

RETAIL CO-OPERATIVE SOCIETIES

These are controlled by their members – that is, the customers. Co-operatives now sell a wide range of products such as furniture, foodstuffs, coal, milk, clothing and electrical goods. They also provide services such as insurance and banking.

Membership

1 Open to all on payment of a small fee. The share list is never closed.
2 Members are allowed only one vote irrespective of shares owned.
3 There is a limit on the value of the investment any one member can make.

Shares

1 Usually worth £1. Each shareholder is given a number which is used for voting purposes.
2 In most societies today, shareholders (members) are given coupons which may be used when purchasing special offers. Emphasis in most societies however is on lower prices.

Management

1 Managed by a Committee of Management and President elected by members.
2 The Committee (who are unpaid) decide on all questions of policy.
3 Decisions are carried out by paid officials, the chief of whom is the Manager or Chief Executive of the local Society.

Advantages of retail co-operatives

1 Trade is encouraged by lower prices and special offers.
2 Co-operatives purchase many of their products in bulk from the co-operative wholesale society (CWS).
3 Members all have an equal voice in the running of the society.
4 The co-operative has traditional social and political objectives as well as economic.
5 Members provide a readily available market for general sales and special promotion.

Disadvantages of retail co-operatives

1 Many of the products sold come from non co-operative firms, in effect their competitiors.
2 In large urban areas such as London there may be more than one society competing one against another.
3 The Committee of Management may have little industrial or commercial experience.
4 Most members do not attend meetings.
5 A traditional and conservative image.

In recent years the Co-operative Movement has tried to counter the claim that it is too conservative and traditional. It has introduced self-service techniques and undertaken nationwide advertising campaigns.

5 ▶ We often speak of 'the Co-op' as if it were one large business instead of a very large number of separate local retail societies and two Co-operative Wholesale Societies (one English and one Scottish).

(*a*) From what source does a local retail society obtain its capital?
(*b*) How is it controlled?
(*c*) How does it dispose of its profits?
(*d*) Who are the members of a co-operative wholesale society?
(*e*) How does the business of the English Co-operative Wholesale Society differ from that of other large wholesale organizations outside the co-operative movement?

MAIL ORDER SELLING

This takes place when products are sold through the post and is a rapidly expanding form of retailing. Most of the mail order business is in the hands of specialist firms such as Freeman's, Littlewoods and Kays. Manufacturers and department stores also attempt to sell products by this method of retailing through press advertisements.

Normally the mail order firms employ an agent in a locality. He or she has a catalogue of the products being sold and receives a commission depending on the value of sales. The commission is a higher percentage if taken in the form of products rather than cash.

Advantages of mail order selling

1 Costs are reduced since fewer staff are needed. The mail order firm often only requires a warehouse and an office.
2 It does not provide other costly services.
3 Consumers can avoid the inconvenience of travel and traffic congestion.
4 Consumers can examine the product in the comfort of their own homes.
5 Credit is available.
6 Products can always be returned by the customer within a certain time, in case of dissatisfaction.

Disadvantages of mail order selling

1 Costs of mail and warehousing are high.
2 Personal service is lacking. Although this can be overcome by an agent with a pleasant personality.
3 Consumers may have to wait days or weeks for the product.
4 Success depends to a certain extent on the agent who is perhaps most interested in profit.
5 The catalogue may give a misleading impression of the product, giving rise to disappointment.

6 ▶ (*a*) Hypermarkets and mail order firms frequently attract large numbers of customers. Why is each of these types of trader so popular with the consumer?
(*b*) How do retail co-operative societies differ from other forms of retail organisation?
(*c*) Give reasons why the share of retail trade achieved by retail co-operatives has fallen.

Vending machines

These are found in a wide variety of places such as rail and coach stations, factories, offices, colleges and schools. An increasing number of products can be sold in this way – cigarettes, sweets, milk, sandwiches and even complete meals. The main **advantage** is that the product can be purchased at any time of the day or night. **Disadvantages** include the risk of vandalism, the risk of mechanical failure, and that the perishability of some products makes them unsuitable to be sold in this way.

Mobile shops

These are mainly concerned with food sales especially grocery products. The **advantage** is that the products are taken to the consumer which is very useful in isolated communities. The **disadvantages** are that only a limited quanitity of products can be carried and the cost of petrol and motoring has increased dramatically in recent years, making it an expensive method of selling products.

Direct selling

This method includes door-to-door retailing popular with many firms selling double-glazing, cosmetics and cavity-wall insulation. This type of sale usually takes place when the manufacturer deals directly with the consumer at home. It reduces many costs such as expensively equipped retail premises and employment of a large sales staff. It is also by its very nature more personal, allowing the sales staff to be trained in a more effective manner. However this could be a disadvantage if staff are too aggressive in their sales technique in order to secure a sale.

Party selling

Manufacturers sometimes arrange a 'party' – usually in someone's home – so that potential customers can gather together to view the product in a relaxed friendly atmosphere. Whilst no obligation or pressure to buy is directly administered it is possible for some consumers to feel 'guilty' at not making a purchase. Examples of this type of selling include Avon cosmetics, Tupperware, etc.

Telephone sales

A recent sales technique by which potential customers are phoned at their home by persuasive salespeople. Some people view this as an invasion of privacy and often results in no sale and less goodwill towards the firm.

Discount warehouses

These organisations (Comet, Supreme, etc) can be found in large premises with minimal fixtures and fittings selling mainly consumer durable goods at discount prices. There is often little personal or after-sales service, customers making their own transport arrangements. A similar type of selling is undertaken using catalogues (Argos), consumers later visiting the centrally placed warehouse. As with other large retailers, discount warehouses attempt to enjoy the economies of large scale retailing.

FRANCHISING

Franchising has existed for many years in activities such as brewery and car distribution, and has expanded rapidly in recent times. This involves a franchisor giving licences to franchisees allowing the latter to use, sell or manufacture a product under a well-known name. A tenant of a public house for example may be granted a franchise by a brewery. Recent developments have included closer involvement, the franchisor providing extensive 'back-up' services. Kentucky Fried Chicken, Little Chef, The Body Shop etc.

Upon purchasing the franchise, the franchisee:

1 receives the right to use the trade name;
2 may receive advice and guidance from the franchisor, e.g. site selection, staff training, assistance in buying and control of stock;
3 may receive the sole right to a particular sales territory;
4 may have the possibility of leasing premises and equipment;
5 receives the benefit of a national advertising campaign or other special services provided by the franchisor;
6 agrees to pay a regular amount to the franchisor – usually a percentage of sales.

MC1. A multiple shop is also known as a

A supermarket
B department store
C hypermarket
D chain store
E voluntary chain

MC2. Which of the following is not an advantage of the supermarket to the customer?

A fast and efficient service
B wide variety of goods
C clear display
D lack of personal assistance
E competitively priced goods

MC3. The main advantage of mail order shopping is

A convenience
B discount buying
C bulk buying
D a wide variety of choice
E goods of high quality

MC4. A loss leader is

A a free gift with a purchase
B a claims manager of an insurance company
C an article sold cheaply to attract customers
D an editorial column in the *Financial Times*
E an advertisement that has had little or no response

In order to answer **MC5** and **MC6** one or more of the options may be correct.

A if 1 only is correct
B if 1, 2 and 3 are correct
C if 2, 3 and 4 are correct
D if 1, 2, 3 and and 4 are correct
E if 3 and 4 are correct

MC5. Which of the following is/are normally characteristic of large supermarkets?

1 bulk buying by the shop owners
2 lack of personal service
3 part of a chain
4 have 'own brand' goods

MC6. Compared with department stores, mail order warehouses tend to spend less on

1 postage
2 advertising
3 rent
4 rates

MC7. A factoring type of business usually differs from other forms of retailing because

A a charge is made for use of company name
B only certain types of business are allowed by law

C sales are restricted to given areas
D there is a restriction of opening hours
E all profits are equally divided between factors

MC8. The main source of finance for the co-operative society is
A its members
B a bank
C the government
D the stock exchange
E its customers

MC9. Which of the following retail outlets have grown because of the increased mobility of consumers?
A retail co-operatives
B hypermarkets
C corner shops
D mail-order businesses
E voluntary chain stores

MC10. Which of the following would *not* be expected to help the small independent retailer?
A a rise in public transport fares
B an increase in trade discounts
C a decrease in bulk-buying discounts
D an increase in rates in inner city areas
E an increase in private car ownership

7 ▶ Usually department stores are found in city centres, multiple stores on local high streets and small retailers on housing estates, and in outlying areas.
(*a*) Explain why this is so.
(*b*) What are the distinctive characteristics of each of these forms of retailing?
(*c*) Why does the small retailer still flourish despite competition from large retailing concerns?

To answer (*a*) department stores are found in city centres because they offer a wide range of goods under one roof and they hope to attract the many people from a very wide area who may visit centres. They offer comparatively luxurious conditions and a high quality service including delivery. Traditionally they have developed in the city centre.

Multiple stores are found in the high street because they offer a narrow range of goods at relatively low prices and they hope to attract the many people in the high street. They will have many shops in different towns.

Small retailers offer a convenience and personal service. They are in the immediate neighbourhood to attract small and convenience purchases from very local consumers.

To answer (*b*) you need to discuss the distinctive features of each type of retail outlet. For instance, department stores offer a wide range of goods under one roof. They tend to be expensive. Multiple stores on the other hand are part of a chain of ten or more branches selling a narrow range of products at relatively low prices. Small retailers offer a personal service and are convenient to the local neighbourhood.

To answer (*c*) you need to discuss the advantages of independent retailers such as personal service, selling in small quantities, long opening hours, etc. They enjoy the economies of small-scale production.

Answers to multiple choice questions

MC1	D	**MC6**	E
MC2	D	**MC7**	C
MC3	A	**MC8**	A
MC4	C	**MC9**	B
MC5	D	**MC10**	E

THE WHOLESALE AND COMMODITY MARKETS

CONTENTS

In this chapter we examine the workings of the wholesale and commodity markets. We shall cover the following topics:

1 The wholesale trade – the functions of the wholesaler; the operation of middlemen such as merchants, agents and brokers; the decline of traditional wholesalers and how they are fighting back.

2 The commodity market – the meaning of markets, methods of dealing, 'spot' markets, 'futures' markets, hedging, the marketing of foodstuffs and commodities.

THE WHOLESALE TRADE

A DEFINITION OF THE WHOLESALER

Wholesalers traditionally act as 'middlemen' between producers and retailers. A wholesaler buys in very large quantities from the producer and sells in smaller quantities to the retailer. The traditional chain of distribution has been:

Producer → wholesaler → retailer → consumer

However, as was shown in Chapter 2, the traditional type of wholesaler has been heavily criticised and these functions often taken over by the producer or indeed the retailer (see page 36). Nevertheless the wholesaler has attempted to fight back by forming voluntary chains and self-service wholesalers (see page 57).

THE FUNCTIONS OF THE WHOLESALER

You should realise that the wholesaler fulfils several useful functions for producers, retailers and consumers. We shall examine the advantages to each of these three groups.

Advantages to the producer

1 Provides the producer with market information – the wholesaler will be able to tell the producer about how well (or badly) a particular commodity is selling; the wholesaler is in close touch with both retailers and consumers and will note any suggestions or criticisms made about a particular commodity.

2 The wholesaler will purchase from the producer in bulk – thus the

wholesaler will allow the producer to keep production lines clear and carry fewer stocks.

3 The wholesaler may create a demand for a particular commodity – this is achieved by bringing it to the attention of both retailers and consumers by means of special offers, advertising campaigns, etc.
4 The wholesaler will even out the flow of commodities and prevent big price changes – when a product is in short supply the wholesaler can put more on the market, when it is in surplus and not selling well perhaps because of seasonal demand, the wholesaler can add to existing stocks and hold until required.
5 The wholesaler will pay the producer promptly – this increases the producers available cash for further investment.

Advantages to the retailer

1 The retailer need only carry small stocks – he or she can easily obtain supplies from the wholesaler and need not keep large stocks.
2 The wholesaler can give the retailer advice and the benefit of marketing methods and in addition he or she may be a specialist in particular commodities. The wholesaler can also let the retailer know about new commodities or changes being introduced by the producer.
3 The wholesaler often gives credit to the retailer – this reduces the amount of liquid capital needed by retailers.
4 The wholesaler will often break up bulk, pre-pack and price certain commodities – this reduces the effort needed by the retailer.
5 The wholesaler will often stock a wide variety and may deliver the commodities to the retailer, or will be situated in close proximity being open at convenient times.

Advantages to the consumer

1 The wholesaler ensures a steady flow of commodities at stable prices for consumers – as we have seen when there is a shortage the wholesaler will release stocks, when there is a surplus stocks will be retained until required.
2 The wholesalers provide commodities for a range of different outlets, including retail shops, keeping them well stocked to the advantage of consumers.
3 The wholesaler will pass on suggestions and complaints to the producers – also if commodities are not popular with consumers the wholesaler can quickly alert the producer.
4 The wholesaler will generally ensure that commodities will reach the consumer in the correct quantity, correct quality at the right price and at the proper time.

You should now consider and be able to answer the following questions. Wholesaling topics are popular with examiners and questions often include aspects of retailing as well. It is advisable therefore that retailing and wholesaling are not treated in isolation from one another.

1 ▶ (*a*) Describe the functions of the wholesaler.
(*b*) Briefly outline three examples or circumstances in which manufacturers might prefer to sell direct to retail firms.

First of all you need to discuss the meaning of the wholesaler. The functions of wholesalers are dealt with on page 53 and you should refer to these.

The circumstances in which manufacturers may deal directly with retail firms are:

(i) When the product is extremely expensive – high-class jewellery for example.
(ii) When the product has a regular demand and is well known to the public, perhaps due to advertising. Branded or specialist type products may come into this category. You should give examples in this part of the answer
(iii) When the retailer, such as Marks and Spencer, is able to undertake its own wholesaling.

2 ▶ Why has the influence of the wholesaler declined in importance in recent years?

3 ▶ Give a brief account of the functions of a wholesaler. Indicate how and why the links between some wholesaler merchants and their customers have become closer since the advent of the hypermarket and superstore.

4 ▶ (*a*) What services does the wholesaler provide for the manufacturer?
(*b*) Why have manufacturers in recent years increasingly bypassed the wholesaler?

Wholesalers have been the subject of criticism

In recent years the words 'wholesaler' and 'middleman' have been given adverse meanings. They are used commonly to suggest someone who is profiteering and taking advantage of the consumer and the producer. It could be true that unscrupulous wholesalers could make vast profits. They are ideally placed to do so since they buy from the producer and sell to the consumer. Since they buy at low prices and sell at higher prices, there may be opportunities to create artificial shortages and push up prices and thus make vast profits.

However, many wholesalers suggest that they do not create shortages but in fact relieve shortages by running down stocks at appropriate times. Wholesalers also point to the fact that they provide many useful functions for producers, retailers and consumers and somebody has to perform these functions even when wholesalers are eliminated.

Whether you consider wholesalers to be profiteers is something on which you must decide. However, the fact remains that wholesalers in some cases have been gradually replaced. For instance, retailers may do their own wholesaling and this is particularly true of the large multiple chain stores (see page 39). Also manufacturers may cut out the wholesaler and deal directly with the retailer or consumer. This is especially so in certain situations. You should refer to page 34 to understand when manufacturers deal directly with retailers or consumers.

Consider the following essay question:

5 ▶ Compare and contrast the services given to the small retailer by:
(*a*) the traditional wholesaler; and
(*b*) the cash and carry warehouse.

We have discussed why wholesalers are dying out and which organisations are taking over their functions. However, you should also be aware that wholesalers have attempted to fight back and there are two ways in which they have tried to do this. Traditional wholesalers may have formed themselves into either:

1 a voluntary chain; or
2 a self-service wholesaler.

Both these innovations have been successful in many parts of the country.

VOLUNTARY CHAIN STORES

Voluntary chain stores must not be confused with variety chain stores, such as Woolworths, selling a wide variety of goods. A voluntary chain organisation is one in which a traditional wholesaler allies himself or herself with many small independent retailers. Examples include Mace, Spar and Wavy Line. They attempt to imitate the best features of multiple chain supermarkets while at the same time retaining the advantages of independent retailing and traditional wholesaling.

Advantages to the wholesaler

The retailers agree to:

1 purchase most of their products from the wholesaler;
2 accept delivery on certain days;
3 adhere to strict credit terms;
4 display the chain's emblem at retail premises, or on letterheads and in all advertising literature;
5 display products recommended by the wholesaler.

As a result the wholesaler's costs are reduced as well as ensuring a ready market for products.

Advantages to the retailer

1 Lower wholesaling costs reduce prices to the retailer.
2 He or she receives advice from the wholesaler on how to display and sell products.
3 The retailer knows when deliveries from the wholesaler will occur.
4 Modern equipment such as display cabinets and refrigerators is made available at reduced prices.

5 The retailer receives credit from the wholesaler.

These factors have enabled the independent retailer, tied closely to a traditional wholesaler, to compete successfully against supermarkets. They achieve the economies of large-scale retailing.

SELF-SERVICE WHOLESALERS

The self-service wholesaler operates on a 'cash and carry' basis. Customers travel to the wholesaler warehouse and provide their own transport. Purchases are usually paid for in cash. These 'cash and carry' warehouses are often available only to retailers but in recent years, private customers have been able to purchase their requirements as well.

Advantages to the retailer

1 Quick and convenient – the retailer can choose the time when purchases need to be made.
2 He or she can purchase the exact requirements.
3 Since wholesaling costs are lower the price of products is likely to be lower than elsewhere.

Disadvantages to the retailer

1 It is usually necessary to pay in cash, no credit is allowed.
2 The costs of transport involved add to overall costs.
3 Time spent in visiting the wholesaler may necessitate closing the shop with the resultant loss of custom.

Advantages to the wholesaler

1 No credit is given, thus immediate cash is available to purchase further supplies.
2 There are no transport expenses involved and no capital invested in transport equipment.
3 Comparatively fewer administrative and other costs incurred e.g. in sending out invoices, statements, etc, and postage.
4 Wage costs are at a minimum since the 'cash and carry' premises employ few people.

Disadvantages to the wholesaler

1 There may be a breakdown of 'goodwill' between wholesaler and retailer.
2 There is little in the way of personal service.
3 High costs of transport may force the retailer out of business.

Consider the following questions:

6 ▶ What are the advantages and disadvantages of 'cash and carry' wholesaling to

(*a*) the retailer;
(*b*) the wholesaler and
(*c*) the consumer?

This can be answered by reference to the previous section on self-service wholesaling.

7 ▶ Why is it that numerous independent grocers now belong to voluntary chains?

8 ▶ 'The work of the wholesaler has been largely eliminated by the increased use of nationally advertised branded goods, and by the growth of hypermarkets, superstores and chain stores.'
(*a*) Discuss this statement; and
(*b*) show what the wholesaler is doing in the grocery trade to overcome the problem.
You should be able to approach part (*a*) of this question with reference to what you have read so far in this unit with some knowledge of the unit on retailing. Part (*b*) can be answered by referring to voluntary chain organisations and self-service wholesaling.

THE COMMODITY MARKET

THE MEANING OF MARKETS

A market is a place where buyers and sellers are in contact with one another and where the price of the commodity in question will be determined by the forces of supply and demand. London has become an important centre of market activities for many reasons. It is the capital of a politically stable country, an important financial and administrative centre and a competent legal centre. Moreover because of its history and geographical position Britain has always been a trading country importing and exporting a variety of commodities. Thus London became well known for its expertise in commodity trading. Later on in this section we shall categorise the markets as follows:

1 Markets in commodities – examples include the London Diamond Market, the London Metal Exchange, the Baltic Exchange.

2 Markets in foodstuffs Billingsgate, renowned for its fish market; Smithfield, for meat and poultry; and New Covent Garden, for fruit and vegetables.
There are of course other markets, such as the Stock Market and the London Money Markets, which are discussed in other chapters.

METHODS OF DEALING

Exchanges Members of the exchange agree to conduct business according to a set of rules. Membership is often restricted. Exchanges exist for those commodities which are of a standardised quality or are easily graded, the London Metal Exchange for example.

Auction sales Where commodities cannot be graded or vary in quality they are sold by auction, for example the London Tea Auctions. The commodity is stored in a warehouse and is available for inspection. Samples may be taken for consideration by the commodity brokers in order to judge the quality and likely bidding price.

Direct sales When an importer of a commodity deals regularly with a customer the commodity may be sold directly to that customer without recourse to the exchange or auction sale, e.g. large-scale imports of produce by the co-operative movement from own farms, plantations, etc.

SPECIALISTS IN THE COMMODITY TRADE

A **merchant** buys commodities on his or her behalf, unlike an agent who is employed by a principal. The merchant pays the supplier promptly and transports, displays and warehouses the commodity, undertaking the risks involved.

A **broker** on the other hand is an agent employed by a principal to make bargains and contracts with other parties for a commission (or brokerage). He or she does not possess the commodities, but is a 'middleman' who brings the two parties to the sale together. The broker is therfore a specialist who brings buyers and sellers together at the right price and time and can advise the principal of possible trends.

A **'del credere' agent** however guarantees payment in any contract for an extra commission. He or she is responsible for any debts which may arise and therfore carries the risks of non-payment by the buyer.

Each of these three dealers performs useful functions in commerce, especially in the commodity trade where problems of distance, language, currency, measurement and expense are apparent. They are all involved in obtaining commodities of the right quality and correct quantity accepting many of the risks and uncertainties involved in the commodity trade. They are specialists on particular markets and are able to use their expertise for the benefit of their clients.

Consider the following question:

9 ▶ What is the difference between a merchant, a 'del credere' agent and a broker? What useful function does each of these persons serve in commerce?

SPOT MARKETS, FUTURES MARKETS AND HEDGING

The spot markets These are markets dealing in commodities for *immediate* delivery. The 'spot' price is the price of the product quoted in the market at the present time.

The futures market The main fear of a seller of a commodity is that the price will fall. Thus the seller may agree a futures price. This means he or she sells for future delivery at present-day prices. If the price falls in the meantime he or she is protected.

Alternatively the main fear of a buyer is that the price will rise. Thus he or she may buy today at a futures price. This means the purchaser buys for future delivery at present day prices. If prices rise in the meantime he or she is protected.

A futures contract is therefore made when a given quantity of a commodity is to be provided at a future date and at a previously agreed price.

Hedging The main problem with futures is obviously that buyers and sellers need some protection from price fluctuations. For instance, if the seller of a commodity fearing a price *fall* agrees a futures price and by that future date the price has *risen*, he or she has missed out on profits. Similarly if the buyer of the commodity fearing a price rise agrees a futures price and by that future date the price has fallen, the buyer has likewise missed out on profits.

Hedging occurs when the futures market is used as a protection against price fluctuations. Consider the following example:

1 January – the 'spot' price for crude oil is £100 for a given quantity. The oil company agrees a futures price for crude oil of £100.

1 March – after refining, oil costs £200 for a given quantity giving a surplus of £100

However, assume that by 1 March the spot price for crude oil is £50 and therefore refined oil is £150. This gives the oil company a surplus of only £50 since they bought the crude oil at 1 January price of £100.

The oil company can hedge against this:

1 January – the company sells crude oil on the futures market at £100 (oil which they do not yet have).

1 March – crude oil has a spot price of £50. The company can buy crude oil at spot price and sell it at the futures price of £100. The company therefore makes a surplus of £50 which compensates for the loss of £50 on the main transaction.

What would have happened if the spot price for crude oil on 1 January was £100 and by 1 March it has risen to £150, forcing up the price of refined oil to £250?

The question of 'futures' and 'hedging' is quite a popular one with examiners. Consider the following:

10 ▶ Why does London continue to be an important centre for the commodity trade? Explain, in relation to the commodity markets, the meaning of the following terms:

(*a*) forward contracts;
(*b*) futures.

You should be able to answer this question with reference to your reading in this chapter.

11 ▶ 'By means of "futures" a manufacturer may obtain protection against losses caused by fluctuations in the price of the commodity in which he or she is dealing.' Explain the meaning of the quotation and state in which commodities future contracts are commonly made.

You should be able to explain the meaning of the statement and describe the time element attached to futures. Also now futures contracts are commonly made for those commodities which over time are fairly standard in quality and are easily graded, e.g. currency, wheat, copper, rubber, etc. A commodity which may vary in quality, e.g. tea, wood, meat, etc, is not suitable for future contracts.

12 ▶ Few people would buy groceries merely on description yet many manufacturers buy a high proportion of their raw materials almost entirely by description. Why is this so? Give examples.

Your reading on futures and the material on commodity markets later in the chapter (page 62) will enable you to answer this question.

THE MARKETING OF FOODSTUFFS

Britain is mainly a manufacturing country and in consequence agriculture is a relatively small (but important) part of the economy. This being so, roughly about half of Britain's food has to be imported.

Some of the most important imported food products include:

Wheat A large volume of Britain's imported wheat comes from the USA, Canada and Australia. This is classified by each of these areas in to different grades whilst supplies from other countries are graded by Corn Trade Associations in this country. Whilst homegrown wheat is sold by samples on both the London and Liverpool Corn Exchanges supplies are also sold on two important exchanges in London:

1 The Baltic Mercantile and Shipping Exchange (known as the Baltic Exchange) – as well as the Grain Market this is the centre of the freight market (cargoes arranged for both ships and aircraft), the Air Freight Market and the Oil (vegetable) and Oilseeds Market. For wheat from overseas no samples are allowed and all grains are sold by description. Futures dealings is an important aspect of this market.

2 The London Corn Exchange – grain dealers buy in large quantities from the Baltic Exchange and sell in smaller quantities on the London Corn Exchange. Homegrown wheat is sold by sample.

Tea Britain imports most of its tea from India, Sri Lanka and East

Africa. On arrival it is stacked according to estate and grade. The tea broker is able to take samples. The product is later sold at auction, London being the tea centre for the whole of Western Europe.

Sugar Britain imports much of its sugar in an unrefined form from sugarcane producing areas including the West Indies and Mauritius. Homegrown sugar beet is also an important source of supply and all the homegrown crop is bought by the British Sugar Corporation. London is one of the most important world markets for sugar and daily 'spot' and 'futures' sales are held.

THE LONDON WHOLESALE FOOD MARKETS

New Covent Garden The largest horticultural market in the country. Sales within the market are undertaken by many specialist wholesalers or growers associations. Some of the produce is sold directly to consumers in the market. Most of the produce is sold after inspection and some selling is by sample. The produce is distributed from the new site in London to all parts of Britain.

Smithfield Both home killed and imported meat is sold. It is owned by the Corporation of London and is one of the oldest markets in Britain. Smithfield supplies London, the South and Midlands with all kinds of meat and poultry.

Billingsgate Fish is often sold by auction at the ports, mainly on the North Sea coast such as Aberdeen. Large quantities, however, are sent to Billingsgate and provincial markets for resale to merchants and caterers. A great deal of fish is also bought by firms such as Birds Eye and Findus for frozen fish products.

THE MARKETING OF COMMODITIES

Britain has traditionally imported the bulk of its raw material requirements which have been used in the manufacture of finished goods for export. Various organisations have developed in order to market these commodities.

Cotton Most of Britain's imported raw cotton is from the United States and is imported mainly through Liverpool near the main cotton manufacturing region of Lancashire. Recent years however have witnessed a marked decline of the domestic cotton industry, due to the development of synthetic fibres and intense competition from abroad.

Wool The centre of the British woollen industry is West Yorkshire. Whilst a great deal of wool is produced in this country, large amounts are imported from countries such as Australia and New Zealand. It is sold by auction at the wool markets in Bradford and London, after inspection, to buyers from Yorkshire and the rest of the world.

Jute Jute is a vegetable fibre grown in Northern India and Bangladesh. It is used in the manufacture of sacks, carpets, linoleum and shoes. The British jute industry is centred on Dundee.

Metals The London Metal Exchange deals mainly in copper, lead and zinc. It is the most important market of its type in the world, and its prices are often regarded as world prices. The stocks are warehoused and official price lists are published for both 'spot' and 'futures' markets. Dealings are conducted by private negotiation between members.

London is also the centre for the marketing of other important commodities, including gold and silver bullion.

Consider the following questions:

MC1. Which of the following is not a function of wholesaling?
A giving credit
B bulk buying
C after-sales service
D advertising
E packaging

MC2. A commodity market is one where its products are
A imported
B standardised
C prepared for sale
D exported
E perishable

13 ▶ Describe the work of two wholesale produce markets or exchanges. Explain why they are mainly centred in London.

14 ▶ Explain, and give the purpose of the following, in relation to organised commodity markets:
(*a*) auctions
(*b*) grading
(*c*) sampling
(*d*) spot transactions
You should be able to answer these questions from your reading in this chapter.

Answers to multiple choice questions
MC1 C **MC2** B

Study the following information carefully.

A large wholesaler has recently sought permission from the *local authority* to build a new warehouse on the outskirts of a large town twenty miles from London. The site chosen is a vacant plot of land with *easy access to the M25* and also to the relevant *commodity markets*. Using their own transport the wholesalers will be able to extend their market of operations to supply numerous *voluntary chain stores* and independent retailers in the district.

(*a*) What do you understand to be the meaning of 'Local Authority'? Why should permission to build have to be obtained?

(*b*) Why is access to the M25 so important?

(*c*) Explain the term *commodity markets* in connection with wholesaling.

(*d*) What are voluntary chain stores? How do they differ from variety chain stores?

BUYING AND SELLING

CONTENTS

This chapter examines aspects of buying and selling in the following sections:

1 **Terms of sale** – the difference between cash discounts and trade discounts, and the documents used between buyer and seller.

2 **Value Added Tax** – what it is and how it is calculated.

3 **Advertising** – the purpose of advertising, types of advertising, advantages and disadvantages.

4 **Credit and hire purchase** – the meaning of credit, forms of credit such as hire purchase, advantages and disadvantages.

5 **Consumer protection** – an analysis of government protection of consumers' interests.

TERMS OF SALE

Questions are frequently set on this topic which covers the function of discounts and the documents which pass between buyer and seller.

TRADE DISCOUNTS AND CASH DISCOUNTS

Trade discount This is given by the manufacturer or wholesaler to the retailer. It is a discount (reduction) on list prices or catalogue prices. Occasionally the catalogue describes the commodities being offered for sale and may give prices. It is, however, usually accompanied by a price list which normally shows current prices separately from the catalogue. To avoid continually reprinting the catalogue or list the wholesaler may vary the trade discount, e.g. if prices rise the discount may be reduced from say 20 per cent to 15 per cent. The amount of trade discount varies according to the commodity in question. Commodities with a quick turnover (confectionery) offer a smaller trade discount than those having a slow turnover (household furniture). It will also depend on the quantity purchased; the larger the amount the greater the probable discount.

Cash discount This is sometimes given by the seller to purchasers who pay promptly for commmodities and therefore improve the 'cash flow' in the business. Giving cash discounts may reduce profits but this is often preferable to allowing debts to increase. The discount is deducted from the **net** price of the goods (i.e. the list prices **less** the trade discount).

THE DOCUMENTS USED IN A TRANSACTION

The order When a buyer is purchasing commodities from a seller for the first time he or she will send a letter of inquiry asking for a price list of commodities required. If the prices are acceptable the buyer will place an order either using the seller's order form, by writing a letter on his or her own notepaper stating what is required, or by using his or her own order form keeping copies for reference.

The invoice This is sent by the seller to the buyer and it gives all details relevant to the order:

1 names and addresses of buyer and seller;
2 date of sale;
3 description of goods, quantity and price;
4 terms of the sale, such as any discount;
5 where applicable Value Added Tax is added to the net price (see page 71 for a description of VAT).

On receipt of the invoice the buyer will check it with the relevant copy of the order. The goods will also be checked for quality, quantity, damage, etc. There are normally **five** copies of the invoice as follows:

1 **top copy** – sent by seller to buyer;
2 **second copy** – kept by seller for his or her own records;
3 **third copy** – kept by seller's stores department or given to the transporter to obtain a signature of receipt from the buyer, often called the **delivery note**;
4 **fourth copy** – kept by buyer's stores department to check the commodities arriving, often termed the **advice note**;
5 **fifth copy** – kept by sales representative of the seller, who deals closely with the buyer. May be used to calculate sales commission (if any).

Many firms include 'E & OE' at the bottom of the invoice which means 'errors and omissions excepted' – if an error or omission has been made it is usual for the seller to correct it.

The credit note This is used when the amount charged on the invoice is greater than the amount due from the buyer. This may occur when:

1 damaged goods are returned by the buyer;
2 the customer has been overcharged;
3 goods are returned, for whatever reason;
4 packing cases are returned which have been charged for on the invoice. Credit notes are usually printed in red ink which makes them easily distinguishable from an invoice. The credit note should give the following information:

1 the names and addresses of buyer and seller;
2 description of commodities returned;
3 the number and total value of commodities being returned.

Two copies are normally made, one for the buyer and one for the seller.

The debit note This is usually sent when it is necessary to **increase** the amount charged on the invoice. This may be required when:

1 commodities have been undercharged;
2 commodities have been sent but not charged on the invoice.

The debit note can be regarded as a supplementary invoice and is usually accompanied by a letter of explanation, particularly as it frequently arises because of an error by the seller.

The statement In business it is not usual for the buyer to pay each invoice as it arrives. He or she may make several purchases from the same seller over a period of time. The seller sends the necessary documents with each delivery and at the end of a certain time period (usually a month) sends a statement of total indebtedness. The buyer checks the statement against the individual invoices taking into account any credit or debit notes.

The receipt On receiving the cash or cheque in settlement of the account the seller will acknowledge payment if the customer so requests. Whilst this is not usually necessary when payment by cheque is made, it is important that receipts are taken as proof of payment for all cash payments. There are several ways of giving a receipt:

1 stamping or acknowledging receipt on the statement itself;
2 some firms keep separate receipt forms, keeping a copy for their records;
3 if the payment is made through the Bank Giro system the bank will stamp the statement which can be used as a receipt;
4 the Cheques Act 1957 renders a separate receipt unnecessary when paying by cheque, but occasionally a receipt form will be printed on the back of the cheque.

MC1. I receive two quotations, one from supplier X who quotes £100 less 20 per cent trade discount and 20 per cent cash discount, and one from supplier Y who quotes £100 less 30 per cent trade discount and 10 per cent cash discount. If I intend to take advantage of trade and cash discount then

A the lower price is quoted by X
B the lower price is quoted by Y
C both suppliers are quoting exactly the same price
D I shall have to allow similar discounts to customers when I re-sell the goods
E I will not be allowed to purchase from another supplier

MC2. I receive statements of account from each of my twenty suppliers on the first of each month. The total of these twenty statements tells me

A how much stock I have on my shelves or in my warehouse
B how much is owed to me by my customers
C how much I owe my creditors for stock
D how much I have sold in the past month
E the amounts owed to me by my suppliers

MC3. The total amount I must pay for goods invoiced at £500 less 20 per cent trade discount and 5 per cent cash discount when receiving both discounts is

A not known from the above data
B £480
C £375
D £475
E £380

MC4. The abbreviated phrase 'E & OE' is likely to be found printed at the bottom of

A a receipt
B an invoice
C a cheque
D a delivery note
E a debit note

MC5. An invoice is a business document which

A must be signed by the receiver of goods
B gives all the details of goods except their price
C must include the letters 'E & OE' if the seller wishes to alter it later
D describes the goods, including the purchase price and terms of sale
E must be returned to the supplier

Questions are sometimes set on the documents used in business. Consider the following:

1 ▶ What are the main documents which pass between buyer and seller in the purchase and sale of goods, and what are their functions?

2 ▶ Distinguish between trade discount and cash discount. Under what circumstances would a trader allow a customer

(*a*) both
(*b*) cash only?

3 ▶ A retailer decides to purchase from a wholesaler with whom he has not previously dealt.

(*a*) Explain the purpose of all the documents involved from the first approach to the final payment.

(*b*) Assume that a part of the delivery is faulty but not replaced.

4 ▶ (*a*) How does cash discount differ from trade discount?
(*b*) Explain the benefits of cash discount to
(i) buyers and
(ii) sellers.

5 ▶ What is the difference between a debit note and a credit note? Under what circumstances and by whom is the latter used?

MARKET RESEARCH

This is a topic that is essential not only to existing firms but also to those about to embark into business of one sort or another. It is, for example, important to know of actual and potential demand for a product or service, existing outlets (if any), likely acceptance of a new or modified product etc. The principal aim therefore is to obtain as much information as possible in order that the management may come to a decision regarding production, sales area, packaging, price, quality etc. This may be undertaken by some or all of the following methods:

(*a*) introducing the product into a defined area, obtaining customer reaction and consideration of expansion in conjunction with a systematic advertising campaign;

(*b*) depending upon the product to be marketed, free samples may be given to households or potential customers.

Researchers need to have detailed knowledge of the likely market to whom they will direct questionnaires, advertising literature, canvas directly either through personal contact or by telephone, etc. Statistics will be drawn up to analyse these findings whilst variables such as seasonal factors, age, sex, occupational classification, etc. will be taken into account. Market research therefore forms an important part in the launch of a product but also takes into account its continued acceptance by the customer. Successful products are thus marketed and re-marketed using up-to-date techniques keeping the customer informed through as many sources as possible.

VALUE ADDED TAX

Value Added Tax (VAT) was introduced by the government in Britain in 1973. It is a tax on the sale of certain commodities. Some goods are exempted, such as most foodstuffs, children's clothes, and services provided by schools and hospitals. In practice the **seller** is required by the government to add on VAT when he or she sells to the buyer and it is levied at each stage of the distribution process. The rate of VAT levied is decided by the government and may be changed at any time. As it is a direct tax, added to the cost of purchases, the government can use it to regulate demand on the home market.

Look at the following table (assuming VAT to be 10 per cent):

(a) Purchase price		(b) Selling price before VAT	(c) VAT liability	(d) VAT credit	(e) VAT paid
£		£	£	£	£
0	Farmer sells to manufacturer	100	10	–	10
110	Manufacturer sells to wholesaler	200	20	10	10
220	Wholesaler sells to retailer	250	25	20	5
275	Retailer sells to consumer	300	30	25	5

Thus the consumer will pay £330 for this commodity [(b) + (e)]. Note that tax is calculated by charging 10 per cent on the selling price but deducting tax already paid. The cost of the article to the consumer will therefore include the total tax of £30 paid by each stage of instalments.

ADVERTISING

The main aim of advertising is to increase the demand for a firm's product and therefore improve its profits. There are, however, a few exceptions to this – the government, for instance, finances anti-smoking advertising in an attempt to reduce demand for cigarettes because of health risks.

The two main types of advertising

Persuasive advertising attempts to persuade people to buy particular products. Various techniques may be used. For example the use of pretty girls to advertise cars, tobacco or alcohol, special ingredients in washing powders or toothpastes, point of sale displays, etc.

Information advertising gives more precise information as regards price, size and technical performance of a product or service. It gives useful information, e.g. advertisements for a film showing at the local cinema, or for a holiday abroad.

Methods of advertising

1 Newspapers The main medium for advertising – includes both national and local daily or weekly newspapers and also magazines and trade journals.

2 Television Very expensive and confined to the Independent Broadcasting Authority and Channel 4. The 'commercial break' is an important form of advertising especially at peak viewing times. Advertising on commercial radio is also important but is more local in character.

3 Circulars and catalogues These are delivered to people's homes and can be wasteful as many people may have no desire to purchase the particular commodity.

4 Posters These aim to give a vivid impression of a commodity or service and are useful in reminding people of their existence.

5 Vans and lorries of the firm may also carry advertisements, along with most other forms of transport in the public sector.

Can you think of any other forms of advertising?

There are various ways in which a firm may wish to promote its products. These include periodic sales, special offers, competitions, window displays, use of plastic bags and mechanical/electrical devices.

Advantages of advertising

1 It creates employment for people involved in the advertising business.

2 Successful advertising increases demand for a commodity. It can then be produced on a large scale and the economies of scale can be enjoyed, reducing cost per unit and prices. Mass production techniques can be employed.

3 Informative advertising gives consumers the information with which they can make a more rational decision. It also promotes competition between firms.

Disadvantages of advertising

1 It may be a waste of money. A great deal of scarce resources and much money are allocated to advertising. These could be used to actually produce the commodity or to spend on improving its performance.

2 The costs of advertising have to be paid for by the consumer therefore the price of the product itself is greater.

3 Consumers are not usually able to make rational decisions because much persuasive advertising uses subtle techniques. It may induce people to buy a particular commodity that they cannot afford.

4 It reduces competition. The largest firms can afford the most advertising. Assuming this to be successful then smaller firms will lose ground and may eventually go out of business altogether. Monopolies or near monopolies may result.

Advertising has now become a necessary cost to most successful products. It is estimated that over £5,000 million is spent annually on advertising in this country. There are of course certain products excluded by law from being advertised. Nevertheless the *Advertising Standards Authority* is directly concerned in the maintenance of acceptable standards in all forms of advertising throughout the UK.

Consider the following typical questions:

6 ▶ Describe the main forms of advertising and state why you think advertising may decrease or increase the costs of goods advertised.

The main forms of advertising have been described in this section but you should also include other examples such as outdoor signs, handbills, free samples, telephone canvassing, etc. The second part of the question can be answered either way – advertising does increase the cost of goods because it is expensive, creates monopolies and takes up valuable resources. But it can also be argued that advertising reduces the cost of goods since it allows mass production and economies of scale. It can also be said to increase competition between firms.

7 ▶ 'Most of the money spent on advertising is wasted.' Discuss this statement and state what steps may be taken by the advertiser in an attempt to make advertising more cost-effective.

8 ▶ (*a*) Give an account of the way in which successful advertising is organised.

(*b*) The manufacturer pays for an advertisement but manufacturer, retailer and consumer may all benefit from advertising. Is this statement totally correct?

MC6. Choose the statement about advertising that is untrue.

A advertising always raises the retail price of goods
B people can be misled by advertisements
C an advertiser cannot say anything he likes about his product
D some advertising is informative, and serves a useful purpose to people other than the advertiser
E it must agree with certain standards

MC7. Retailers often advertise their products by offering

A a free gift with every purchase of all goods
B special price reductions at certain times of the year
C an article sold at any inflated price to attract customers
D advertisements in the *Financial Times*
E the services of their competitors

CREDIT AND HIRE PURCHASE

This topic is a favourite with examiners and all aspects should be known thoroughly.

THE MEANING OF CREDIT

Credit is often granted in the business world and it reflects confidence in a person's ability to pay sometime in the future for the commodities immediately provided. This is known as trade credit.

Credit may be granted in the form of a verbal agreement between businessmen and payment is not forthcoming until later. Other agreements may be in writing. A Bill of Exchange is a good example and actual payment may take place many months after the sale depending upon the agreement. Commercial banks also give credit in the form of loans and overdrafts, whilst finance houses lend money to consumers enabling them to buy consumer durables such as cars, record players and washing machines. Credit agreements are important in providing evidence of debt which in addition to bank loans and hire purchase, include credit sales, leases, rental, contract hire.

The creation of too much credit is often critizised for providing too much purchasing power and contributing to inflation. This aspect is dealt with on page 194 together with government attempts to restrict credit. We shall now examine the main types of agreement.

HIRE PURCHASE

A student of commerce is not expected to study law to any great extent. There are, however, certain legal principles involved in credit and credit sales. They are as follows:

1 Hire purchase usually requires the initial payment of a deposit, the customer receiving the commodity immediately. He or she agrees to pay the balance, plus interest and service charges, by regular instalments – either weekly or monthly for a stated time.

2 The retailer often cannot afford to finance the transaction and may act as an agent for a finance house which will grant the required credit direct to the consumer.

3 The commodity is legally the property of the seller or finance company until the last instalment has been paid. Thus the instalments can be regarded as hire payments and in some cases such as the non-payment of instalments the commodity can be reclaimed by the seller or finance company.

4 A customer who signs an agreement at his or her home can cancel it within five days in the case of a change of mind. This does not apply to agreements signed elsewhere.

5 A customer who no longer wishes to pay the remaining instalments can cease payment and return the commodity to the seller providing at least 50 per cent of the purchase price has been paid.

6 Where the customer has paid more than one third of the payments the commodity can only be claimed by the seller or finance company through a Court Order.

7 The cash sale price and the hire purchase price must both be stated separately on the agreement in order that the customer may calculate the additional costs involved.

The government may wish to control the amount of hire purchase available at any one time since credit may increase demand and contribute to inflation. In order to do this it may increase the amount of deposit required, increase the interest rate or shorten the period of repayment. Any, or all, of these measures should discourage consumers from entering into hire purchase agreements thus reducing demand. This may also control output on the home market, reduce imports from abroad or divert home produced products towards the export trade.

CREDIT SALES

This is another type of credit offered to customers – note the differences between this agreement and hire purchase agreements.

1 The customer receives the commodity upon payment of the first instalment.
2 The commodity is the property of the purchaser after the payment of the **first** instalment.
3 Payment of further instalments is agreed at regular intervals.
4 If the customer refuses or is unable to pay further instalments the commodity cannot be claimed back by the seller or finance company. Instead it must sue the customer in a Court of Law for the outstanding amount.
5 This method of credit is frequently offered in place of hire purchase when the commodity would not be worth reselling. For instance clothes, carpets, car tyres.

Conditional sales agreement

Similar to hire purchase but the sale of the commodity is conditional upon the instalments being completed. On completion of all payments the purchaser is charged a nominal amount (usually £1) for cancellation of agreement and transfer of ownership into purchaser's name.

Lease, contract hire or rental

Legally this is not a sale since the commodity rarely becomes the property of the person renting. The customer rents or leases the commodity for a period of time making regular payments for the privilege of its use. This type of agreement is found where the commodity is very expensive or depreciates rapidly in value such as lorries and builders' equipment. It may also be used by firms where certain tax advantages occur.

ADVANTAGES OF HIRE PURCHASE

To the seller and manufacturer

1 It increases the sales of commodities which are expensive to purchase in one lump sum. For instance motorcars and televisions sell in much greater numbers when payment is spread over a number of months than if full payment is required immediately on sale.
2 Stock is turned over constantly, avoiding the risks of damage and changes in fashion.

To the consumer

1 He or she enjoys the use of the commodity whilst paying for it.
2 It is easier to pay by regular instalments than attempting to save the full amount in order to pay in cash.
3 The purchaser is in a strong position should the commodity prove faulty.

To the finance company

The finance company finds hire purchase to be a very profitable form of business. The interest rates charged for the finance is usually higher than that charged by banks for bank loans. In addition a commission is charged on the sale as well as a small transfer fee at the completion of payment.

DISADVANTAGES OF HIRE PURCHASE

To the seller

1 If the seller has to take possession of the commodity in the event of non-payment, it may not be worth reselling because of its poor condition.
2 There may be a considerable amount of time and expense involved in suing a customer for the return of goods in a Court of Law.

To the consumer

1 Some may be tempted to enter into too many hire purchase agreements and may not be able to afford the instalments.
2 The purchaser is charged a high rate of interest and commission adding a substantial amount to the overall cost.
3 The purchaser is not in such a good bargaining position when purchasing the commodity by this method compared to cash payment when he or she may be able to claim a discount for cash or preferential treatment.

To the finance company

The disadvantages to the finance company are much the same as those facing the seller.

THE CONSUMER CREDIT ACT, 1974

This Act was introduced to protect the consumer from any malpractice as regards consumer credit. The following are points to note:

1 The upper limit of value of goods covered by this Act is £15,000. There is a lower limit on credit sales agreements of £50.
2 There must be a declaration of cash price.
3 The memorandum available in writing should contain such information as a statement of cash price and total hire purchase price, instalment particulars, list of commodities and a notice of the consumer's rights.

4 There are rights to cancel the agreement if signed on business premises or if signed elsewhere, e.g. at home, but the cancellation must take place within five days.
5 The consumer may terminate the agreement after 50 per cent of the total price is paid.
6 There is a restriction on the seller's rights to retake the commodity (see page 75).

MC8. If a washing machine costing £240 is bought for three monthly instalments of £80 each, this is
A a credit sale and the machine is mine immediately
B a hire purchase transaction, and the machine is not mine until the payments are completed
C legal, but I must not sell until I have finished paying for it
D illegal, since there must be a deposit at the time of purchase
E none of these

MC9. If the government decreases the minimum deposit required for hire purchase, the number of hire purchase transactions is likely to
A create unemployment
B remain the same
C decrease
D be uncertain
E increase

MC10. Under a hire purchase contract the purchaser must receive
A a written guarantee
B a copy of the contract
C free maintenance of the goods
D a copy of the hire purchase company's profit and loss account
E none of these

MC11. During the period of a hire purchase agreement, the goods legally belong to
A the buyer
B the government
C the person who has possession of them
D the owner of the shop from which they were purchased
E the hire purchase company

Consider the following questions:

9 ▶ What is the meaning of the term 'hire purchase'? Describe
(*a*) the advantages; and
(*b*) the disadvantages of hire purchase to buyers.

10 ▶ Consumers who purchase on instalments are protected by law:
(*a*) as to the total price paid;
(*b*) as to the place where the purchase is made;

(*c*) as to the right of the seller to repossess the goods.

Summarise these rules on behalf of one of your customers.

11 ▶ Account for the expansion of the hire purchase system of purchasing goods during recent years. Are there any disadvantages to this method of selling goods?

In accounting for the expansion of hire purchase you should outline the advantages to sellers, consumers and finance companies. Then set out the disadvantages to all parties involved, i.e. the seller, the consumer and the hire purchase company. Also mention that too much hire purchase can cause inflation and needs to be restricted by government legislation. Alternatively, the government may encourage credit buying in order to boost a flagging economy.

CONSUMER PROTECTION

In recent years selling and advertising have become more sophisticated with the result that consumers have increasing difficulty in anticipating the quality or reliability of a product. The consumer needs protection from advertising which may distract him or her from real needs. It is for these reasons that the consumer is protected by government legislation and by both government and independent agencies.

LEGISLATION PROTECTING THE CONSUMER

Below is a brief summary of the principal Acts of Parliament designed to protect the consumer:

Sale of Goods Act 1893

1 Amended by the Supply of Goods (Implied terms) Act, 1973 and the Fair Trading Act, 1973.
2 The shopkeeper undertakes that the goods sold are of merchantable quality.
3 The goods must be fit for the purpose for which they are normally used.
4 The goods must meet the description applied to them.

If any of these conditions fail to be met, the retailer has broken his or her agreement or contract with the customer and the customer is entitled to return the goods for replacement or a refund of the money paid.

These legal rights cannot be taken away from the customer, and do not depend on any guarantee given with the goods. If the goods are faulty it is the *seller's* responsibility to put things right. There is no point therefore in the seller recommending the buyer to contact the manufacturer. However, the customer will not be entitled to a refund if he or she examined the goods before buying them and should have seen that they were faulty, or if the faults were pointed out at the time of sale or sold at an auction.

Food and Drugs Act, 1955 and 1956

It is an offence to describe food falsely, or to mislead people about its nature, substance or quality (including nutritional value). This Act is designed to ensure that premises selling food are both clean and hygienic. Ingredients must be shown on packets or jars together with the name and address of the packer or labeller.

Consumer Safety Act, 1978

Gives the Home Secretary power to regulate sale of goods which may be unsafe or cause death or serious injury. Numerous regulations have been made in this context including electrical appliance colour codes, safety of carrycot stands, electric blankets, oil heaters, fireguards and lead content in pencils and paints.

Weights and Measures Act, 1963 and 1979

The weight, or some indication of quantity, must be marked on certain packets. This affects meat, fish, cheese, sausages and other prepacked foods. It is an offence to give short weight or inadequate quantities or to mark goods with a wrong indication of their amount. Local Authorities are responsible for enforcement and that traders' scales, weights and measures are accurate and readily seen by the consumer.

Trade Descriptions Act, 1968 and 1972

It is an offence for goods or services to be inaccurately described. In addition some types of price reductions carried out by disreputable firms are against the law. In order to comply with the law a trader wishing to display a price reduction must have offered the goods at the higher price for at least twenty-eight days in the previous six months. Local Authorities are empowered to enter premises in order to enforce this during normal shopping hours.

Unsolicited Goods and Services Act, 1971

It is an offence to demand payment for goods which have been sent to people who have not requested, or ordered them. If a consumer receives goods in this way and does not wish to keep them it is the sender's responsibility to retrieve them within the next six months. If the sender does not collect the goods, they become the receiver's absolute property and can be used or disposed of as if they were a gift.

Consumer Credit Act, 1974 (see page 77)

This Act is concerned mainly with credit provision and hiring facilities. It includes:

1 The licensing of all business concerned with credit or hire transactions.

2 The prohibition of canvassing for business outside the usual trade premises of the business unless the customer specifically requests information.

3 A requirement that the consumer should be advised of the true annual rate of interest on any loan.

The Prices Act, 1974

Requires prices or unit prices to be marked on goods offered for sale and also the price at which they are commonly sold, if this is different. Other Acts of Parliament connected with protection of the consumer include the Restrictive Trade Practices Act, 1976, the Estate Agents Act, 1979, Competition Act, 1980, Access to Information Act, 1985, Data Protection Act, 1987, in addition to the appropriate directives of the Health and Safety Executive, etc.

PROTECTION BY GOVERNMENT AGENCIES

The Office of Fair Trading

This government department is mainly responsible for protective legislation dealing with laws affecting consumers concerning trading practices, consumer credit, mergers and anti-competitive matters. It also:

1 publishes information for consumers so that they may be aware of their legal rights and whom to consult for advice;
2 encourages trading organisations to prepare and publish voluntary codes of practice which member firms accept (e.g. for dealing with complaints);
3 proposes new laws to stop unfair trading methods;
4 tracks down persistent offenders and, if necessary, takes them to court.

The Department of Trade

Responsible for general policy towards many aspects of trade including legislation affecting patents and company legislation. Works in close collaboration with the Office of Fair Trading, being responsible for competition and consumer affairs. It also has an interest in respect of **policy** on consumer credit and safety, quality assurance, weights and measures.

The Ministry of Agriculture, Fisheries and Food

Responsible for enforcing proper standards especially in connection with the Food and Drugs Act. Slaughterhouse cleanliness, the use of fertilizers and chemicals are included in the Ministry's concern. The Ministry is also responsible for administration of the EC common agricultural and fisheries policy in addition to national standards of food quality, hygiene, labelling and advertising.

The Department of Health and Social Security

Concerned with the Food and Drugs Act in relation to food hygiene. Local Authorities undertake much of the work, such as inspecting shops and restaurants.

The Department of the Environment

Responsible for controlling the conditions in which people live and work. In close contact with Local Authorities on such matters as pollution, sewerage, water supply, land use, inner city areas, etc.

The Home Office

Responsible for safety requirements of many consumer goods and control over dangerous drugs and poisons, in addition to general policy on shop licensing laws.

Local Government

Trading Standards and Consumer Protection Departments investigate complaints from the general public and advise traders, etc., where possible breaches of the law may occur.They are particularly concerned with matters relating to Trade Description and Consumer Protection.

INDEPENDENT ORGANIZATIONS

The Consumer's Association

The largest private organisation of its kind in the country. It buys, compares and tests all manner of goods and reports on services, publishing its findings as to product performance, quality and cost in its monthly magazine *Which?* It finances its organisation through members' subscriptions.

The Citizens Advice Bureaux

A 'walk-in' service with independent, confidential, free help and guidance. Deals with any inquiry, e.g. health, housing, legal, social and consumer problems. It can act as a 'referee' between consumer and trader.

British Standards Institution

Financed by voluntary subscriptions and a government grant. Concerned with setting up standards acceptable to both manufacturer and consumer. Goods reaching the required standard are given a 'kite' mark which is the trade symbol of the BSI.

Consumer consultative councils

These advise the boards of nationalised industries and consist of representatives of consumer interests (see page 120).

MC12. *Which?* is a magazine circulated mainly for the purpose of

A advertising new consumer goods
B providing consumer protection
C promoting new and yet untried products
D recommending home produced products
E controlling home expenditure

You can expect examiners to set questions on consumer protection. Consider the following:

12 ▶ Briefly describe how:
(*a*) the Advertising Standards Authority; and
(*b*) the Trade Description Acts
protect the interest of consumers.

13 ▶ Outline briefly the ways in which Parliament attempts to control the advertising, price and health and safety aspects of products sold to the public.

14 ▶ What are consumer associations? Describe the work and purpose of independent consumer associations and given an account of any modern developments of these associations.

15 ▶ Consumer protection has been slow of growth but is now extensive. What are the chief ways in which consumers are protected?

16 ▶ Explain the arrangement and financing of hire purchase transactions and show how they differ from credit sales. What are the advantages of hire purchase to both retailer and customer?

Answers to multiple choice questions

MC1	B	**MC7**	B
MC2	C	**MC8**	A
MC3	E	**MC9**	E
MC4	B	**MC10**	B
MC5	D	**MC11**	E
MC6	A	**MC12**	B

The following advertisement appeared in a national newspaper

FOR SALE

Detached house near cliff edge
Large garden – freehold
View any time
ENQUIRIES PHONE 987654

(*a*) What important details are missing?
(*b*) What is meant by freehold?
(*c*) Would this advertisement come under the Trades Description Act if
(i) the property was being sold through an estate agent;
(ii) it was being sold privately?

FIRMS IN PRIVATE ENTERPRISE

CONTENTS

The British economy is a **mixed economy** in that it is made up of two types of industries, those which are owned by private individuals and those owned by the state. You must be aware of this fundamental and important distinction and be prepared for questions which require comparison of the different aspects of **private** and **public enterprise** – often called the private and public sectors.

This chapter concentrates on private enterprise; public enterprise will be dealt with in Chapter 6. The discussion will take the form of:

1 An examination of **each type of private enterprise** business in respect of such distinguishing features as raising capital, disposal of profits, ownership and control, their advantages and disadvantages.
2 An examination of the trend towards **increasing size** of firms, illustrating the advantages and disadvantages of large and small firms. Integration and conglomerates.
3 An examination of where firms and industries are geographically located, factors influencing location and government regional policy.

TYPES OF BUSINESS IN PRIVATE ENTERPRISE

All firms in the private sector have one objective: to make profits.

SOLE TRADERS OR PROPRIETORS

The **sole trader** is a one-man business, for example, some retail shops (newsagents, greengrocers, etc) and window cleaners. Sole traders are found particularly in the areas of business where a personal service is desirable, or quick decisions need to be made.

Advantages

1 They keep all the profit for themselves.
2 They are their own boss and have independence.
3 They are able to make quick decisions.
4 They provide a personal service for customers.
5 They enjoy the economies of small-scale production.

Disadvantages

1 They are often not able to take holidays and there may be problems if they are ill.
2 There is no limited liability (see page 92).
3 They cannot enjoy the advantages or economies of large-scale production.

The raising of capital Money is needed to buy equipment for the running of the business. The sole trader could raise this from his own savings, with loans from relatives or friends, by 'ploughing back' profits into the firm, or by small bank loans.

PARTNERSHIPS

If a sole trader wishes to expand the firm he or she may form a partnership. There are two types – an **ordinary** (or **general partnership**) and **limited partnership**.

THE ORDINARY PARTNERSHIP

An ordinary partnership usually consists of between two and twenty partners. However where large amounts of capital investment or expertise are required, e.g. accountants' practice, more than twenty partners are permitted.

Advantages

1 Partnerships can usually raise more capital than sole traders.
2 The different partners can contribute different skills and experience.
3 Business affairs still remain private.

Disadvantages

1 They do not have **limited liability** (see below).
2 They still tend to be quite small and cannot enjoy the economies of large-scale production.
3 All the partners have to be consulted when decisions are made.
4 Profits have to be shared (usually equally unless otherwise stated).
5 Decisions are binding on all partners.

THE LIMITED PARTNERSHIP

This consists of between two and twenty partners with limited liability. However, at least one partner in a limited partnership must be a general or ordinary partner. This means that he or she will not have limited liability and will therefore carry the full burden of paying off debts, even out of personal belongings if the partnership fails. Limited partnerships are not popular nowadays except perhaps in France. Most firms if they wish to raise capital will form a **private company** (see page 92).

Advantages

1 Because the limited partner has limited liability that partner is taking less of a risk and therefore may contribute more capital.
2 He or she still takes a share in the profits.

Disadvantages

1 Only the general partners have a say in the running of the part-

nership and making decisions. ('Sleeping' partners take no part in decision making but still enjoy a share of the profits.)

2 The limited partners' share of the profits will probably be less because they are taking less of a risk.

3 The limited partners are unable to withdraw even part of their capital unless the general ordinary partners agree.

Partnerships are most evident in the professions, e.g. doctors, dentists, barristers and solicitors, because the rules of the professional bodies (British Medical Association, the Law Society, etc.) prohibit their members from forming themselves into private limited companies. They may however be found in a wide area of business including estate agents, jobbing builders, etc.

Because there are so many variations it is advisable that every partnership is controlled by a formal document known as a **Deed of Partnership** signed by all partners. This will contain details relating to the business as a whole and include matters such as capital structure, division of profits, duties of partners, etc. In cases of dispute therefore reference can easily be made to this source.

THE CO-OPERATIVE MOVEMENT

In Britain there are two broad types of co-operative societies:

I CONSUMER CO-OPERATIVES

(a) The Co-operative Retail Societies

This dates back to the 'Rochdale Pioneers' of 1844 when a group of people in that Lancashire town co-operated together to buy goods in bulk. These were then sold to consumers in the area at prices below those charged elsewhere. This important principle can still be seen today in the co-operative movement, there being about a hundred and twenty separate societies in the country with some ten million members.

Raising of capital An important aspect of the movement is its open membership. The share lists never close and shares (usually of £1 denominations) may be purchased by anyone. There is however a maximum share ownership but whatever the holding a shareholder is only entitled to one vote per resolution at meetings. Further important points include:

1 Shares may be redeemed at their face value – their purchase price – as and when required.

2 The liability of all members is limited.

3 The shares are not sold on the Stock Exchange, share certificates are not issued, and they can only be purchased at the local societies.

Disposal of profits A proportion of available profits are ploughed back into the business, the remainder being distributed amongst the members in proportion to their purchases. This used to be by way of 'dividend stamps' which may be later redeemed for cash though these are being phased out for lower prices and special offers (see page 43).

Ownership Each of the retail societies has a separate existence although some have **merged** to form a larger unit known as the **Co-operative Retail Services Ltd** in order to reap the benefits of large-scale enterprise. Nevertheless each society is owned by its members who are able to appoint its own Committee of Management.

(b) The Co-operative Wholesale Society (CWS)

This was formed in 1863 to supply retail societies with products for re-sale. Today the retail societies purchase about two thirds of their supplies from this source – the remainder from the private and public sectors. Other activities of the CWS include:

1 manufacturing their own goods and food products;
2 farming both in this country and overseas;
3 travel agencies and hotels, printing, publishing, laundries, etc;
4 controlling the operation of CWS based banking and insurance offices;
5 assisting the retail societies by undertaking national advertising campaigns, research projects, etc.

Control of the CWS is in the hands of the retail societies themselves. They contribute most of the capital and elect the Board of Directors. Their voting power is proportional to the value of their purchases from the CWS.

Changes in the co-operative movement over recent years include:

1 less emphasis and concentration on food sales and a move to other areas of retailing;
2 a growth through amalgamations of larger societies in order to compete on a more equal footing with the other large retail organisations, hypermarkets, etc;
3 a greater amount of local and national advertising – particularly through the press and television;
4 the introduction of modern retailing to members and non-members.

II PRODUCER CO-OPERATIVE

These are less numerous than consumer co-operatives. In this form of co-operation it is the employees who provide the capital and take the risks. The company is owned by the workers who provide the capital and profits are shared. There have been numerous schemes set up in recent years with varying degrees of success, varying from motor cycle production to light engineering. Government assistance and tax incentives have played an important part in start-up schemes. This type of co-operation is more widespread on the Continent.

MC1. A retail co-operative society
A sells only to members of the society
B is controlled by the CWS
C sells only goods provided by the CWS
D pays a dividend in some form or other on most sales to members of the society
E issues shares on the Stock Exchange

MC2. Co-operative retail societies pass on their profits to
A their customers
B their employees
C their directors
D the CWS
E their bankers

You should consider the following question which compares retail co-operatives with a public company. Public companies are **public joint stock** companies which are dealt with in detail on page 92.

1 ▶ (*a*) What are the special features of a co-operative retail society?
(*b*) Why has the number of retail societies declined?
(*c*) How have the retail co-operatives benefited from this reduction in numbers?

In order to answer this question the special features which should be mentioned include:

(*a*) How the retail society raises capital: shares worth £1; maximum holding allowed; shares cannot be sold on the Stock Exchange but can be redeemed at face value from local society when required. The way in which the society disposes of profits: interest payments; some ploughed back; rest returned to members according to amount of their purchases.

(*b*) Ownership and control: member ownership; only one vote irrespective of capital invested; elect own committee of management; democratic control.

(*c*) Number of societies declined because of rationalisation, amalgamations and changes in pattern of retailing. Expansion of large organisations including Sainsbury's, Tesco, etc., led to greatly increased competition: smaller societies unable to compete, therefore tendency to amalgamate with neighbouring society or societies. Also change in shopping habits of present-day consumer who is more mobile, 'bargain orientated', and has less loyalty to a particular store or shop than previously.

(*d*) Present retail societies increasingly enjoy benefits of economies of large-scale units, greater efficiency in buying, growth in number of superstores and hypermarkets.

2 ▶ (*a*) (i) Explain how a retail co-operative society obtains its capital.
(ii) How is the profit disposed of?

(iii) How is the business managed?

(*b*) (i) What are the functions of a co-operative wholesale society?

(ii) Who are its members?

Although firms such as sole traders and partnerships are numerous within the economy another important type of firm is the **joint stock company**.

JOINT STOCK COMPANIES (OR LIMITED COMPANIES)

The distinguishing feature of joint stock companies is that they issue shares and have **limited liability**. This means that in the event of a company going out of business, shareholders will only lose the money they have invested in the company, and not their personal assets. (Compare this with a sole trader or partnership.)

Limited liability is a great advantage to Joint Stock Companies. It enables them to raise more capital since investors are more willing to buy shares in the knowledge that at the worst they only lose their investment and not personal possessions as well.

TYPES OF JOINT STOCK COMPANY

There are two types: a private joint stock company and a public joint stock company. Examiners often refer to these as limited companies, or private companies, or public companies. The latter may also be termed PLCs. (The operations of companies have been affected by the 1980 Companies Act.)

The private joint stock company has five distinguishing features:

1 At least two shareholders with no maximum.
2 Shares are not offered to the public on the Stock Enchange.
3 The transfer of shares can only take place with the agreement of all the shareholders.
4 Smaller but more numerous than public companies – it is often a family-run business.
5 It is free from many of the legal requirements of the public company.

A public company has the following distinguishing features:

1 It must have a minimum of two shareholders – there is no limit to the maximum number.
2 It issues shares to the public on the Stock Exchange.
3 It tends to be larger and not so numerous as private companies.
4 The public company's affairs are public – that is its accounts are filed at Companies House (London or Edinburgh) and it makes an annual report to shareholders.
5 It has the words Public Limited Company or plc after the company's name.
6 The minimum share issue is £50,000.

Advantages of public companies

1 Large amounts of capital can be raised.
2 Each shareholder has limited liability.
3 Shares are easily transferable.
4 There are legal requirements to be satisfied, safeguarding the shareholder.
5 Accounts are made public.
6 It may enjoy economies of scale.

Disadvantages of public companies

1 It suffers the diseconomies and disadvantages of large-scale production.
2 There may be a divorce between ownership and control.

How joint stock companies are formed

The company must prepare the following documents in the interest of shareholders:

The Memorandum of Association This must be sent to the **Registrar of Companies**. It would include:

1 the name of the company, with 'limited' (or plc if public) as the last word;
2 the situation of the registered office;
3 the objects of the company;
4 a statement that liability is limited;
5 amounts of shares and types of shares to be issued.

This Memorandum must be signed by at least two people and they must agree to take shares in the company.

The Articles of Association This would explain how the internal running of the company would be controlled and it would include:

1 the powers of the managing director;
2 how meetings are to be organised
3 how shares are to be issued and transferred;
4 how profit will be divided.

The Memorandum and Articles of Association, together with a statement of authorised capital (i.e. the amount of shares it might issue) are sent to the Registrar of Companies. If all is in order the Registrar will issue a Certificate of Incorporation.

The Certificate of Incorporation Issued by the Registrar of Companies, this recognises the company and gives it permission to begin trading. It must be displayed in the company's registered office.

The Prospectus This applies only to public companies when they are about to set up in business. It invites the public to take shares in the company. A copy is filed with the Registrar. It contains the names and addresses of directors with all details likely to be of interest to investors so that they can assess the prospects of the company.

3 ▶ (*a*) Explain the significance of plc (public limited company) after the name of a business.
(*b*) Discuss the importance of this term to
(i) the company's shareholders; and
(ii) the expansion of the business.
(*c*) What are the main differences between a plc and a private limited company?

The answers would include the following points:
(*a*) The term plc shows that the firm is a public joint stock company with limited liability. You should now explain the meaning of limited liability. The firm is a public company (*not* a public corporation): discuss the main features including the number of shareholders, ownership, control, raising of capital, disposal of profits.
(*b*) (i) Discuss the significance of limited liability to shareholders – the advantages – the ability to buy and sell shares at known (quoted) prices on the Stock Exchange.
(ii) The company will find it easier to raise capital in order to expand. Investors will be more willing to risk their capital.
(*c*) To answer this you need to discuss the distinguishing features of a plc compared with a private company. For instance shares in a plc are bought and sold on the Stock Exchange, plc's tend to be larger (minimum share issue of £50,000), shareholders have to be invited to purchase shares in a private company, the financial affairs of a private company are not so readily available to the general public.

MC3. The word 'limited' at the end of a firm's name means
A it can only carry out certain activities
B shareholders are not liable for paying all the debts of the company
C the capital is limited
D shareholders cannot lose the money they have paid for their shares
E there can only be fifty shareholders

MC4. The capital of a limited company is provided by
A the partners
B the debtors
C the creditors
D the directors
E the shareholders

MC5. An important advantage of the limited company is
A it cannot be sued in law
B it is not bound by any Act of Parliament
C it can have any number of shareholders between two and twenty

D	it continues to exist even though its shares change hands
E	it is owned by the government

MC6. When the public are invited to subscribe to a new share issue information concerning the issue is given in the
A	Memorandum
B	Articles
C	Prospectus
D	Debenture
E	Certificate of Incorporation

4 ▶ Set out in two columns the difference between a private limited company and an ordinary partnership under the following headings:
(*a*)	method of formation
(*b*)	division of profits
(*c*)	inability of the business to meet its debts
(*d*)	death of a member

To answer (note the question requires two columns):
(*a*) An ordinary partnership is formed between *two* and *twenty* partners and a Deed of Partnership is drawn up stating partners' powers and method of profit disposal. A private limited company needs to issue a Memorandum and (if required) Articles of Association, forwarding these to the Registrar of Companies for acceptance and issue of Certificate of Incorporation.
(*b*) Profits are divided amongst the partners – not necessarily in accordance with proportion of capital invested – depending upon Deeds of Partnership. Shareholders dividend share of company profit depends upon amount and type of shares held.
(*c*) A partnership unable to meet its debts would call upon the ordinary partners to settle the outstanding amounts from their personal assets should the capital invested prove insufficient. Shareholders on the other hand have limited liability and in case of company default lose only the capital invested in the now worthless shares.
(*d*) A partnership legally ceases on the death of a partner and a new deed is required. The death of a shareholder has no effect whatsoever on the running of the company as the shares can be either sold privately or passed to the deceased person's executors.

RAISING CAPITAL

In this section we examine the four main ways by which joint stock companies raise capital: issue shares, issue debentures, plough-back of profits, and bank loans.

Shares

There are various types of shares which can be issued but the company must follow the Memorandum of Association. A shareholder may receive a share in the profits depending upon company policy; this reward being called a **dividend**. There are the following types of shares: ordinary shares, preference shares, cumulative preference shares, participating preference shares and deferred or founders' shares. A company may issue different types of shares to attract different types of shareholder and raise more capital. Some investors are cautious and have only a small amount to invest. These people are likely to purchase cumulative preference shares where the risks are less. Other investors are willing to take a risk in their pursuit of big dividends. These people would probably purchase ordinary shares. As well as individuals purchasing shares, the institutions are important purchasers of shares, including banks, insurance companies, investment trusts, pension funds and, indeed, other companies. These are called institutional investors.

Ordinary shares – Advantages

1 In years of very good profits they may achieve large dividends because they do not have fixed interest rates limiting their dividend payment.

2 Owners of ordinary shares are often the only type of shareholder who can vote at the **annual general meeting** (AGM) of the board of directors and shareholders.

Disadvantages

1 They are last in the queue of shareholders when dividends are being paid out.

2 In bad years when only small profits are made the ordinary shareholder may not receive any dividend at all – for this reason ordinary shares are often called **risk capital**.

Preference shares – Advantages

1 The preference shareholder has a claim on profits before the ordinary shareholder.

2 They are fixed interest dividend shares, which is a guaranteed dividend, assuming there is sufficient profit.

Disadvantages

1 They carry fixed interest dividends – this could be a disadvantage when very good profits are made and dividend going to the preference shares is small in relation to that being paid on ordinary shares.

2 Preference shareholders often cannot vote at the AGM and therefore have no say in the running of the company.

Cumulative preference shares – Advantages

(The word cumulative means increasingly adding together.) As for preference shares above. Nowadays all preference shares are cumulative unless otherwise stated; when they do not receive the correct amount of dividend in any one year or years of poor profits they would catch up on these missed dividends eventually in a year of good profits.

Disadvantages

As for preference shares.

Participating preference shares

Their advantages and disadvantages are the same as for preference shares. However, they have the additional advantages of their entitlement to a **bonus** from profits in good profit years and after the ordinary shareholders have received sufficient dividend.

Deferred or founders' shares

These are usually taken up by the founders of the company. They would receive a dividend after all the claims of all the other shareholders have been met. In practice their shares are transferred to one of the other types of shares described above after the company has become established.

Why buy shares?

1 In order to earn a dividend.
2 To gain control of the company by buying the shares entitling the holder to a vote.
3 To speculate – hope that the market price of the share will rise so that it may be sold later at a profit.

Debentures

These are loans to the company mainly from banks and other financal institutions as well as private investors. They carry a fixed rate of interest and this must be paid out whether the company makes a profit or loss. They carry a low risk and are bought by investors who are cautious and looking for not only low, but safe, returns. Like shares, they can be purchased on the Stock Exchange.

5 ▶ (*a*) Name and describe the different types of shares issued by public companies.
(*b*) Explain the advantages of each type of share to
(i) the shareholders; and
(ii) the company.
(*c*) How may shareholders in
(i) a plc and
(ii) a private limited company sell their shares?

Plough-back of profits

When profits are made the company might pay all of these in dividends to shareholders. It could, and usually does, retain some to finance spending on machinery, to provide for further production, employment, etc. This is the most usual way of financing expansion.

Borrowing from the bank

Joint stock companies may be able to raise money by borrowing on a loan account from a bank. They may also be able to borrow on a short-term basis from the bank by going into **overdraft** on their current account. For more details on the loan account, overdraft and current account see the chapter on banking.

MC7. The ordinary shares of a company are known as
A working capital
B equity capital
C reserve capital
D fixed capital
E circulating capital

MC8. A share which carries a fixed rate of dividend is known as
A a debenture
B a preference share
C an ordinary share
D a founder's share
E a gilt-edged security

MC9. Shareholders receive a share of the profits of a company in the form of
A interest
B dividends
C premiums
D rent
E salaries

The final aspect of joint stock companies you need to be aware of concerns who owns and who controls them.

OWNERSHIP AND CONTROL OF A JOINT STOCK COMPANY

The owners of the company are its shareholders. These elect a **board of directors** headed by a **chairman**. The Board may meet regularly and make broad decisions applying to the running of the company. The directors and chairman are often some of the largest shareholders. However, the day-to-day running of the joint stock company may be in the hands of a **managing director**. He need not be a shareholder and is appointed by the Board.

Thus there could be a situation where the owners of the company may not be in day-to-day control of its affairs. Indeed the mass of shareholders may meet only once a year, many not even bothering to turn up, at the AGM. This often leads to a situation where there is a divorce between ownership and control.

Joint stock companies are an extremely important part of the syllabus and you can expect questions to be set on this topic. It has already been noted that a comparison is often required between public companies and public corporations. Sometimes a comparison is also required between joint stock companies and other private enterprise firms.

MC10. The members of the board of a public company are chosen by
A a government minister
B the managing director
C the founders of the company
D the registrar of companies
E the shareholders

6 ▶ (*a*) In what ways does the position of a partner actively involved in a partnership differ from that of a shareholder in a private limited company running a business of the same size?
(*b*) What is the reason why in most partnerships today the partners are either members of the same family or professional people like solicitors and accountants?
(*c*) What resemblance is there between the function of the Partnership Deed and that of a company's Articles of Association?

7 ▶ Consider a business owned by a single proprietor and a business owned by a public limited company.
(*a*) How might each business obtain the necessary capital?
(*b*) How is each business managed?
(*c*) What happens in each case to any profits which are made?
(*d*) The single proprietor may decide to form a private limited company to run his business. Give reasons why he might do so.

8 ▶ (*a*) What is a Memorandum of Association?
(*b*) Name *five* facts a Memorandum of Association would contain.
(*c*) What other documents must a company produce on formation?
(*d*) Which government official authorises the formation of a company?
(*e*) State *three* ways in which public and private companies differ.

HOLDING COMPANIES

An important aspect of ownership and control of joint stock companies which you need to be able to discuss is the **holding company**. These are companies which gain control of other companies. They can do this by gaining over half of the ordinary shares in the other company (known subsequently as a **subsidiary**). Indeed if only a small percentage of ordinary shareholders turn up at the AGM it could be possible to pass resolutions not in the interest of the shareholders in that company, particularly if a few hold a large number of shares.

Reasons for forming holding companies There may be three advantages in forming a holding company:

1 It would allow the firms to achieve the economies of large scale production.
2 It could prevent competition and form a **monopoly**. A monopoly is a firm that dominates an industry and can set prices without fear of competition. This may be an advantage for the company but it may result in high prices for consumers.
3 The firm could through a process known as **rationalisation** close down the loss making sectors and concentrate on those sectors which produce the highest return.

Criticisms of holding companies The most important points made against them are:

1 They could form monopolies which might be against consumers' interests.
2 They can gain control of a whole group of companies for a relatively small amount of money, e.g.
Company A: Capital includes £1 million worth of ordinary shares and debentures worth £1 million. Controls
Company B: Capital includes £500,000 worth of ordinary shares and debentures worth £250,000.
Another company may be able to gain control of Company A by purchasing over half of its ordinary shares for over £500,000. For this amount it could have control of Company B as well.
3 A company may be bought by purchasing over half of its ordinary shares. Then its assets (premises, furniture, machinery) may be sold off – called **asset stripping**. This would create unemployment. Holding companies are required to make clear to the public their control of subsidiaries. Examples of holding companies: Sears (Holdings) plc, Unilever plc, Imperial Chemical Industries Ltd, etc.

THE INCREASING SIZE OF FIRMS

Production is carried on by many firms varying in size from sole trader to huge joint stock companies with thousands of shareholders. The trend has been for firms to become bigger and bigger. Some firms are taken over by others, others amalgamate. It is not unusual for entire industries to be dominated by a few large firms which may monopolise a particular sector of production, e.g.

Banking: Barclays, Lloyds, Midland, National Westminster, The TSB Group, Girobank and the Royal Bank of Scotland.
Vehicle production: Ford, General Motors (Vauxhall), Peugot/Talbot etc.

Some firms may form a **cartel** which occurs when a group of firms get together with the aim of fixing prices and output in a particular industry. They aim to act as a **monopolist** dominating the market thus increasing prices and reducing output against the interest of consumers. A monopolistic situation is often seen as undesirable to the extent that the government has set up the **Monopolies and Mergers Commission** to investigate possible mergers leading to a monopoly. If such a likelihood occurs the government may prohibit such a move.

Both in private enterprise and public enterprise the main reason for the trend toward increasing size has been the economies of large-scale production. You should be fully aware of these economies.

The economies of large-scale production

Internal economies of scale are the advantages which come to a firm as a result of its decision to increase its size. All of these will reduce the costs of production for the larger firms and make its products cheaper to consumers. There are several types of internal economies of scale for you to consider. They are:

Technical economies

1 A greater division of labour.
2 Large and expensive machinery can be purchased. Some machinery is indivisible which means that it can only be used economically with large outputs.
3 Large machines can sometimes cut the costs per unit of output. They cater for a much larger output at only a slight increase in costs. This is called the economy of increased dimensions.
4 Large firms can afford to link processes so that production goes on as efficiently and economically as possible.
5 Large firms can afford to have the right size machinery at all stages of production so that there are no hold-ups.

Financial economies

1 It is easier to obtain large bank loans.
2 The issue of shares and debentures in larger amounts and range is possible.
3 Purchase of goods and materials in bulk (large quantities) at cheaper prices.

Marketing economies

1 Advertising on television or in the national newspapers at home or overseas.
2 Good packaging and free gifts and competitions to help sell the goods – although small firms also introduce such marketing practices.

Research economies

It is possible to afford research laboratories, employ scientists and make grants to universities to develop new and better techniques.

Welfare economies

Large firms can afford good working conditions, canteens and social and leisure facilities for the employees (small firms may also introduce such welfare facilities).

Despite all these advantages of size however, there are disadvantages in being so large, known as the **dis-economies of large-scale production**.

The dis-economies of large-scale production

1 Personal contact with staff and customers is lost.
2 Workers and managers may not work so hard, regarding themselves as being less important in a large firm.
3 There are the disadvantages of division of labour
4 Decision making is more difficult because of the larger management structure of the firm.

Although the trend has been for firms to get larger in recent years, small firms still exist and indeed are more numerous than large firms. This is an important point for you to remember, and the following reasons for the continuing existence of small firms should be considered.

Reasons why small firms still exist

The economies of small-scale production The advantages of being small can be found on page 87 under the 'advantages of the sole proprietor'.

Other reasons In addition to the advantages of small-scale production:

1 they may not be able to raise the capital to expand;
2 demand for the product they produce may be small;
3 they cannot attract the good managers away from large firms;
4 sometimes there is a need to adapt quickly to changes in demand; small firms tend to be found in those industries where quick decisions may have to be made (e.g. in agriculture because of changes in the weather) or where a variety of goods produced is required (e.g. fashion) or where a personal service is needed (e.g. small retail shops).

HORIZONTAL AND VERTICAL INTEGRATION

• Firms may become bigger by amalgamation or integration. There are two forms of integration: **horizontal** and **vertical**.

Horizontal integration Firms may become bigger by amalgamating with other firms which are at the same stage of the same production process. For instance the National Provincial Bank and the Westminster Bank amalgamated to become the National Westminster Bank.

Vertical integration Firms may become bigger by amalgamating with other firms which are at different stages of the same production process. For instance a brewery may own the hop fields and the public houses. Also a chocolate manufacturer may own a cocoa plantation. There are two types of vertical integration:

1 **Backward integration** This occurs when a firm amalgamates with the suppliers of its materials or component parts.
2 **Forward integration** This occurs when a firm amalgamates with those which sell and market its products.

Advantages of integration

1 Achieves economies of scale.
2 May achieve a larger share of the market. Current opinion suggests that this is often undesirable for the consumer.
3 Vertical integration backwards will ensure the firm gets its materials at the right time, in the right place, the right quality and in the right quantity.
4 Vertical integration forwards will likewise ensure the firm can sell its goods at the right time, etc.
5 Integration is likely to prevent suppliers making a large profit.
6 The firms become large so that they can compete with large multinational firms. These are large firms based in many countries of the world, e.g. Ford, IBM, Shell, Beecham, etc.

Disadvantages of integration

1 Large firms suffer from the diseconomies of large-scale production.
2 They may form monopolies which may not be in the consumers' interests.
3 In recent years the performance of large firms has not always been impressive. A feeling may be growing that 'big is bad' and 'small is beautiful'.

CONGLOMERATES (DIVERSIFICATION)

A conglomerate is one in which a firm integrates with others and very often there is no conceivable direct link. The British Match Corporation for example owns Wilkinson Sword, while Lloyds Bank owns a finance house, an estate agent and has interests in subsidiary firms both in this country and abroad. However, with some conglomerate mergers there is often an agreement that enables products to be sold in common outlets (Cadbury Schweppes) or have a common source of materials (Dunlop) or have similar products (Dixons).

Apart from the advantage of achieving the economies of scale, the conglomerate can diversify its product range and not rely on one specific type of goods. This would apply particularly where a firm has already absorbed a large proportion of the available market.

MULTI-NATIONAL FIRMS

These are organisations which are based in many different countries. It is likely that the parent company is based in one country and has subsidiaries in numerous other countries, e.g. Ford, Beechams, General Motors, Unilever, etc. Multi-nationals achieve the economies of large-scale production by having more than one market to satisfy, often with a wide range of products suiting 'local' needs. They are frequently criticised for damaging the 'home firms' and it is possible they may accumulate undesirable political strength in that country. Thus the wealth and power of the multi-national may be used in its own selfish interest with the attendant risk of meddling in a country's politics.

MC11. In which of the following would large scale production *not* be suitable? Where

A a personal service is required
B mass production techniques are used
C large amounts of capital investment is required
D there is a large demand
E standardised production techniques are established

MC12. A tyre company taking control over a rubber plantation would be an example of:

A economies of scale
B a cartel
C vertical integration
D horizontal integration
E diversification

MC13. A multi-national organisation is one which is/has:

A branches in more than one country
B shareholders in more than one country
C nationalised
D based in Britain but employs many nationalities
E based in the European community

9 ▶ (*a*) Give the main features of a multi-national corporation.
(*b*) Why have businesses been developed in this form?
(*c*) How may their existence create problems for national governments?

10 ▶ (*a*) What is the meaning of the term 'economies of scale'? Illustrate your answers with examples.
(*b*) Why do small firms continue to survive?
(*c*) How can firms increase their size?
(*d*) Why do firms increase their size?

THE LOCATION OF FIRMS AND INDUSTRIES

Another type of specialisation (discussed on page 19 – in relation to specialisation by individuals) is regional specialisation. This occurs when certain industries tend to be located in certain regions. There are many examples in the UK, such as the car industry in the West Midlands, textiles in Lancashire and Yorkshire and pottery in Staffordshire. The theory of comparative advantage (costs) determines in which commodities a region should specialise (see page 156).

FACTORS INFLUENCING THE LOCATION OF INDUSTRY

Firms will locate where costs of production per unit of output are at their lowest and where the firm is, as a result, more profitable. There are several factors which the firm will take into account.

1 Transport costs

The firm will want to locate itself where transport costs are at their lowest. Much will depend on the situation of the **market** and **raw materials**. Firms will not want to be located too far away from either their raw materials or their market. However there could be a problem when the raw material is in one area and the market in another.

Material-orientated industries. If the raw material is more expensive to transport than the finished commodity then the firm will locate nearer to the raw materials, e.g. the brick-making industries in Bedfordshire.

Market-orientated industries. If the finished commodity is more expensive to transport than the raw material then the firm will locate nearer to the market, e.g. Ravenscraig steelworks (Scotland) using imported iron-ore.

In some industries it does not matter whether they are located near to the market or the raw material. These are termed 'footloose' industries.

2 Power Supplies

Firms need power to provide heat and light and drive machinery. Before the development of the national grid system, being near a coalfield was very important because coal provided power. This is why many old and traditional industries are located in the coalfield areas of the UK, such as South Wales and Central Scotland. With the development of the national grid, firms can be located anywhere in the UK and yet still receive power.

3 Nearness to Factors of Production

Firms will require land, labour, capital and enterprise in the correct quantity and quality.

4 The external economies of scale

The external economies of scale are those advantages which apply to all firms in the industry as a result of being located in a particular area. The other category of economies of scale is the internal economies of scale discussed on page 101. The external economies of scale are developed over a period of time in a particular region. All firms can enjoy them, but large firms can take advantage of these economies to a proportionately greater extent.

External economies of scale include:

a pool of skilled labour that will develop in a particular area. For instance many workers in the Stoke-on-Trent area are skilled at pottery work;
subsidiary or ancillary firms develop which provide the main industry with components. For instance, in the West Midlands many car-component firms can be found;
local services and educational facilities will develop dominated by the needs of the main industry in the area;
transport and communications systems develop to the advantage of all firms in the area.

5 Inertia

This occurs when a certain area becomes traditionally famous for producing a certain commodity. This tradition will be a factor to take into account by the firm when choosing where to locate.

6 Special factors

There may be special influences on location for industries such as:
climate. This was important in determining the location of textiles in Lancashire and Yorkshire. Cotton needed a damp environment. It is also important in determining the location of agricultural activities;
plenty of cheap, flat land. Important in locating oil refineries;
safety factors. Nuclear power stations need to be located away from the main areas of population;
personal factors. The entrepreneur may have a personal preference for a certain part of the country. It may be, like Lord Nuffield who as William Morris developed Morris cars in Oxford, that the entrepreneur will locate the firm in his/her home town.

7 Government regional policy

The government has developed a regional policy to help regionally depressed areas such as Scotland, Northern Ireland, Wales and Northern England. These are termed the assisted areas. Regional policy is discussed in the next section.

REGIONALLY DEPRESSED AREAS

Government regional policy is an attempt by national government to overcome the economic problems – notably unemployment – to be found in the assisted areas.

1 Where are the depressed areas?

The government differentiates between two types of depressed area: Intermediate areas and Development areas.

Great Britain – Assisted Areas (as defined by the Department of Trade and Industry)

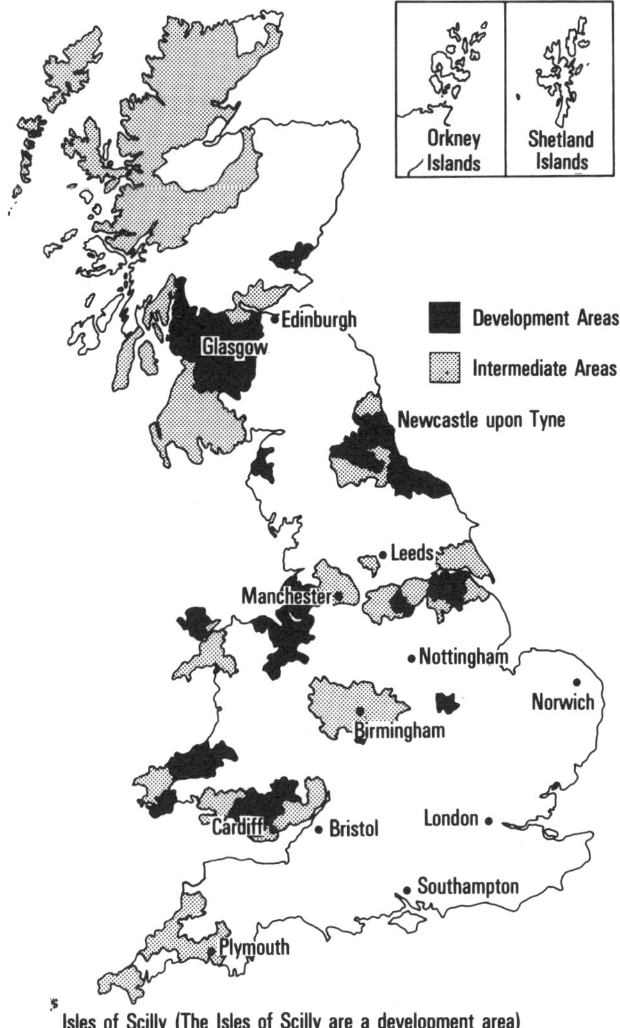

More recently, the government has identified a number of **Enterprise Zones**, which are derelict areas, lacking in industrial development, mainly to be found in Inner City areas. Firms in these zones receive a range of government aid such as simplified planning procedures for factory building, tax allowances and other grants.

2 Why are there assisted areas?

The depressed areas overspecialised in one (or in some cases a few) industry which is now in decline. South Wales concentrated on coal and steel both of which are in decline owing to competition from other countries and from new products. Similarly, the North of England concentrated on textiles, Tyneside and Clydeside on shipbuilding. These old traditional (or staple) industries of coal, shipbuilding, steel and textiles are now in decline and so too are the regions which they previously dominated. This has led to the existence of structural unemployment in the depressed areas, that is unemployment within an industry owing to a lack of demand for the industry's products.

3 What are the problems to be found in the assisted areas?

All of the assisted areas have certain common characteristics. The main problem is one of high unemployment which is above the UK national average. Other problems include a poor regional capital infrastructure (i.e. roads, hospitals, schools,); lower income per head than the national average; an ageing population as young people leave to find work elsewhere; lower levels of educational achievement and a higher level of social problems.

4 Government concern about assisted areas

The government is concerned to do something for these areas not least because there is a waste of scarce factors of production (resources are unemployed) and because of the financial costs of supporting unemployed labour. Of course, there is also a social argument (as opposed to economic) in favour of helping the assisted areas to alleviate the misery and unhappiness which unemployment brings to the worker and his/her family.

GOVERNMENT REGIONAL POLICY

Government regional policy is based on the Industrial Development Act, 1984. Regional policy is an attempt by government to persuade firms to move to the assisted areas, thereby creating jobs and incomes in those areas. This policy is called 'taking the work to the workers'. The policy consists of two different approaches. Firstly, financial inducements to firms to move into the assisted areas such as loans, grants, payment of removal expenses. Advance factories built and provided rent free, and retraining of workers. The main form of assistance is the regional development grant which is available only to those firms operating within development areas. Secondly, measures to persuade firms to move out of so-called growth areas (i.e. the more prosperous areas in the south and south-east of England) such as refusal to allow development of buildings.

The government itself has set a lead to private industry by moving many of its departments out to the assisted areas. For instance the Royal Mint in Llantrisant (South Wales) and National Giro in Bootle (Merseyside). The government has also built new towns, including Washington (Tyne and Wear), Milton Keynes and Telford, to attract firms out of the large urban areas.

Since joining the European Community, in 1973, Britain can also call on resources from the community's regional fund set up to help assisted areas throughout the community.

MC14. Where bulk is decreased during the production of a good, a firm is likely to produce near to
A its source of power
B its source of raw materials
C its market
D good motorways
E component firms

MC15. Which of the following characteristics is common to all the Development Areas?
A levels of unemployment above the national average
B poor transport facilities
C low levels of population
D too much dependence on textiles
E too much dependence on primary industries

11 ▶ (*a*) Select two major industries.
(i) State their locations
(ii) Compare the factors determining their locations.
(*b*) (i) Why and
(ii) how does the government attempt to influence the location of industry?

Data response question 1
Study the passage below and then answer questions (*a*) to (*e*).

Havant plc is one of two toy manufacturers in Portsmouth. The company has capital from investors of £450,000 divided into:

600,000 ordinary shares of 50p each.
100,000 cumulative preference shares of £1 each, attracting 7 per cent return.
£50,000 of loan capital in 6 per cent debentures of £1 each.

After all other payments have been made the company has the following amounts available for distribution to shareholders over a three year period.

Year 1	£9,000
Year 2	£15,500
Year 3	£43,000

The company encouraged by its good performance in Year 3 is considering expanding. There are two possibilities.

1 Take-over Emsworth plc, the other local toy manufacturer.
2 Establish a new toy manufacturing company in a development area over 100 miles away in South Wales.

(*a*) What is the type of integration being considered by the company?
(*b*) What is the main advantage for shareholders of Havant plc of having limited liability?
(*c*) If Havant plc decides to take over Emsworth plc, give two advantages which may be expected.
(*d*) What factors should be considered by the directors of Havant plc when deciding whether to build a new factory in South Wales (a development area)?
(*e*) Calculate how much the debenture holders, cumulative preference shareholders and ordinary shareholders receive in each year.

Data response question 2

The table below refers to changes in the percentage level of regional unemployment in 1982 and 1986.

Region	1982 percentage unemployed	1986 percentage unemployed
United Kingdom	12.1	13.5
South East	8.5	9.9
East Anglia	9.7	10.7
East Midlands	11.0	12.7
West Midlands	14.7	15.5
Yorkshire and Humberside	13.2	15.1
South West	10.6	12.0
North West	14.7	16.3
Wales	15.4	16.9
Scotland	14.0	15.6
North	16.6	18.9
Northern Ireland	18.7	21.0

Source: *Department of Employment Gazette*

(*a*) Define unemployment.
(*b*) (i) Which region had the highest unemployment rate in 1985?
(ii) Which region had the lowest unemployment rate in 1985?
(*c*) How do you account for these regional variations in unemployment?
(*d*) Briefly explain the different types of assistance now available to firms which locate in assisted areas.

Answer

(*a*) Unemployment is now officially defined as all those people who are registered as unemployed and in receipt of unemployment benefits. See page 106 for a detailed definition and criticisms of this definition.
(*b*) (i) Northern Ireland with 21 per cent of the labour force registered as unemployed.
(ii) South East England with 9.9 per cent of the labour force registered unemployed.
(*c*) Some regions have unemployment rates above the national average mainy because of structural unemployment which has

developed into regional unemployment. These regions were dominated by a few industries now in decline because of foreign competition (at home and abroad) and technological innovations. There are few alternative sources of employment in these areas. The problem is compounded by geographical and occupational immobility of labour (see page 108). Refer to specific regions and their particular problems, e.g. the decline of motor vehicle manufacture in the West Midlands.

Other regions have suffered less badly because the newer and more technologically based industries are expanding in these regions, e.g. South East England. These areas are more populated (larger market) and nearer to UK's main markets (i.e. the European Community).

(*d*) You need to discuss the various types of aid available to the Assisted Areas. Make special reference to the Enterprise Zones. The main method of regional aid is the regional development grant. Also include other grants, allowances and help such as advance factories. Differentiate between development areas and intermediate areas – more help is available to development areas.

Answers to multiple choice questions

MC1	D	MC9	B
MC2	A	MC10	E
MC3	B	MC11	A
MC4	E	MC12	C
MC5	D	MC13	A
MC6	C	MC14	B
MC7	B	MC15	A
MC8	B		

THE PUBLIC SECTOR

CONTENTS

In this chapter the following topics will be discussed:

1 What is meant by the **public sector.**
2 Arguments in favour and against **nationalisation** and **privatisation.**
3 How **nationalised industries** raise **capital** and dispose of **profits**: the ownership and control of nationalised industries.
4 **Public sector finance**: taxation, government spending and the public sector borrowing requirement.
5 **Local authorities**: functions, ownership and control, the raising of capital and disposal of profits. Rates and alternatives to rates.
6 **Privatisation.**

WHAT IS THE PUBLIC SECTOR?

The public sector is that part of the company owned by the state and controlled by the government. It is different from the private sector which includes firms and businesses owned by private individuals (or **entrepreneurs**) and which is often called private enterprise. Britain is said to be a mixed economy because it consists of both public and private sectors. Students should be able to compare public enterprise with private enterprise; this is a favourite examination question and will be dealt with later in this chapter.

The public sector includes:

1 Those public services provided by government such as the armed forces, police, education, health and social security services which are run by government departments.
2 Nationalised industries – also termed public corporations or public enterprises, e.g. British Rail. Students should note that examiners may use the terms nationalised industry or public corporation in questions under this heading. The comparison of public corporation and public companies is popular with examiners and is dealt with later in this chapter.

   The following are examples of nationalised industries: *power:* Central Electricity Generating Board; *banking:* Bank of England; *industry:* British Steel Corporation; *transport:* British Rail.
3 Services provided by local authorities.
4 Bodies and agencies set up by the government, e.g. the Monopolies and Mergers Commission and the Office of Fair Trading.
5 The government also has large shareholdings in some public companies, e.g. British Petroleum.

MC1. A public enterprise is distinguished from a private enterprise by whether
A it is making a profit
B it has issued fixed interest capital
C it is owned by more than twenty persons
D it is owned by the government
E it makes a loss

MC2. The main difference between a public company and a public corporation is that:
A the public company is always small, the latter usually much larger
B the former only raises capital through the Stock Exchange, the latter only through the taxpayer
C the former is controlled by the government, the latter by the shareholders
D the former is privately owned whilst the latter is publicly owned
E there is no difference since both organisations are the same

You are probably aware that nationalisation is a controversial topic and people may be strongly in favour of or against state involvement in industry, etc. The purpose of the following section is to outline the most commonly used arguments.

FOR AND AGAINST NATIONALISATION

When an industry is nationalised this does not mean that the holdings of existing shareholders are confiscated. These shareholders are given compensation by the exchange of their shares for government stocks in the newly formed nationalised industry. The main period of nationalisation was between 1945 and 1951 when the Labour government took over the control of coal mines, railways, some British airlines, electricity, gas, steel and some transport. Nationalisation still takes place from time to time but depending upon the type of government in power. There has in recent years been a move towards de-nationalisation or privatisation, e.g. British Telecom.

ARGUMENTS IN FAVOUR OF NATIONALISATION

1 To achieve economies of large-scale production

Nationalised industries tend to be large and can enjoy the advantages of size. For economies of scale see page 101.

2 The 'commanding heights of the economy' argument

Certain industries are very important to the economy, e.g. power, steel, transport and coal. If the government wishes to gain and keep control over the economy then these industries may well need to be nationalised.

3 To avoid private monopolies

One of the disadvantages of private enterprise is that it may lead to a private monopoly. Such a development has disadvantages to the consumer. Prices are said to be higher, output and investment may be of lower quality and there may be no variety or choice open to consumers.

4 Where much capital is needed

Certain industries need to provide millions of pounds worth of specialist buildings and machinery, e.g. a modern steelworks or power station. Private enterprise may not be able to afford such large undertakings for an industry of prime importance to the economy.

5 Certain industries are operated better when organised on a national basis

When railways began in the 1830s they were controlled by over a hunded small companies. This had disadvantages including passengers having frequently to change trains and many different rail gauges, etc. Thus it is better to run railways on a national basis to avoid such inefficiencies. A similar argument applies to electricity, and other service industries such as the Post Office, Bank of England, etc.

6 It may be unwise from the point of view of national security for an industry to be in the hands of private enterprise

The provision of nuclear power should not be in the hands of private individuals or organisations for obvious reasons.

7 Social reasons

The government may wish to nationalise an industry which may have run into financial problems and is in danger of closing down. For instance if well-known firms such as British Leyland (now Austin Rover) and Rolls-Royce Aero-engines (privatised in 1987) were to have closed down this would have caused much undesirable unemployment (and loss of potential export earnings).

8 Political reasons

When in power, the Labour governments tend to be in favour of nationalisation. This is usually part of their political programme which contends that the basic industries should be in government rather than private control.

ARGUMENTS AGAINST NATIONALISATION

1 Political reasons

Conservative governments tend to be against state intervention and nationalisation. Consequently some previously nationalised industries have been returned to the private sector e.g. The National Freight Corporation (now the National Freight Consortium), Sealink (now British Ferries), Amersham International, British Telecom, etc.

2 Nationalised industries suffer from the dis-economies of large-scale production

By their very nature they tend to be big and therefore may suffer from the disadvantages of being too large.

3 Nationalised industries form State or public monopolies

They may suffer from the same disadvantages as private monopolies and because of their size these are more pronounced.

4 Public accountability

Nationalised industries are always in the public eye and their results are investigated by both Parliament and the media. This may make managers over-cautious and therefore decisions will never be exciting or imaginative because of the risks of criticism involved.

THE RAISING OF CAPITAL, DISPOSAL OF PROFITS, OWNERSHIP AND CONTROL

This discusses how nationalised industries raise the capital to carry on business, and in the event of a profit being made it illustrates what in fact happens to that profit. Finally it examines who in fact owns the nationalised industries and how these are controlled.

Students should be aware that questions set requiring a comparison on public and private enterprise (or public corporations and public companies) would require knowledge of this section.

The raising of capital and disposal of profits

The nationalised industries receive their finance from the government. In order to raise this capital the government may sell stocks in the nationalised industries on the Stock Exchange. These usually earn a fixed interest and can be bought by foreign firms and governments as well as British investors. Nationalised industries may also receive subsidies and grants from the government which will be financed out of taxation. Of course, if the industry makes a profit (as many do) then some of this may be 'ploughed back' into the industry. Profits may also be used to pay interest to stockholders or even be paid to the Chancellor of the Exchequer, thus leading to lower taxes than would otherwise exist.

DO NATIONALISED INDUSTRIES MAKE PROFITS?

Nationalised industries do not all make losses. However, there are industries such as Austin Rover and British Rail which tend to make losses more often than profits. On the other hand they do provide employment for many workers whilst other industries and areas of the country depend upon them. They are also often engaged in providing a basic commodity or service essential to the nation as a whole.

Nationalised industries are increasingly under pressure from government to make profits. However this may be frustrated by other objectives of nationalised industries. These are:

1 The social role of nationalised industries

This may require nationalised industries to provide unprofitable services because of public need. For example an unprofitable power station or railway line may be vital to a small community in the Scottish Highlands.

2 The government has other economic objectives

The nationalised industry may be prevented from increasing its prices because this may cause inflation. The industry may also be forced to buy British to 'prop up' another industry, even if it wished to purchase from elsewhere. An uneconomic coal mine may be kept open to prevent increases in unemployment in regionally depressed areas such as South Wales.

Ideally a nationalised industry should be left to be run by its managers. However, management can be obstructed by interference from the government and this may harm its aim to make a profit.

Ownership of nationalised industries

Nationalised industries 'belong' to the government and people. They are organised and controlled, on behalf of the community, by the government through various boards and committees.

Organisation and control

Each nationalised industry is controlled by its Act of Parliament which aims at setting up an organisation most suited to that particular industry.

A Minister (a member of the government) is appointed to control policy. He or she represents the public and is in charge of overall policy applying to the industry and is subject to questions in Parliament.

A board will be appointed by the Minister The board has a chairperson at its head. These Boards are in charge of the day-to-day running of the industry. They are required to submit annual reports to Parliament and an annual debate normally takes place in Parliament to discuss the industry's affairs.

Financial and staffing affairs Boards are free from control but they are expected to pay their way taking one year with another. They employ their own staff and deal directly with trade unions over pay and conditions.

Consumer participation Consumers' councils have been set up to ensure direct consumer participation in the affairs of the nationalised industry e.g. the Transport Users Consultative Committee, the Post Office Users National Council. These consumer members are unpaid and nominated by bodies such as trade unions and local authorities. The councils deal with any complaints by and suggestions from consumers and advise both the boards and minister about consumer views.

Public accountability of the nationalised industries is achieved by the overall control of Parliament and consumer participation.

1 ▶ (*a*) What is a public corporation?
(*b*) How does the position of the chairman of the board of such an industry differ from that of the managing director of a large plc?
(*c*) If heavy losses were made over a long period, in what ways would a public corporation be in a different situation from that of a private enterprise company?

For part (*a*) a brief analysis of the meaning of nationalised industries or public corporations is required. Give examples and discuss how it is set up together with ownership and control and how revenue is raised.

For (*b*) this should mention that the chairman of the board of a nationalised industry is appointed by the responsible government minister whilst the managing director of a large private enterprise company is appointed by the chairman and board of that company. The managing director is the chief salaried employee and may (or may not be) a shareholder. You should mention their responsibilities and powers drawing direct comparisons between the two.

For (*c*) it should be stated that nationalised industries have the backing of government resources, receiving subsidies and grants raised from taxes, etc. A private company however might arrange for the sale of shares or debentures or might obtain a bank loan. In the long term though the company would either have to severely curtail its operations or go into liquidation and sell off its assets. This is unlikely to happen to a nationalised industry.

2 ▶ 'It must be right to press ahead with the transfer of ownership from the state to private enterprise of as many public sector businesses as possible.'
(*a*) What is meant by the public sector of the economy?
(*b*) Why are some industries nationalised?
(*c*) What are the arguments in favour of denationalisation?
(*d*) What arguments can be used against transferring the ownership of public sector businesses to the private enterprise sector?

3 ▶ (*a*) Explain the main differences between a public corporation and a plc in respect of
(i) ownership

(ii) finance
(iii) control
(iv) objectives.

(*b*) What are the advantages of public corporations?

(*c*) Should the size of a public corporation's surplus determine whether or not it has been successful?

(*d*) What advantages might be expected if a previously nationalised industry is privatised?

MC3. A public corporation comes into existence by means of

A registration under the Companies Acts
B a separate Act of Parliament for each one
C A Royal Charter
D a decision made by shareholders of the company concerned
E a national referendum

MC4. The members of the Board of a public corporation are appointed by

A shareholders
B ratepayers
C a government minister
D the registrar of companies
E taxpayers

PUBLIC SECTOR FINANCE (OR CENTRAL GOVERNMENT FINANCE)

Public sector finance refers to government's policies towards taxation and government (or public) spending. This policy is often referred to as *fiscal policy* and can be used to influence the level of demand in the economy.

TAXATION

The principal aims of taxation are to achieve the government's economic and social objectives. The former includes the creation of jobs, control of inflation, the achievement of a balance of payments surplus and the achievement of economic growth. The latter includes the redistribution of income and wealth from the rich to the poor and the development of a welfare state to assist the old, sick and unemployed. Taxation also raises money to finance government spending and can be used to discourage consumption of certain commodities such as alcohol, tobacco, etc.

There are two main types of taxation: direct and indirect.

DIRECT TAXATION

Direct taxation is levied on incomes and includes Income Tax, Capital

Gains Tax, Inheritance Tax and Corporation Tax. Direct taxes are collected by the Inland Revenue.

Advantages of direct taxation

1. It tends to be *progressive* which means that the rich pay a higher percentage of their income than the poor;
2. It tends to be easy and cheap to collect, e.g. Pay As You Earn (PAYE) applies to income tax;
3. It is easy to manipulate to achieve government economic and social objectives, e.g. higher levels of income tax will reduce demand (spending power).

Disadvantages of direct taxation

1. It tends to be a disincentive to work and effort;
2. There is no element of choice – the tax cannot be avoided;
3. It discourages savings and investment.

INDIRECT TAXATION

Indirect taxes are taxes on spending and are collected by the Customs and Excise Department. The most significant indirect tax is Value Added Tax (VAT), see page 71.

Advantages of indirect taxation

1. It can be used to discourage certain spending, e.g. smoking and drinking;
2. Consumers have a choice – they can forego the spending and avoid the tax;
3. It is not a disincentive to hard work.

Disadvantages of indirect taxation

1. It is *regressive*, which means it takes a bigger percentage of poor people's incomes than those of rich people;
2. Certain groups of consumers complain that they are hit hardest, e.g. smokers and drinkers.
3. It may contribute to inflation by raising prices.

GOVERNMENT (PUBLIC) SPENDING

This is the money spent by the government on behalf of the community as a whole, e.g. on defence, education, health, social security, industry and housing. The aims of government spending apart from providing public goods and services are the same as for taxation, as shown by the following statistics.

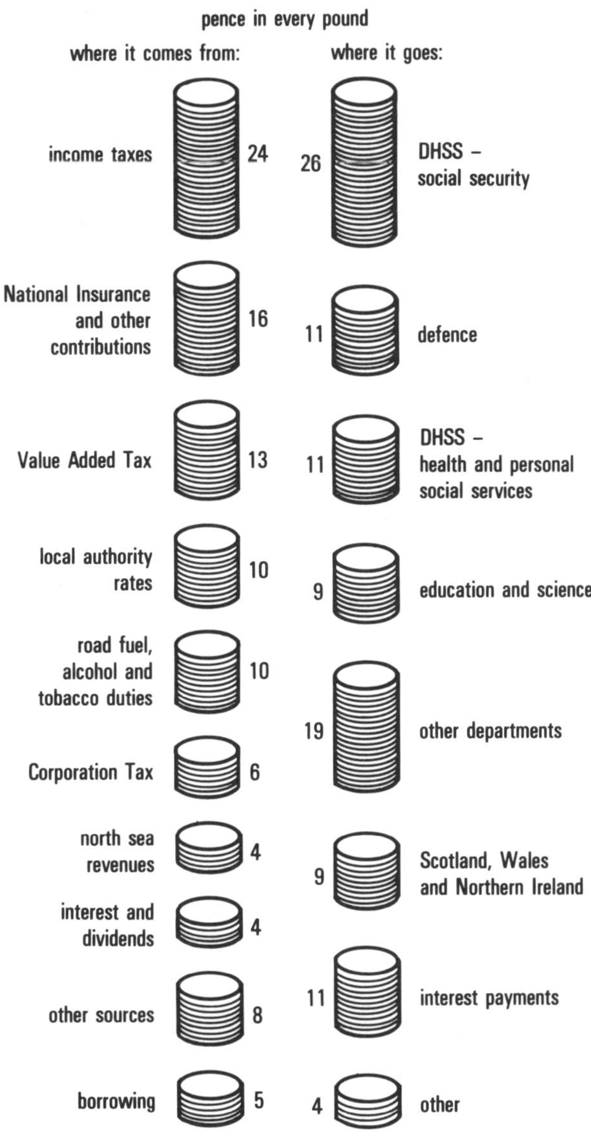

BUDGETARY POLICY

The government could spend more than it receives in revenue from taxation, etc. This is called a **budget deficit** and is financed by borrowing. This borrowing is termed the *Public Sector Borrowing Requirement* (PSBR) and consists of sales of interest bearing debt (gilt-edged securities). The effects of a budget deficit will be to increase demand

and create jobs, incomes and economic growth. However, there is a danger of inflation if the budget deficit is too large.

The government could spend less than it receives in revenue from taxation, etc. This is called a **budget surplus.** It will reduce inflationary tendencies but may cause unemployment and less economic growth.

Every spring the Chancellor of the Exchequer prepares a **budget statement** where changes in taxation, government spending and PSBR are concerned.

Consider the following questions.

4 ▶ (*a*) Why does the government levy taxes?
(*b*) Using examples, distinguish betwen direct and indirect taxes.
(*c*) What are the advantages and disadvantages of both types of taxation?

5 ▶ (*a*) What are the main objectives of public expenditure?
(*b*) Why might a government increase public expenditure?
(*c*) What forms might the increase in government spending take?

LOCAL AUTHORITIES

We have so far considered the role and functions of public corporations which are activities controlled by central government. You should also be aware of the role and functions of local authorities.

Functions

Local authorities consist of city councils and county councils, and for local affairs, borough and district councils. They have responsibility for essential services such as drainage, cleaning, street lighting, recreation, education, police, fire service and roads, etc.

Control

Control is exercised through a committee of council representatives (elected by local people) who in turn employ a full-time official to run affairs on a day-to-day basis. This person will be answerable to the committee for all matters affecting the local authority's undertakings.

Financing

1 Stock They issue stock through the Stock Exchange, borrow from the Public Works Loans Board at low interest rates and also from the London money market and the commercial banks. This provides capital to finance long-term expenditure such as a new road construction or new school buildings.

2 Sales of goods and services Include sea-front trading enterprises, entry fees to swimming pools and municipal golf courses and the hire of tennis courts in public parks. The idea is that those people who use these facilities should pay for or contribute to the cost of their upkeep.

3 Central government grants Central government (Parliament in London) makes grants towards the cost of local authority spending. Additional grants may be made for specific projects or inner city areas having acute social problems.

4 Rates A rate is a tax which is levied by the local authority on the value of land and buildings. Each parcel of land and every building is given a 'rateable value' which is roughly equal to its annual letting value. The local authority calculates how much money it needs from the rates to support its expenditure and it will levy a rate of so many pence in the pound of rateable value, e.g. if the rateable value of a house is £1,000 a rate of 20 pence in the pound is levied, then the householder's annual rate bill will be £200. Note: agricultural land is not subject to rates.

Advantages of rates

1 They provide a stable source of revenue from householders, industry and commerce.
2 It is difficult to avoid payment.
3 Wealthier home-owning citizens pay a higher contribution than those who do not own such property, e.g. tenants.

Disadvantages of rates

1 The household may never use many of the services, e.g. parks and recreational services.
2 Rates vary from area to area depending on the total spending of the local authority and the number of householders, etc., who can contribute.
3 A householder's rates may increase if the property is improved (e.g. by adding a garage or central heating). This may discourage necessary improvements.
4 The present system takes no account of household income. Similar properties in the same area pay the same annual rates yet the income of one household may be many times greater than the other.
5 Rates are often criticised for being an unsatisfactory method of raising revenue. Alternatives however, such as a local income tax, also have disadvantages.

THREE POSSIBLE ALTERNATIVES TO RATES

A local income tax

This could be collected either by the Inland Revenue (through PAYE – see page 122) or by the local authority.

Problems may arise however where a firm's workforce comes from different local authority areas – there will be different levels of local income tax to be paid and deducted by employers through PAYE. It will also add to the 'poverty trap' – i.e. when an employer becomes 'worse off' when receiving a pay rise – being equivalent to an increase in the basic rate of tax. It will discourage people finding jobs. However, compared to the present rating system it will be progressive for those people who are unemployed or very low income earners.

A local sales tax

This may be a percentage tax in addition to VAT (see page 71) but would only be levied at the retail stage (unlike VAT which is levied at all stages). The problems here include the fact that it may be regressive to someone who does not pay rates at the moment or who is a low income earner or unemployed.

Another problem is that it will encourage cross border shopping as consumers in high local sales tax areas go to shop in low local sales tax areas. This will involve a waste of time and energy (petrol, etc) for consumers and in addition the revenues going to the local authority will be difficult to calculate. It will also lead to higher prices (inflation).

A poll tax (or community charge)

In this case every adult in a local authority pays the same lump sum amount of tax. It cannot be avoided but there may be exemptions or rebates for old people and people on social security. However, it can be regarded as regressive and households with many adults will pay more compared to the present system. It may also be difficult to collect from people who frequently change their accommodation.

6 ► (*a*) What are the main differences between the public sector and the private sector?
(*b*) How does central government control and finance nationalised industries?
(*c*) How do these methods differ from those methods employed by local authorities to control and finance local government activities?

To answer part (*a*) discuss the main differences between public sector and private sector enterprises. Note that the question is not a direct comparison between public corporations and plc's. Briefly discuss objectives, raising of revenue, disposal of profits, ownership and control, etc.

Part (*b*) requires an analysis of how central government controls public enterprises through appropriate ministers, appointing the chairman of the board, the annual parliamentary debate and the questioning of the chairman by parliamentary committees. In addition an Act of Parliament lays down in broad outline the 'rules' for operating the public corporation. Finance is directly controlled by central government by means of grants and subsidies, thus a great deal of reliance is placed upon the government of the day for revenue.

Part (*c*) needs a brief discussion of the differences between central and local government control and the ways by which they finance their respective services. A reference to rates and local trading would be required as well as government grants and loans available to authorities at preferential rates of interest.

7 ▶ (*a*) Describe the main features of local authority revenue.
(*b*) Why has there been public criticism about the way in which local people contribute to the cost of local government services?
(*c*) Give two arguments against replacing the revenue from domestic rates by extra central government grants.
(*d*) Discuss one alternative to rates (other than extra grants) as a source of revenue for local authorities.

8 ▶ (*a*) What are local authority enterprises? Give examples.
(*b*) Indicate the main sources of finance for
(i) central government and
(ii) local government.
(*c*) What is the interrelationship between central government and local authority finance?

PRIVATISATION

In 1987 a Conservative government was elected committed to reducing the size of the public sector. This policy included the privatisation of many nationalised industries.

Publicly owned assets which have been sold or are to be sold (as at Summer 1987)

Already sold (in whole or part)		To be sold (in whole or part)
British Petroleum	Wytch Farm (British Gas)	British Shipbuilders
British Aerospace	Enterprise Oil	Royal Ordnance Factories
British Sugar Corporation	Sealink	National Bus Company
Cable and Wireless	Jaguar	BL Unipart
Amersham International	British Technology Assets	British Steel
National Freight Corporation	British Telecom	Water Authorities
Britoil	British Airways	Electricity
Associated British Ports	British Gas	
Inter Airadio	Rolls Royce Aero-engines	
British Rail Hotels	British Airports Authority	

Arguments for privatisation

1 These nationalised industries are returned to competitive market conditions and are driven by the profit motive. This leads to more efficiency. Public monopolies are destroyed.

2 Management is freed from government interference in decision making.
3 As part of the private enterprise sector these industries are able to raise more finance from private investors.
4 Trade unions have in the past treated nationalised industries as a 'soft touch' and have been able to operate restrictive practices and gain high wage increases.
5 The financial burden on the government is reduced because of revenue gained from the sale. The government's public sector borrowing requirement (PSBR) can be made smaller. This means lower interest rates as the government needs to borrow less. See page 123 for an analysis of PSBR.
6 The market mechanism is allowed to operate more freely to allocate resources.

Arguments against privatisation

The Labour party has been opposed to the policy of privatisation and is committed to re-nationalisation where appropriate.

1 Public monopolies are merely being replaced by private monopolies. Thus the problem with monopoly still applies – high prices for less variety and choice of product.
2 Returning these industries back to private enterprise may mean more unemployment as the industry is driven only by the profit motive.
3 It is sometimes said that only the profitable parts of the public sector will successfully be sold to private enterprise e.g. British Telecom.
4 The manner in which the nationalised industries have been sold are often criticised. Some people feel that they have been sold too cheaply allowing private investors large capital gains, e.g. British Telecom and Amersham International.

MC5. Which of the following is more likely to be provided by a local authority rather than a nationalised concern?

A motorways
B power
C railway transport
D education
E postal service

MC6. The major source of capital for a nationalised industry is from

A a commercial bank
B building societies
C shareholders
D overseas investors
E taxpayers

MC7. Nationalisation is best defined as

A taking over a company which is run by foreign nationals
B the acquisition by government of an industry or organisation to serve the interests of the nation as a whole

C the selling of national assets to private entrepreneurs
D government buying shares in private companies
E the conversion of private companies into public companies

MC8. One of the greatest problems of a nationalised business is that
A the government has no control
B they cannot raise capital
C they are always inefficient
D they are too profitable
E workers and managers often lack incentives

MC9. Which one of the following statements is an argument in favour of rates?
A They are one main source of revenue for local authorities
B They ensure an equal level of income to local authorities throughout the country
C They provide local authorities with an independent source of revenue
D They are a progressive form of taxation
E They keep pace with inflation as they increase with property values

MC10. Which of the following is *not* a part of the private enterprise sector?
A sole proprietors
B limited partnerships
C public corporations
D public companies
E private companies

9 ▶ Some people are strongly in favour of the privatisation of the nationalised industries in the UK and of returning them to the private sector of industry and commerce.
(*a*) Distinguish between the public sector and the private sector.
(*b*) Name two previously nationalised industries which have been privatised.
(*c*) Explain what is meant by privatisation.
(*d*) Analyse the likely consequences of privatisation on
(i) prices for the consumer
(ii) Ownership of the company
(iii) the raising of capital
(iv) the disposal of profits
(*e*) Assess the arguments for and against the transfer of public assets to the private sector.

Data response questions

Newspaper extracts on Budget proposals given to Parliament by the Chancellor of the Exchequer.

A cut of one per cent in the basic rate of income tax is the big surprise in this year's Budget.

It comes down from 30 per cent to 29 per cent and the Chancellor promised further cuts next year and the year after with the eventual aim of bringing the rate down to 25 per cent.

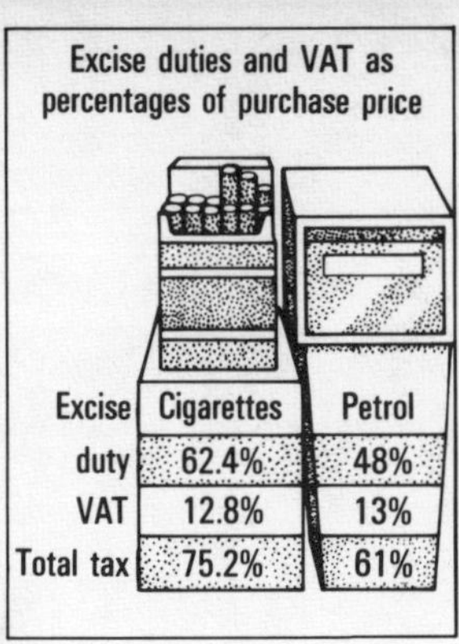

NEW INCOME TAX BANDS

NEW		OLD	
Taxable income		Taxable income	
Up to £17,200	29%	Up to £16,200	30%
£17,201 to £20,200	40%	£16,201 to £19,200	40%
£20,201 to £25,400	45%	£19,201 to £24,400	45%
£25,401 to £33,300	50%	£24,401 to £32,300	50%
£33,301 to £41,200	55%	£32,301 to £40,200	55%
£41,201 and over	60%	£40,201 and over	60%

(*a*) (i) Give one example of a direct tax and one example of an indirect tax referred to in the newspaper extracts.
(ii) Distinguish between direct and indirect taxes.

(*b*) Give two reasons why you think the proportion of tax in the purchase price of cigarettes and petrol is so high. (75.2 per cent and 61 per cent respectively).

(*c*) (i) Explain how the item of 'new income tax bands' indicates progressive taxation.
(ii) Why is Value Added Tax regarded as regressive?

(*d*) Examine the likely economic consequences of a fall in the basic rate of income tax from 30 per cent to 29 per cent.

(*e*) The Chancellor has increased taxation on cigarettes by 11p on a packet of twenty. Examine the likely effects on
(i) cigarette prices
(ii) taxation revenue gained from cigarettes
(iii) employment prospects in the tobacco industry.

Answers

(*a*) (i) Direct tax: income tax (personal tax).
Indirect tax: VAT or excise duty on petrol or cigarettes.
(ii) Direct tax is any tax on income and is collected by the Inland Revenue. Examples include income tax, inheritance tax, capital gains tax and corporation tax.

Indirect tax is any tax on expenditure on goods and services. VAT and any excise duty would be examples. Indirect tax is collected by the Customs and Excise Department.

(*b*) (i) Good revenue raisers because of inelastic demand.
(ii) The government may wish to discourage consumption of these products (for different reasons).

(*c*) (i) Progressive tax is levied when higher income earners pay a greater percentage of tax. The bands illustrate this. High income earners will have higher marginal and average rates of tax.
(ii) Any consumer purchasing a specific commodity will pay the same percentage VAT. However, the tax as a percentage of income will be greater for the poor man than the rich. This illustrates regressive taxation.

(*d*) (i) Higher demand in the economy because people have more money (higher disposable income).
(ii) Reflationary effects on jobs and prices.
(iii) More money spent on imports.
(iv) Stimulates more effort and more motivation.
(v) Reduces the poverty trap.
(vi) Large PSBR.

Of course much depends on the level of government spending and other taxes – the answer assumes that they remain unchanged.

(*e*) (i) Increase price by as much as 11p because of inelastic demand. Most of the tax (if not all of it) will be passed on to consumers.
(ii) Cigarettes are a good tax revenue raiser because of inelastic demand.
(iii) Whilst the demand for cigarettes tends to be inelastic, in the long term there may be some small drop in demand, thus reducing jobs in the tobacco industry.

Answers to multiple choice questions

MC1	D	**MC6**	E
MC2	D	**MC7**	B
MC3	B	**MC8**	E
MC4	C	**MC9**	C
MC5	D	**MC10**	C

TRANSPORT AND COMMUNICATIONS

CONTENTS

There is little doubt that today an economy needs a fast, efficient and cost-effective transport system and it is for this reason that so much of the nation's resources are spent on this sector. Consider the cost of building a motorway, electrifying the rail network, building an airport, etc and furthermore maintaining them all to modern standard.

The following are considered to be the **advantages of transport**:

1 No country in the world need be isolated from other countries.
2 Bulk movement of food, raw materials and finished goods from areas of surplus to areas of shortage is possible.
3 Quick and easy movement of people giving a high rate of personal mobility.
4 Raw materials more easily exploited and new markets for finished manufactures opened up.
5 Different peoples have been brought into contact with each other, fostering friendship and greater understanding.
6 The standard of living for people all over the world has been and is being improved.

There are four major methods of transport to be examined in this chapter: road, rail, water and air.

ROAD TRANSPORT

Between the Roman period in Britain (from approximately AD 65 to AD 400) and the eighteenth century, the condition of roads was very poor indeed. However, the Industrial Revolution brought about a rapid expansion in industry, agriculture and commerce; this meant that not only had the *number* of roads in Britain to be increased but equally important the *quality* of roads had to be improved. This work was left to such famous road builders as Metcalfe, Telford and Macadam.

Development of the canal and railway systems in the mid-nineteenth century eased the burden on the road network. However with the invention of the internal combustion engine by Daimler in 1884, the introduction of motor vehicles again made roads increasingly important. So much so that today some 80% of goods are transported by road over a distance of under 200 kms.

CATEGORIES OF ROAD TRANSPORT

The types of road transport are set out in order of importance calculated by traffic value:

1 Motorways These are part of a programme to provide a national network of modern through-routes. It is estimated that there are about 2,600 km of completed motorways in Britain which provide industry and commerce with quick, direct links with their markets, raw materials, ports and airports. They have improved communications considerably and allowed the population to become highly mobile. They are administered and financed by central government (the Department of Transport).

2 Trunk roads These are the secondary arteries of the road transport system. Britain has about 15,000 km of such roads. Much of the trunk road system links up the major motorways and is also administered and financed by central government.

3 Classified roads There are about 34,000 km of classified roads in Britain, administered by the local authority within which they lie. The county council or local authority receives grants from central government to help with their upkeep and maintenance.

4 Unclassified roads Over 291,000 km of such roads exist in Britain and they are entirely the responsibility of the local authority.

ROAD CARRIERS

The carriage of commodities by road is done by three different types of road carriers:

1 Local carriers Small carriers who operate in limited areas and can be found all over Britain. They connect local communities, industries and commerce with neighbouring areas. They are used frequently to transport products from the retailer to the consumer's home which will probably be in the locality.

2 General carriers These organisations collect and deliver commodities by road all over Britain. They have depots and agents throughout the country. Some of them may specialise in the carriage of a particular type of commodity. A few provide an international service between Britain and Europe using the Ro/Ro (roll on, roll off) ferries such as those at Hull, Dover, Harwich and Southampton. NB If the supplier does not provide transport a general carrier will be employed to transport goods from say the wholesale warehouse to retail shops throughout Britain. British road carriers are members of either the *Freight Transport Association* or the *Road Haulage Association*. The two organisations, together with their European counterparts, have drawn up acceptable international rules and regulations governing road carriage. These are the *Transports Internationales Routiers* (TIR) rules which cover such matters as guarantees to customs authorities, the security of loads and the road worthiness of vehicles. Certificates are given, which are renewable every two years and allow the distinctive TIR plates to be placed on the vehicle.

The largest privately owned road transport carrier and distributor is the worker owned *National Freight Consortium* which has changed considerably in recent years from general haulage to specialist business. In addition to its British Road Services subsidiary a large volume of its trade is concerned with contract hire operating vehicles under the company names. These include Renault, Kellogg's, Zanussi, Habitat, Hoover, etc.

3 Firms undertaking their own transport Many businesses organise their own collection and delivery of commodities. This has the advantage of being cheaper and probably quicker (provided the volume of business is sufficient), of allowing personal contact with customers and providing advertising on their own vehicles. The following factors are taken into account when the road carrier determines the prices to be charged: depreciation of vehicles; maintenance of vehicles and the depot; wages and running costs; the weight of the load; the distance to be covered; the liability of the commodities to damage and the likelihood of a return load.

Compare these with the **economic** cost of rail or air transport – which do you think is the most efficient? What are the problems one meets when making comparative costs?

GOVERNMENT INVOLVEMENT WITH ROAD TRANSPORT

As a member of the European Community Britain has followed a policy of integration of all transport services. In addition to road transport legislation it is directly concerned with the operation of the following:

Passenger Transport Executives cover large centres of population outside London in order to integrate public transport as much as possible, particularly road and rail, e.g. Tyne and Wear, Lothian Transport, etc.

Each Executive (and local council) having a bus undertaking is required to operate its fleet as a separate limited company established on a sound commercial footing. Subject to minimum operational standards private operators are allowed to compete for the available business. Where uneconomic services are necessary on social grounds, a subsidy is payable by the local authority.

London Transport Control over central bus and underground services is in the hands of the London Regional Transport. This works closely with British Rail which also provides commuter services. London Transport is one of the largest public transport undertakings in the world carrying over one and a half million passengers daily on the Underground network alone.

The Post Bus is a service operated by the Post Office in country areas for both passengers and mail collection/delivery.

Express Coach Services are operated throughout the country using the motorway network wherever possible in direct competition with British Rail on timing and price.

Advantages of road transport

1 Very flexible – unlike other means of transport roads lead almost everywhere.
2 Quick and comparatively cheap over short distances.
3 No timetable required – vehicles can be sent at any time.
4 No transhipments necessary therefore less damage or pilferage.
5 Heavy costs of police, traffic control and track maintenance paid by the state, therefore prices likely to be cheaper.
6 Suitable for the transport of perishables and occasions where rapid transport is required.
7 Most other forms of transport rely upon road to deliver or collect commodities or passengers.

Disadvantages of road transport

1 Not as speedy as air or rail for long-distance travel.
2 Unable to carry bulky commodities as cheaply as rail over long hauls.
3 Charges may include costs of driver who could be away from home for a long time.
4 A road vehicle often has to return empty to its depot.
5 Road transport is more easily disrupted by poor weather conditions.
6 Some people think road transport contributes to high social costs such as congestion, pollution and damage to road surface, etc.
7 Large numbers of people are killed or injured on the roads every year.

You can expect essays to be set on road transport, particularly those requiring a comparison; for instance between road and other forms of transport (notably railways, see below). Consider the following:

1 ▶ 'A mail-order business which sells its goods over the whole of Britain uses the rail transport services for sending its goods to customers. What would be the advantages and disadvantages of changing to a system of delivering goods by road using its own vehicles?

Obviously to answer this question you need some knowledge about rail transport but depending upon the type, weight, urgency, size, etc, the goods may be sent immediately to customers by various means of road transport. Discuss the advantages and disadvantages of this change, finishing off with a conclusion.

2 ▶ What considerations ought to determine the mode of transport to be adopted in the following cases?

(*a*) Distribution of goods from wholesale warehouse to retailers' shops.
(*b*) Distribution to consumer from retail shop.

RAILWAYS

The rail network in Britain is under government control and comprises about 16,000 km of track linking the main centres of population. In addition to fast InterCity passenger trains, it is the principal carrier of bulk commodities including coal, grain, limestone, oil, cement, etc. Despite this, however, considerable government financial support is required to operate the system as a public service. Hence the government is constantly looking at ways to improve the efficiency of the railways before further large-scale investment such as electrification or new rolling stock is authorised. Control of the network is in the hands of the British Railways Board which has delegated many of its powers to five regional boards – Eastern, Midland, Southern, Western and Scottish.

Freightliners

The Freightliner Company, owned by British Rail, is responsible for the marketing, routing and control of the national freightliner services. It operates high speed, high capacity container services on specially designed rail wagons. Over two hundred long-haul fixed formation trains run daily between numerous terminals throughout the country from which road vehicles complete the door-to-door container delivery service. The containers which are of standard sizes are either privately owned or the property of the Freightliner Company. The network links the principal industrial areas of the country with ports such as London (Tilbury), Southampton, Harwich, etc, which have specially constructed berths to allow the speedy transfer from ship to lorry or train.

Source of freightliner traffic (percentages)

	1979	1983	1986
Deep sea	35	48	51
Domestic	42	29	26
Europe	16	15	15
Ireland	7	8	8

Speedlink

British Rail also operates a timetabled service for express freight in wagon or lorry load quantities between certain important centres with guaranteed delivery times. The network is also extensively used by *'merry-go-round'* trains transporting coal between pit-head and power-station. Other freight services include the regular movement of Royal Mail, newspapers and the important *Red Star* service guaranteeing dispatch by nominated train to regional stations throughout Britain.

Advantages of railways

1 Suitable for the carriage of bulky commodities over long distances.
2 Freightliner, Speedlink and 'Red Star' services guarantee delivery of commodities by certain times.
3 Not so badly affected by poor weather conditions as road transport.
4 Relieves road congestion to a considerable extent and has an excellent record of safety.

Disadvantages of railways

1 An inflexible method of transport since routes are determined by track.
2 Expensive track equipment, signalling, stations, fencing, etc. add to costs – compare this with road transport.
3 Necessary transhipments often mean delays and damage.
4 A strong lobby of road transport interests in parliament and with the Press that often ridicules rail transport.

Consider the following essay question:

3 ▶ Give the advantages and disadvantages of sending goods (*a*) by air and (*b*) by rail. Give two examples where you would use air transport in preference to rail and two examples where you would use rail transport in preference to air transport.

Containerisation

This is a system of transporting goods which came into general use in the 1950s, and now extends to a variety of products and forms of transport including road, rail and air. It reduces handling – the goods are carefully packed into containers at the departure point and not unpacked until they reach their destination. The containers can be transferred relatively easily from one form of transport to another, e.g. aircraft or ship to lorry or train (freightliner) by simply lifting the container. The system has several **advantages**:

1 Saves manpower at airport or docks.
2 It is quicker than unloading separate items.
3 It has a high degree of mechanization because of the standardised sizes of containers and lifting points – specialised lifting gear transfers containers from and to the transporter.
4 Enjoys the economies of scale resulting in lower costs.

There are some **limitations** to their use including:

1 some opposition from labour and trade unions regarding their use;
2 financial costs of adapting ports, railways and rolling stock;
3 cost of specialist machinery necessary for lifting and transferring.

MC1 The container revolution in the transport of goods refers to
A a larger consumption of tinned foods, e.g. fish, fruit, meat
B plastic bags replacing paper
C refrigerated counters and shop fittings
D sealed, standard boxes to load on vehicles
E none of these

Consider this question:

5 ▶ What are the effects of containerisation in transport?

WATER TRANSPORT

There are three types: river, canal and sea.

River transport

Rivers have been used for transport from the earliest times. There are disadvantages: some areas are not served by extensive river patterns, some rivers are subject to silting up and tidal flows. Only a small percentage of traffic can be carried on rivers and the largest ships would not be able to progress far on most. However, in Britain such rivers as the Thames, Forth, Trent and Clyde still carry much traffic and serve as principal means of transport, whilst overseas important rivers such as the Amazon, Niger, Danube, Rhine, Seine and Mississippi come readily to mind.

Canals

Rivers have obvious disadvantages, and in the middle of the eighteenth century, before the development of railways, businessmen built canals to help them transport raw materials and finished commodities. The period 1780–1830 was the height of canal building and the most famous of canals still in regular use include the Grand Union Canal, Caledonian Canal, Trent Navigation, etc.

Some examples of canals in Britain include the Aire and Calder Navigation Canal linking parts of Humberside with industrial West Yorkshire whilst the Caledonian Canal is a most important link between Inverness and Fort William enabling small craft to bypass the northern tip of Scotland. The Grand Union Canal connects the Thames at Brentford with the Regent's Canal Dock at Southall. Most canals (an exception is the Manchester Ship Canal) are administered by the British Waterways Board.

The advantages and disadvantages of canal transport Canals have advantages compared with rivers and roads especially in the carriage of bulk products which are not easily damaged. Many canals are to be found in West Yorkshire, linking that region with ports on the east coast.

They reach areas not served by rivers and are relatively cheap. Canals are capable of reducing transport costs per tonne kilometre since the power required to move a string of barges is small compared to the load it can carry. It must be said that the canal network in Britain is at the moment small scale and badly in need of modernisation compared with European canals such as those linking the Rhine to the river Seine.

Compared to modern road, air and rail transport canals have disadvantages. Above all it is a slow method of transport, and the volume of traffic which can be carried is very small. (There are some exceptions to this such as the Corinth, Suez and Panama canals which are important waterways.) Canals are subject to adverse weather conditions such as ice and need continuing maintenance to keep them clear from weeds and debris. With the coming of railways, canals in Britain began to decline and in recent years they have been increasingly used for leisure. However, with congestion on roads and the economic losses involved in running railways canals may again become a financial proposition in the carriage of certain types of freight.

As in the other areas of transport, examiners tend to set comparative questions on canals – for example:

5 ▶ What factors would a business take into account when considering the use of inland water or canal transport for the carriage of goods?

In answering this question you would be expected to expand on the advantages and disadvantages of canals. Moreover the nature of the goods to be carried would also be important as well as the desirability of speed in carrying the goods. In addition, do not restrict your essay or examples to Britain – consider the extensive use of canals in Western Europe and other parts of the world.

6 ▶ Give examples of cases where canal or river transport might still be used in preference to rail or road transport.

Sea

Britain is an island and shipping has traditionally been very important. In 1987 Britain had the eighth largest fleet after Liberia, Japan, Panama and Greece and about one twelfth of total world tonnage. Nearly all the British fleet is modern and privately owned, amounting to about eleven million tonnes. However, Britain has this century had a declining share of world shipping tonnage for the following reasons:

1 Losses of shipping in two world wars.
2 Outdated shipyards unable to replace tonnage quickly.
3 Other countries have developed their own merchant fleets.
4 The use of 'flags of convenience' allows ships to register with foreign

countries (e.g. Liberia) and, by doing so, receive tax and other advantages.

5 The construction of large tankers and bulk carriers – these have been built mainly in Japanese yards.
6 Increased use of container ships – one modern containers ship carries the equivalent cargo of four traditional cargo ships.
7 The competition of air travel, especially since 1945.
8 High wages and other costs compared with other countries.

The earnings received from shipping are still important and Britain receives invisible earnings (see page 161). It also provides employment for approximately 30,000 people.

Types of vessels

Ocean liners These consist of several decks for passenger accommodation and limited cargo space; they also carry mail. They keep regular timetables (a disadvantage as far as carrying cargo is concerned as they have to take what is available at the time of departure). Passenger liners travel all over the world to places such as the Far East and Australia – they have however declined considerably with the development of air travel and now mostly concentrate on leisure cruises.

Passenger cargo liners These are concerned with the carriage of cargo to and from the world's ports. They carry only a few passengers and in consequence have only a few cabins. The holds of the vessel are the largest part of the ship.

Container vessels operate between the container ports of the world carrying a large proportion of world trade in finished goods. The ease of loading and unloading ensures a quick turn-round time at the destination and hence reduced costs (see page 140).

Tramps This is the name given to cargo ships which travel anywhere in the world to earn an income. They have no home port and carry all types of products. They have no set routes or timetables being 'hired' to shippers for set periods through the Baltic Exchange (see page 61).

Bulk carriers Bulk carrying ships are built for specific types of cargo. In recent years they have become larger to achieve the economies of scale and lower costs. A good example is the oil tanker. These tend to be massive ships which carry huge amounts of oil. They are relatively speedy and turn around quickly at purpose-built terminals such as Europort, Milford Haven, Sullom Voe (Scotland).

Ro-Ro ferries are especially important in the transport of road vehicles between this country and the Continent. In addition to cars they are able to accommodate large lorries and trailers on routes such as Harwich–Esbjerg, Dover–Calais, Southampton–Le Havre, Newcastle–Bergen, etc.

You should consider answering essay questions such as the following:

7 ▶ British merchant shipping may be broadly classified into bulk carriers, tramp ships, cargo liners and container vessels. Discuss the purpose of each type of vessel.

PORTS

Requirements of a good port A good port requires most of the following facilities: deep water, shelter from the weather and sea, a clear channel, supplies of oil and water, wharves, good communications with the road and rail, government offices for customs, etc, warehouses, refrigerator stores and dry docks.

Free ports are areas in which imported goods are processed free of all taxes and customs levies provided they are then re-exported. Examples include Southampton, Prestwick, Belfast, Cardiff, Liverpool, Singapore, Hong Kong, etc.

Britain's major ports

London (Tilbury) The largest port in Britain in terms of visible trade and one of the most important in the world. Tilbury has developed as an important tanker and container port and has good connections with the national freightliner and motorway networks.

Liverpool This is the major export outlet for British goods such as vehicles, chemicals and electrical components. Its principal imports include wool, cotton, grain and raw materials for the industrial North West.

Harwich Situated on the east coast with extensive 'roll on, roll off' facilities to continental ports including Zeebrugge and Ostend. It is now being challenged by **Felixstowe** which also offers 'roll on, roll off' facilities for both passengers and commercial traffic. Such ports have become increasingly important since Britain joined the Common Market and the subsequent increase in traffic needing such facilities.

Tees and Hartlepool in common with the Shetlands (**Sullom Voe**) and Orkneys (**Flotten**) has developed into one of the largest ports in Britain largely because of traffic in North Sea oil. These areas have become major European oil terminals and together deal with a greater volume of oil than **Milford Haven** on the west coast.

Southampton An important container port linking Britain with other world ports particularly the Far East and USA and connected to the freightliner networks. Also has a large amount of Ro/Ro trading with the continent of Europe through Le Havre and Cherbourg.

Clydeport The main Scottish port serving as an outlet for the exports of industrial, Central Scotland. The area is well known for shipbuilding and repair services.

Leith An important port serving the East coast and Lothian regions of Scotland. Considerable trade is generated between this country, Scandinavia and EC countries.

Hull This port is on the Humber estuary, serving Yorkshire and the East Midlands. It has developed 'roll on, roll off' facilities for containers.

Advantages of sea transport

1 No costs of tracks, etc, and access to most of the world.
2 Very suitable for both heavy and bulky commodities.
3 Small amounts of power are needed to move large cargoes and is therefore comparatively cheap.
4 Ships can be very large and easily carry huge loads, or alternatively relatively small but specially adapted to carry goods vehicles.
5 It has good links with inland systems when containers are used.

Disadvantages of sea transport

1 Relatively slow – both passengers and goods have been lost to airlines.
2 Delays at some ports may occur because of inadequate facilities or labour troubles.
3 Deterioration of cargo possible due to corrosive qualities of seawater.
4 Pilfering may take place, although this has been reduced by increased use of containers.
5 Dependent upon tides and weather conditions.

MC2 'Tramp' vessels are those ships that.

A provide a coastal service only, i.e. not ocean-going
B provide a service that is at owner's risk, i.e. no marine insurance company will undertake to insure the cargo being carried
C provide a regular schedule service between ports, i.e. to a published timetable
D provide a service that can be chartered, i.e. the rate is negotiated by shipping agent through the Baltic Exchange
E are entirely engaged on the cross-channel routes

Consider the following essay questions on sea transport:

8 ▶ (*a*) State three main facilities which you would expect to find in the docks at a large port.
(*b*) Why is the efficiency of the docks important to shipping?
(*c*) What is a container-port? How does this differ from a free-port?

9 ▶ Explain carefully the circumstances in which a manufacturer might send goods by sea rather than by air.

Your answer should stress the reasons for choosing this method of transport, concentrating on the advantages of sea transport and disadvantages of air. Mention also the type of product likely to be carried coupled with cost per tonne/kilometre, volume, destination, regularity of shipment, insurance costs, etc.

AIR TRANSPORT

The transport of freight and passengers by air has been an important development in recent years. Its great advantage is that it can cover long distances in very short periods of time.

Civil Aviation Authority This has general responsibility for the operational regulations of civil aviation in Britain, which includes licensing control over both nationalised and independent airlines, civil airports, passenger safety, aircrew training, etc.

In Britain today the carriers are entirely privately-owned and independent organisations. The largest is British Airways – the former state airline which operates both passenger and cargo routes. These cover overseas long-haul routes, short-haul flights to Europe and domestic services including regular flights to and from London, Edinburgh, Glasgow, Belfast, Isle of Man, etc.

Other independent airlines include Britania Airways, Dan Air and British Midland. They operate a wide range of domestic and international services and provide numerous charter services for civilian holiday traffic. In addition a large volume of first class mail is carried every day between the principal airports of Britain centred on East Midlands airport.

Well over forty million passengers each year enter or leave Britain by air transport. This easily exceeds the number of passengers travelling by sea. The volume of freight traffic to over one million tonnes per annum has increased over recent years with this development of specialised overseas trade. Chief imports include diamonds, out-of-season fruits and pallets containing high-value goods. Exports include machinery, chemicals, medicines and precious stones.

Advantages of air transport

1 A very speedy form of transport essential for business.
2 Danger of damage to goods is reduced.
3 Less chance of pilferage since the commodities are rarely handled.
4 Ideal transport for perishables, expensive products with low weight, urgently required articles and first-class mail.

5 Particularly advantageous over long distances, which are covered in very short times.

Disadvantages of air transport

1 Costs of equipment and machines are high.
2 Running costs are the most expensive of all transport.
3 The size and weight of products which can be carried is limited.
4 Weather conditions may affect services as may landing conditions at airports.
5 Airports are usually on the fringes of large cities which adds to travelling time.
6 Social problems of noise and pollution.

Consider the following essay questions on air transport:

10 ▶ When will a businessperson prefer to use air transport for the movement of (*a*) passengers (*b*) goods?

11 ▶ Consider the main reasons why some products are transported by air rather than by sea. Give two examples for each reason.

12 ▶ Describe (*a*) the advantages; and (*b*) the disadvantages of air transport for the carriage of goods between London and New York.

Pipelines

Increasing use is being made of pipelines for the movement of important products – both liquid and gaseous. Most of Britain's oil and gas for example are transported by pipeline from the North Sea fields. Other examples include octane fuel from the Fawley refinery near Southampton to Heathrow and water supplies from Wales to Birmingham and from the Lake District to Manchester.

Factors to be considered when deciding whether to adopt 'own transport' policy

1 Comparative costs of purchasing own fleet, hiring/leasing, putting contract out to tender, using a professional carrier.
2 Distance and frequency of loads – local, national, international markets.
3 Proximity of motorway, railhead, airport, seaport and co-ordination with other transport modes.
4 Need to control physical distribution, e.g. in speed of delivery, security of load, etc.
5 Advisability in setting up a separate transport department within the firm.

MC3 Valuable goods (such as diamonds from Amsterdam to London) are usually transported by

A air

B Ro-Ro ferry
C specially adapted security lorry
D hovercraft
E container ship

MC4 The best way of transporting spring flowers from Jersey to London is by
A air/rail
B sea/air
C air/road/rail
D sea/road
E air/road

COMMUNICATIONS

Apart from transport you are expected to have a knowledge of communications. Here are some of the ideas of which you should be aware. A good network of communications is essential for the smooth running of industry and commerce. There is always a constant need for a fast and efficient transmission of information at reasonable cost to the user. In Britain because of its importance to national security the government is at the centre of the communications industry having an overall interest in the services of the Post Office Corporation (state owned) and British Telecommunications (independent).

These include the postal services of both home and overseas mail, telephones, telex, Datel, Confravision, Telemessages, overseas telegrams, Prestel, Intelfax and other means of electronic/satellite communication.

Some of the communication services provided by the Post Office Corporation

1 Inland post This ensures the delivery through the ordinary post within a few days of posting, of letters, postcards, printed papers, newspapers, parcels, etc, by either the first or second class services.

2 Business-reply post A licence allows the licensee to send out reply paid envelopes/cards to customer by either class, but only to pay postage on those returned.

3 Franking machines A licence allows the use of special machines at approved premises which frank letters with the postage charges so saving time spent sticking on stamps and obtaining them from the Post Office.

4 Recorded delivery The delivery of a letter or packet where proof of delivery is necesary. By using the **registered post**, compensation may be paid as well if the mail is lost.

5 Free post An organisation such as a large-scale retailer may with the approval of the Post Office arrange for a special address to be included in advertisments to which all customers' replies are directed. All costs for this second class only service are paid by the recipient.

6 Datapost A door-to-door overnight collection and delivery service on a contractual basis for items such as computers tapes, important documents, samples, etc.

7 PO boxes Business firms often make arrangements to rent private post boxes at main Post Offices in order to collect mail at any time during the day.

8 Cash on delivery Enables goods up to a certain value to be sent to any address in Britain and for the postman to collect the amount due on behalf of the consignor.

9 Air mail services operate for all classes of mail from this country to most countries in the world. An increasing amount of internal first class mail also travels overnight by this method of transport.

10 Electronic post A service offered by the Post Office relying on a combination of computer transmission, laser printing and postal delivery of messages, statements, bills, invoices, etc, to many thousands of addresses (see also page 150).

You should be able to answer this essay question:

13 ▶ A large international organisation with many branches needs to have an efficient means of communication with its customers. Describe four methods of communication they could use.

MC5 If you have to post £20 in notes to a person, which service should you use?

A special delivery
B recorded delivery
C registered letter
D first class mail
E cash on delivery

Some of the communication services provided by British Telecommunications

1 Telephone This is often the cheapest, quickest and most direct method of communication. There are about twenty-seven million subscribers in Britain who through the **Subscriber Trunk Dialling** (STD) system are able to dial direct to other subscribers in Britain and through the International Exchange to many subscribers abroad.

2 Telex A fully automatic system of sending or receiving messages with subscribers both at home and abroad using specialist equipment.

3 Datel This service is used for the transmission of coded information such as details of cheques, invoices, orders, etc, between computer centres or Head Office and branches. Varying speeds of transmission are possible up to many thousands of 'bits' per second.

4 Telemessages may be sent to home and addresses overseas through the telephone or telex network. **Overseas telegrams** may also be sent from this country to most parts of the world.

5 Prestel A method of transmitting computerised information on to specially adapted television screens through the telephone network. In addition to the BBC and ITV regular transmission, the television screen is also used as a method of communication by way of *Ceefax* (BBC) and *Oracle* (ITV).

6 Confravision A service that enables a commercial firm to hold meetings simultaneously in different centres or studios.

7 Private Mobile Radio A privately funded civil national radio and paging system using certain radio bands or frequencies previously used by black and white television. They system is increasingly used by business and service industries giving a two-way link between Head Offices and branch networks.

8 Electronic mail is increasingly being used as a means of communication by transmitting computer information over the telephone line network. Teletex allows point-to-point communication between dedicated printers or word processors. Telecom Gold is a similar system using a central computer mail-box. Users are able to transmit information over the system for later collection and storage at the terminal in the recipient's office.
Many questions are set requiring the student to distinguish between teletext and telex and you should be able to answer such questions. You can also expect essays to be set on transport which are of a more general nature and not specific to one or two types.

Examples would include:

14 ▶ (*a*) What general considerations does a manufacturing firm have to take into account in deciding which type of transport to use when distributing its products?

(*b*) Why might a market gardener use road transport for distribution within the country and use air transport when selling abroad?

15 ▶ Several forms of transport are available in the world of commerce.

What considerations will a trader bear in mind when deciding upon the most suitable method?

16 ▶ Which form of transport would you expect to be used for each of the following? In each case briefly give your reasons and indicate the main alternative method.
(*a*) Newspapers sent daily from London to Birmingham.
(*b*) A large quantity of timber at Stockholm to be sent to London.
(*c*) Medical products in Amersham to be despatched to Hong Kong.
(*d*) Spare parts of office machinery in New York urgently required in Singapore.

17 ▶ (*a*) Why is it that the majority of freight carried within Britain is moved by road transport?
(*b*) Describe two ways in which the railways have sought to improve their freight services in order to meet this competition.

18 ▶ (*a*) Describe the facilities provided by the Post Office Corporation and British Telecom for the communication of information.
(*b*) State with two reasons in each case, which method of communication you would use for:
(i) placing an urgent order for equipment
(ii) sending a credit note
(iii) discovering whether a firm stocked an item which you needed urgently.

Data response question

You have recently been appointed as Product Manager of a large chemical company with worldwide interests. It has been agreed that your principal area of operation is throughout the Far East excluding Japan. Your first task is to arrange the itinerary of your journey by air from London to Singapore, Hong Kong, Seoul (Korea) and return direct, staying a minimum of two days in each visiting potential customers. Write a memorandum to your Senior Manager giving details of travel costs (in sterling) – economy class – together with sources of your costing information.

Answers to multiple choice questions

MC1	D	MC4	E
MC2	D	MC5	C
MC3	A		

INTERNATIONAL TRADE

CONTENTS

This chapter on international trade covers the following topics:

1 International trade and protection – the importance of this form of trade to Britain, the advantages of international trade, the instruments of protection, the reasons for introducing protectionist methods and situations where protection might not succeed in achieving its objectives and General Agreement on Tariffs and Trade (GATT).

2 The balance of payments – an analysis of the structure of balance of payments such as current account, visibles and invisibles, investment and other capital flows and official financing; Britain's imports and exports; how a balance of payments deficit may be corrected.

3 The European Community – origins and membership, control of the EC, advantages and disadvantages of British membership.

4 The import and export trade – the export trade: problems facing exporters, methods of gaining orders, government assistance to exporters, Export Credits Guarantee Department. The import trade: specialists in the import trade, the bill of lading, Customs and Excise duties, bonded warehouses.

INTERNATIONAL TRADE AND PROTECTION

It is most important that you are aware of the importance of trade and in particular the importance of international trade. You should also know the arguments in favour of restricting trade in favour of protection.

What is international trade?

International trade is concerned with the buying and selling of commodities between the different countries of the world. Some countries, such as the USA and Russia, could provide most of the produce they need themselves; other countries including Britain rely heavily on other countries for their supplies of foodstuffs and raw materials.

The advantages of international trade

1 Many countries do not produce enough food to feed their populations. Home-produced foodstuffs have to be supplemented by imports (purchases from abroad). For instance Britain will import tea, coffee, wines, meat, etc.

2 Countries such as Britain cannot supply enough raw materials to support their industries. Britain can no longer produce sufficient iron ore to safisfy the steel industry and has therefore to rely on imports.
3 A large number of jobs in Britain depend on the export (selling to other countries) of goods and services. Many manufactured goods produced in this country such as cars, buses, scientific instruments, etc, are sold abroad. Also many foreign countries involved in trade use British ships, aircraft, banks and insurance companies. Without international trade much of this employment would be lost.
4 A larger market for home produced commodities is possible.
5 Competition from abroad will often create greater efficiency in UK industry.
6 A world wide market in commodities may result in the economies of scale (see page 101) and thereby lower costs and prices.
7 The prosperity of all countries depends on their being able to sell goods abroad and purchase products which perhaps they cannot produce themselves. If international trade did not exist people in all countries would suffer a lower standard of living.
8 Because of international trade countries specialise in producing fewer commodities in larger quantity at lower prices.
9 Political advantages. International trade is beneficial because by trading with other countries, friendship and understanding will result.

HOW COUNTRIES DECIDE WHICH COMMODITIES TO PRODUCE

1 A country can produce some commodities but not other goods This may be due to difference in climate or the distribution of raw materials. For instance, Britain is unable to grow oranges or mine gold and therefore had to import these commodities.

2 A country can produce one commodity better than another country and vice versa Country A may be able to produce a commodity better than Country B, Country A therefore decides to specialise in this commodity. Country B may be able to produce another commodity better than Country A, Country B therefore decides to specialise in this other commodity. After specialising in (or concentrating on) producing the commodity to which each country is best suited, the countries will decide to trade with each other. Britain, for instance, can produce wine but perhaps not as cheaply or in such quantities as France. Therefore Britain will import most of the wine it requires, mainly from France and export high quality Scotch beef.

3 A country can produce both commodities better than another country A country may be able to produce two commodities better than another country. However, it will decide to produce only the commodity in which its comparative advantage is greatest and allow the other country to produce the other commodity. This is called the **Theory of Comparative Costs.**

Example

	Output per person	
	Oranges	Lemons
Country A	1	2
Country B	3	4

Here we can see that Country B has the absolute advantage in producing both oranges and lemons.

But what does each country have to give up if it specialises in producing just either oranges or lemons?

	Oranges given up to produce one lemon	Lemons given up to produce one orange
Country A	½	2
Country B	¾	1⅓

Here Country A has the comparative advantage in the production of lemons because to produce a lemon Country A has to give up half an orange, whereas country B has to give up three quarters of an orange. It is much better for Country A to produce lemons than for Country B to do so, because it has to give up less. Why does Country B specialise in oranges?

After deciding in which commodity they have a comparative advantage each country will specialise in the production of that good; the production of both oranges and lemons will increase, trade will take place and people in both countries will enjoy a better standard of living.

TRADE RESTRICTIONS OR PROTECTION

Trade restrictions are implemented by governments to discourage international trade. There are several methods of protection for you to learn:

1 Tariffs (customs duties or import duties) This is a type of tax placed on certain commodities imported into the country. Tariffs may be levied on an *ad-valorem* basis (i.e. as a percentage of value), or on a specific basis (i.e. as an amount per unit). Thus if a car was imported worth £4,000 and the *ad-valorem* tariff was 10 per cent then the tax would raise £400; if the car increased in price to £5,000 then the tax would raise £500. Tariffs serve two purposes: they raise money for the government and raise the price of imports.

2 Import quotas This is a direct restriction on the quantity of imports allowed into a country. It is a more certain way of reducing imports but on the other hand raises no tax. Nevertheless, this method of controlling imports is necessary in certain instances, for example drugs are imported on a quota basis only through certain ports or airports in Britain.

3 Subsidies This occurs when Britain's domestic (home) production is subsidised (or given finance) which allows it to sell at lower prices. Thus when importers try to compete with British domestic producers, they will find that their goods are more expensive and therefore demand for imported goods will be lower.

4 Exchange controls If an importer wants to purchase commodities for import he or she may do so by using the currency of the exporting nation. Thus, if a government wishes to restrict imports it will restrict the availabilty of foreign currencies. (Exchange controls were abolished in Britain in 1979.)

5 Embargo This is a straightforward ban on trading with another country and is usually for political reasons.

6 Discrimination by the government in favour of home producers e.g. a nationalised industry may be instructed to buy British coal even though foreign coal may be cheaper.

7 Health and safety regulations designed to keep out imports.

8 Voluntary export restraint agreements whereby two countries agree to limit the volume of exports to each other.

WHY ARE TRADE RESTRICTIONS INTRODUCED?

Now that you know what the different weapons of protection are, you need to know the reasons why they may be introduced.

1 To correct a balance of payments deficit Normally if Britain exports less than she imports, a **balance of payments** deficit (or loss) is the result. This means more money goes out of the country to pay for imports than comes in from foreigners paying for Britain's goods. Tariffs and other such restrictions will, in the short term, discourage imports and correct Britain's balance of payments.

2 To protect infant industries A country may be trying to build up a new industry. Such an industry could not survive if it was expected to compete with the imports of countries already established in that industry.

3 To protect declining industries and safeguard jobs Certain industries in Britain, such as textiles, are in decline. One of the main reasons for this is that foreign imports are cheaper and consumers do not buy

British goods. By making imports more expensive this could help Britain's declining industries and maintain jobs.

4 The prevention of 'dumping' Some foreign firms may choose to **dump** their surplus production in Britain and sell it at a price just enough to cover costs or give a very small profit. This may be below the prices of British producers and drive them out of business.

5 To protect strategic industries Certain industries are so important that, just in case of an international crisis for instance, they must not be allowed to decline or die. Examples would include agriculture, steel, shipbuilding and coal mining.

6 To protect jobs By protecting domestic industry then jobs are also protected.

When protection might not work

Protection may not be successful in achieving its objectives for the following reasons:

1 British Consumers may still purchase imports Even if tariffs have been put on them to make them more expensive, certain necessities may still be bought as imports, e.g. foodstuffs and raw materials.

2 Other countries may retaliate If Britain prevents imports entering this country, then other countries may prevent British goods entering their country.

3 Protects inefficient industries Perhaps restrictions are just protecting inefficient industries anyway and these industries will eventually decline and die in the face of competition.

4 The advantages of international trade are lost

MC1. A duty which is based on the percentage of the price of goods is known as:

A ad-valorem duty
B specific duty
C percentage duty
D a tariff
E excise duty

1 ▶ (*a*) What economic benefits can a country derive from international trade?
(*b*) How does the UK government
(i) encourage international trade; and
(ii) discourage international trade?
(*c*) Explain the workings of the General Agreement on Tariffs and Trade (GATT).

To answer (*a*), show how international trade is important to improving a country's standard of living. Countries specialise in producing goods in which they have a comparative advantage so that all countries will be better off. International trade also enables countries to obtain raw material, foodstuffs and finished goods which they are unable to produce themselves. Many jobs are heavily dependent on industries involved in international trade. To answer (*b*): (i) discuss the operations of the Department of Trade and the Export Credit Guarantee Department; (ii) mention the various methods of protection available.

To answer (*c*): The General Agreement on Tariffs and Trade is a regular meeting of countries intent on promoting more free trade and reducing protectionist measures. There have been successive 'rounds' of agreements to reduce protectionist measures like tariffs and quotas. GATT also seeks to gain preferential treatment for less-developed countries (underdeveloped or subsistence economies). It has however influenced problems in reducing non-tariff barriers (such as some governments giving preference to domestic suppliers) and with some countries (e.g. Japan) which have complicated internal laws (e.g. anti-pollution requirements) which may reduce imports from other countries.

2 ► (*a*) What is the theory of comparative costs?

(*b*) How does the theory of comparative costs explain international specialisation?

(*c*) Why does international specialisation require international exchange?

(*d*) Despite the advantages of trade most countries introduce protectionist measures such as tariffs. Why is this so?

THE BALANCE OF PAYMENTS

An understanding of balance of payments is essential in our study of international trade. You also need to know the meaning of the **balance of trade**, the meaning of terms such as **current account**, **visibles**, **invisibles** and **investment** and other capital flows. You need to be able to distinguish these terms from one another and to understand their inter-relationship.

The balance of payments is a record of transactions between countries involved in international trade. It is a record of receipts from exports and spending on imports. If a country's receipts are greater than its expenditure then it will have a balance of payments **surplus**. If a country's receipts are less than its spending then it will have a balance of payments **deficit**. Countries obviously prefer to be in surplus on their balance of payments because this means they are earning more than is being spent in international trade.

Balance of payments statistics

£m	Visible balance	Invisible balance	Current balance	Official financing
1970	−34	+857	+823	−1,420
1975	−3,333	+1,810	−1,523	+1,465
1980	+1,361	+2,116	+3,477	−1,372
1981	+3,360	+3,569	+6,929	+687
1982	+2,055	+2,868	+4,923	+1,284
1983	−1,165	+4,411	+3,246	+816
1984	−4,255	+4,879	+624	+1,321
1985	−2,068	+5,020	+2,952	+ 927
1986	−8,300	+7,200	−1,100	−788

Terms used in balance of payments statistics
The current account is divided into two parts:

1 Visible trade balance This includes the imports and exports of *goods*. The difference between these is called the **balance of (visible) trade**. These figures are publicised each month and must not be confused with the balance of payments proper.

2 Invisible trade balance Includes the import and export of *services* such as aviation; interest, profits and dividends; shipping; tourism; banking and insurance and the government services. Here are some examples:

If an American company uses a British ship to transport its goods from the USA to Brazil this is an invisible export because they have paid for the use of that British ship with American money.

If Britain maintains an Embassy in West Germany, this is an invisible import (on government services) because staff are paid wages etc, and that money is spent, not in Britain, but in West Germany.

If a British company with a factory in New Zealand earns interest, profits and dividends on its investment this is an invisible export because that money enters Britain to pay British shareholders.

If the Nissan Motor Company build a factory in the North East of England to produce cars for sale in this country is this an import or an export?

The balance of visible trade and the balance of invisible trade are taken together and make up the balance on current account.

Investment and other capital flows This includes the import and export of capital for investment purposes. If capital flows into Britain because foreign firms or governments have purchased stocks or shares or built a factory, then this is regarded as an export because money has been transferred from abroad into Britain. On the other hand if capital leaves Britain because British firms or the Government have purchases foreign stocks or shares or built a factory abroad, then this is regarded as an import because money has flowed out of Britain.

In future years, of course, those investments abroad may earn interest, profits and dividends for British companies and this would mean an inflow of money on invisibles.

The balancing item It is not always possible to keep an accurate record of the balance of payments because of errors and omissions. However the Bank of England is aware of trends by changes in the official reserves it holds. A negative balancing items means that the balance of payments has been over valued.

The current account and the balance on investment and other capital flows plus the balancing item gives the *balance for official financing*, which is the balance of payments in reality.

However there is one more section of the accounts to describe:

Official financing The balance of payments always balances. This refers to the fact that every penny of a deficit must be financed by borrowing or running down reserves of foreign currency. Likewise every penny of a surplus must be allocated to paying off loans or adding to reserves of foreign currency.

How has Britain performed on its balance of payments in recent years?

Visibles In the early 1980s Britain did well on the visible part of current account. Generally Britain's exports in terms of value has been more than the value of imports. What reasons can be put forward?

1 The relatively lower price of British goods due to higher rates of inflation in *some* foreign countries.
2 Increased trade with Common Market countries.
3 Britain sells a large volume of high quality North Sea oil to overseas markets (particularly Europe) accounting for a substantial surplus on visible trading items. The contribution of North Sea oil has been a major positive influence on both the visibles and the balance of payments. Despite the surplus of oil revenues Britain has a deficit on manufactured goods with the rest of the world. This is worrying because Britain is traditionally a manufacturing country and will once again rely on manufacturing when North Sea oil runs out. The surplus on visibles gave way in the mid 1980s to a deficit. The reasons for this may be explained by the decline in oil prices which meant that the value of Britains oil exports declined. Also there occurred a deficit on manufacturing during the mid 1980s for the first time since the Industrial Revolution of the early nineteenth century.

Invisibles There has always been a surplus on Britain's invisible transactions taken as a whole. This includes the banking and insurance services of the City of London together with profits on other services provided by Britain to the rest of the world.

Investment and other capital flows This may vary from year to year but there is normally an inflow of money and funds depending to a large extent on comparative interest rates between London and other world financial centres, political pressures, market trends, etc.

BRITAIN'S IMPORTS AND EXPORTS: THE PATTERN OF TRADE

This is an important section on what goods Britain imports and exports. It is a popular essay topic with examiners.

The goods which Britain imports and exports

Analysis of visible trade 1985 by commodity	Exports % share	Imports % share
Food and drink	6.5	10.9
Crude materials and oils	2.7	6.4
Fuels	21.3	12.4
Chemicals	12.0	8.1
Manufactures	23.5	28.9
Machinery and transport equipment	31.5	31.7
Other	2.5	1.6
	100	100

Recent changes in Britain's imports and exports

Imports In terms of value, the importation of crude oil was the largest single item in Britain's imports. However, this has been severely reduced following the discovery and exploitation of North Sea Oil and gas. In addition recent years have seen a sharp rise in total imports of manufactures reflecting higher demand for these products and machinery, etc, particularly from Japan.

There has also been a decline in the proportion of imported foodstuffs largely due to the greater output of Britain's farmers.

Exports The largest share is taken by high-quality finished manufactures which account for nearly half the total, e.g. electronic products, engines, vehicles, books and sports equipment. Semi-manufactures are the next most important category of exports.

Who bought and sold?

Analysis of visible trade 1986 by area	Exports % share	Imports % share
EC	48.9	48.8
Other Western Europe	9.5	14.2
North America	17.0	13.8
Other developed	4.8	7.5
Latin America	1.4	1.9
Middle East and North Africa	7.9	3.2
Other developing	8.5	8.3
Centrally planned economies	2.0	2.3
	100	100

Oil and chemical exports have become increasingly important, whereas exports of textiles, metals and coal have diminished. Foodstuffs account for roughly the same proportion of exports as in previous years.

Recent changes in countries from whom we import and to whom we export

There are three major changes:

1 Britain's trade with her partners in the Common Market has increased markedly over the last few years.

2 Trade with the rest of Western Europe has also expanded over the same period.

3 Trade with the members of the Commonwealth such as Australia, Canada and India is proportionately less important now than twenty years ago as is trade with the USA (though still important).

How balance of payments deficits can be corrected

When a country makes a deficit on balance of payments it will try and remedy this in one of the following ways:

Borrowing To finance the deficit on balance of payments the country may have to borrow, usually from the **International Monetary Fund** (an international bank with member countries as depositors) or from other countries. This is only a short-term measure of help and the deficit may appear again.

Impose tariffs and other methods of protection This may be attempted but it may not work and it does have its disadvantages – particularly retaliation by other countries.

Deflationary policies

Deflation means attempting to reduce home demand thereby keeping prices down and leading to less demand for imports. Such a policy may include:

Increasing interest rates The government may raise interest rates in the City which will cause all other interest rates to rise. This will attract money into Britain, on investment and other capital flows.

Preventing banks from creating credit Banks may give people loans which they use to purchase imports and also cause prices to rise. If the government restricts the banks from doing this then imports will fall. For further details see the banking section.

Hire purchase By imposing restrictions such as larger deposit requirements, etc., this could be made more difficult and expensive to obtain. Again, this would lessen imports.

Taxes Taxation could be increased. Thus consumers would have less money in their pockets with which to buy imports.

Government spending A policy to reduce government spending will reduce demand in the UK economy.

Currency devaluation If the country is operating a system of fixed exchange rates (where a country's currency has a fixed value in comparison to other countries), e.g. £1 = $2, then it may choose to devalue the value of its currency against other currencies. This would make imports more expensive, and therefore less imports will be bought; it would also mean exports are cheaper and in consequence more exports will be made.

Example

Before devaluation: £1 = $4 After devaluation: £1 = $2

Assume Britain wants to export a car worth £10,000 to the USA: before devaluation the Americans had to spend $40,000 (10,000×$4) on the car. After devaluation they will have to spend $20,000 (10,000×$2). Hopefully, given the right conditions, more exports will be sold in the USA.

What will happen to the price of American imports to Britain? There are disadvantages, and devaluation may not work because:

1 the Americans may not buy more British goods even if they have become cheaper;
2 other countries may also devalue their currencies and make their exports cheaper;
3 Britain may not be able to produce the amount of cars that the USA requires because of strikes, etc;
4 because of the higher price of imports it may cause inflation in Britain which may counteract the effects of devaluation, i.e. export prices may rise again.

Allowing the pound to float downwards A country may not keep its currency fixed to another currency as on a fixed exchange rate. It may allow its currency to float downwards and this would have the same effect as a devaluation. Britain has had a floating pound since 1972; before that she tried to keep a fixed exchange rate.

3 ▶ (*a*) What are the differences between the visible account, invisible account and current account of a country's balance of payments?
(*b*) How do banks provide direct help with visible trade?
(*c*) Explain how their work also affects the invisible account.

To answer (*a*) discuss the following: Visibles and Invisibles are both part of the current account section of the balance of payments. Visible items are those dealing with actual import and export of *goods* such as food, raw material, etc. The resultant balance of imported and exported goods is known as the balance of trade. Invisibles are concerned with the transfer of *services* between countries and includes shipping, banking, insurance, tourism, etc. (*b*) The commercial banks help directly with visible trade by acting as agents for payment (see Chapter 9). They provide drafts, credits and accept bills of exchange together with advice and reports on potential export markets. Other financial institutions such as merchant banks in the City of London also provide services to British exporters. (*c*) Banking services to the rest of the world is an important category of the invisible trade as the profit earned by this sector is a considerable amount each year. The banks also act as intermediaries and agents for payment for all the other categories of invisible trade.

4 ▶ (*a*) Explain the differences between visible and invisible exports and imports, giving an example of each.
(*b*) Distinguish between a surplus and a deficit on the current account of the balance of payments.
(*c*) Why is this trade so important to the UK?
(*d*) What services are provided to exporters by commercial banks?

5 ▶ (*a*) Outline, using examples, the meaning of invisible trade.
(*b*) Why is a deficit on current account more serious than a deficit on the balance of trade?
(*c*) Explain how a fall in the value of the pound may correct the UK's balance of payments deficit.
(*d*) What factors determine the external exchange rate for the pound?

MC2. Which of the following items in the balance of payments account are invisibles?
(i) imports
(ii) aviation
(iii) tourism
(iv) private investment overseas
(v) interest, profits, and dividends
A (i), (ii) and (iii)
B (ii), (iii) and (iv)
C (ii), (iv) and (v)
D (ii), (iii) and (v)
E (i), (iii) and (v)

MC3. In what section of the balance of payments would an increase in overseas investment in the UK be recorded?
A private transfers of money
B investment and other capital flows
C invisible imports
D interest, profits and dividends
E balance of trade

Match the definitions given in MC4–6 with the terms lettered A–E. Each letter may be used once, more than once or not at all.

A the surplus on current account is less than the deficit on investment and other capital flow account
B visible exports exceed visible imports
C the surplus on invisible items exceeds the deficit on visible items
D imports exceed exports and re-exports
E the deficit on investment and other capital flows is less than the surplus on current account

MC4. a deficit on balance of trade

MC5. visible trade is in deficit

MC6. a surplus on balance of payments

MC7. Concerning Britain's international trade which of the following is not true?
A the largest import, by value, is foodstuffs
B the largest export, by value, is manufactured goods
C Britain usually has a favourable invisible balance
D Britain's trade with the Common Market countries is increasing
E Britain has a deficit on its manufacturing trade

MC8. If the demand for pounds exceeds the supply of pounds
A the demand for pounds is fixed
B the supply of pounds is increasing
C the price of sterling will rise
D the price of sterling will drop
E the pound will be devalued

MC9. Which of the following is *not* an invisible item in the balance of payment figures?
A the cost of carrying mail for foreign countries
B charges for freight carried by aircraft
C charges for passenger travel by sea
D expenditure on machinery imported
E dividends payable to foreign shareholders

MC10. A country's visible balance is the difference between the
A volume of goods imported and exported
B value of capital goods exported and imported
C volume of consumer products imported and exported
D value of goods imported and exported
E value of goods and services exported and imported

MC11. The following figures relate to a country's dealings with other countries in a particular year

	£ m.
Imports of goods	1,000
Exports of goods	900
Invisible imports	4,000
Invisible exports	3,500

That country's balance of trade is

A £500m deficit
B £100m deficit
C £100m surplus
D £500m surplus
E £400m deficit

THE EUROPEAN COMMUNITY (OR THE COMMON MARKET)

You have probably heard of the Common Market or European Community. You should know what it is, its aims and objectives, how it is controlled and the arguments for and against Britain's membership.

Origins and membership

The EC was formed in 1958 by the Treaty of Rome. It originally consisted of six founder members: Belgium, Luxembourg, the Netherlands, France, West Germany and Italy. In 1973 three other countries joined: Britain, Eire and Denmark. Its objectives are full economic, monetary and political union between the member countries. By 1979 some of these aims had been achieved including the abolition of tariffs within the area (a common external tariff exists), a common agricultural policy, greater co-operation in fields of transport, law reform, etc. In 1981 Greece also joined whilst Portugal and Spain joined in 1986 making twelve member states in all.

CONTROL OF THE EC

The Council of Ministers Consists of at least one minister from each member state. On matters of vital importance a unanimous vote is required, thus any one country has the power to veto any proposal in its own national interest. On other matters a qualified majority of voters is required and a system of weighted voting exists with the larger countries having a greater number of votes.

The Commission This consists of commissioners appointed by member countries for a period of four years. Britain, France, Italy and West Germany provide two members each. Commissioners act independently of their own national interest and formulate proposals for consideration by Council. It is the largest of the four main EC institutions and is regarded as the 'Civil Service' of the Community.

The Court of Justice The Court is situated in Luxembourg and consists of judges representing each member country. The judges are appointed for six-year terms and they settle disputes and interpret rules and regulations made by both the council and commission. The Court is able to award damages and impose sanctions on cases brought before it.

The European Parliament Based in Strasbourg, its representatives are elected by member countries for a period of five years. Its role is mainly to consult and debate. Members can question policies made by the council and the commission. It has the power, by a two-thirds majority vote, to force the entire commission to resign.

THE ADVANTAGES AND DISADVANTAGES OF EC MEMBERSHIP TO BRITAIN

Britain joined the Common Market in 1973 after two previous attempts to join had failed. The following are some of the arguments put forward for and against Britain's continued Common Market membership.

Advantages

1 Opens up a wide market with a very large population (*c* 350m).
2 There are no tariff barriers between members.
3 The members of the EC have all enjoyed a high rate of economic growth and improvements in their standard of living.
4 Britain's position in the world was becoming less important – by joining with other European countries this forms an important voice in world affairs.
5 Most of Britain's trade is with the EC.
6 Competition should encourage British firms to become more efficient.

Disadvantages

1 Britain's contribution to the community budget is often greater than any aid she receives.
2 The common agricultural policy has meant that food prices are higher than previously.
3 Britain has lost her very close links with the Commonwealth countries such as Australia and Canada.
4 Britain has lost a great deal of her independence and control over her own affairs.
5 Since British agriculture is highly efficient much of the agricultural budget funds is spent on the inefficient farms abroad.

6 ▶ (*a*) What is the European Community?
(*b*) For what economic reasons was it formed?
(*c*) How has membership of the EC, effected the UK's pattern of foreign trade?
(*d*) What are the arguments
(i) in favour and

(ii) against the UK's continued membership of the EC?

THE IMPORT AND EXPORT TRADE

An extremely important section in this unit is a detailed analysis of the import and export trade.

THE EXPORT TRADE

PROBLEMS FACING THE EXPORTER

Language When a country exports to another country it must expect to translate all information into the language of the country, and employ salesmen who speak the language.

Standardised units Different countries of the world use different units of length, weight, capacity, etc. They may also use different systems of electrical wiring.

Currency The different currencies have an exchange rate with other currencies. Prices have to be converted into currency of the other country. If exchange rates are constantly fluctuating then pricing, etc, becomes very difficult.

Licences and documentation The importing country may have a list of rules and regulations with which all goods have to conform.

Risks of export trade These are numerous, e.g. fire, damage, theft or non-payment by the buyer.

Payment problems affecting exporters

1 Difficulties in obtaining payments from overseas.
2 Exchange control regulations prohibiting the transfer of funds.
3 Movements in exchange rates.
4 Insolvency of the foreign buyer.
5 Loss of interest on capital outlay when payment is delayed.

Methods of gaining export orders

Advertisement and circulars Goods can be advertised in trade journals of the importing country. However, care has to be taken in the use of words (these are often difficult to translate into another language or have different meanings). Another problem is that there is little personal element in this method.

Representatives Firms may employ a representative in the foreign country. These representatives can build up personal contacts. They must be fluent with the language and customs of the country as well as being knowledgeable about the product.

Visits of foreign buyers Foreign buyers and missions representing foreign governments may visit the firm. The advantage of this method is that it builds up personal contacts.

Foreign depots A firm may open a depot abroad which may keep stocks and spare parts. The depot can also act as a showroom.

Trade fairs and exhibitions Trade fairs are held regularly every year in different countries. These attract large numbers of buyers and sellers and firms are eager to gain orders at this time. There are also specialised 'British Weeks' held abroad when British products are promoted.

GOVERNMENT ASSISTANCE TO EXPORTERS

The Department of Trade This Department has responsibility for the development of British industry, commerce and trade. It determines commercial relations, services, promotions, finance and planning. It compiles statistics giving details of imports and exports, and issues journals detailing trade conditions in other countries.

The British Overseas Trade Board Provides information on Commonwealth and Common Market countries and also other foreign countries. The information available may include general trade information such as reports on contracts available and market conditions. It informs exporters about the existence of trade fairs and exhibitions and organises the 'British Weeks' and publishes annual reports about its activities.

The Export Credits Guarantee Department (ECGD) An undertaking run by the government for British exporters; it provides insurance for exporters against the main risks of selling abroad and is expected to run on a self-supporting basis. The exporter may insure against: protracted default of payment; action of foreign governments preventing payment; the outbreak of hostilities between Britain and the importing country; seizure of assets by foreign governments and any other cause of loss occurring outside Britain and not normally insurable. The ECGD also provides financial guarantees for British banks and firms who lend money to British exporters (refer also to page 190).

7 ▶ Many firms prefer to sell in the home market because of the extra problems and difficulties involved in exporting.

(*a*) What are these problems and difficulties?

(*b*) Explain how

(i) commercial organisations and

(ii) the government can help exporters overcome these problems.

(*c*) Why is exporting so important to the UK?

(*d*) State the usual methods by which overseas export orders are obtained.

THE IMPORT TRADE

Specialists in the import trade

Specialists can be found in most markets but they are especially useful in import and export trade because of the difficulties which are encountered.

Merchants As principals they deal on their own behalf and accept all the risk.

Agents Work on behalf of and under instructions from the principal for a commission. A 'del credere' agent for an extra commission will guarantee payment.

Factor Is an agent who has possession of the goods and has a great deal of authority in deciding selling price, method of sale, etc.

Broker Is the 'middleman' who is able to find buyers, has detailed knowledge of the market and works on commission.

DOCUMENTS USED IN OVERSEAS TRADE

1 The Bill of Lading This is a very important document as it confers a right to the goods to the holder of the bill. The bill presents the following information: the quantity, quality, weight and calculated value of the produce, the name of the ship carrying the goods and ports of loading and destination, and a statement that the shipowner is responsible for loss or damage due to employees.

When the produce is loaded it is checked by a tally clerk and if free of damage or deficiency a **clean bill** is issued. The ship's master or agent then signs the bill. There are three copies: one is retained by the shipping company and two are sent to the importer by different routes. The bill serves three useful functions: as an acknowledgement of receipt by the carrier, it is an agreement to carry the goods and it is negotiable and transferable by endorsement (signature) – i.e. the produce can be sold to another importer whilst still at sea.

2 Airway Bill Is similar to the Bill of Lading but deals with the shipment of goods by air. Whilst it is issued in triplicate however it is not a title of ownership nor is it transferable.

3 Consular Invoice A document signed by the consul of the importing country in the exporting country affirming the price of the products as quoted on the invoice.

4 Certificate of Origin A certificate confirming the export of goods from a particular country. This may be necessary if say goods are exported to a tariff-free area or where they are exported to a country giving reciprocal arrangements with import duties.

Customs duties and Excise duties

Customs duties are imposed on commodities entering the country from abroad. Excise duties are charged on commodities produced within the home country with a view to raising revenue for the State and reducing the consumption of certain goods.

Bonded warehouses

Customs authorities are required to levy duties on certain imported produce on arrival. However, the importer may not be willing or able to pay at that time. The produce is therefore placed in bonded warehouses by the customs until the duty is paid. Whilst the produce is in bond it can still be prepared for sale by the importer. The produce can even be sold while still in this state but duty must still be paid. If produce on which duty has been paid is subsequently re-exported then the duty will be refunded by the Customs (known as Customs Drawback).

MC12. The Export Credits Guarantee Department (ECGD) provides insurance cover for UK exporters against some of the risks of overseas trade.
It is a department of
A HM Customs & Excise
B the Treasury
C the Department of Trade and Industry
D Lloyd's of London
E the Bank of England

MC13. The necessary document required by an importer to claim goods on arrival is
A a Ship's Manifest
B Certificate of Origin
C Customs specification
D Bill of Exchange
E Bill of Lading

8 ▶ (*a*) A consignment is sent from Norway to Britain and a Bill of Exchange is prepared for the total amount due.
(i) Briefly explain the purpose of a Bill of Exchange,
(ii) who prepares it and
(iii) who are the signatories.

(*b*) 'When goods are sent by sea a Bill of Lading is always required, a charter party is sometimes required, a consignment note is never required.

(i) Explain why this is so,

(ii) indicate the use and importance of these three documents.

Methods of making payments in International Trade

1 Open account transactions This type of transaction takes place when the exporter and importer are well known to each other and the importer pays directly to a named bank account either in this country or abroad where the exporter keeps accounts.

2 By Bill of Exchange – known as 'the currency of international trade' (see page 201).

3 The merchant and commercial banks assist importers and exporters by making credit available (sometimes through government schemes), documentary credits, bank drafts, etc.

Data response question

The following figures relate to the UK balance of payments:

Year	Visible balance £ bn	Invisible balance £ bn	Current balance £ bn	Balance for official financing £ bn
1980	....	+2028	+3206	−1372
1985	−2068	+5020	....	+927

From the above statistics

(*a*) (i) What was the visible balance in 1980?

(ii) What was the current balance in 1985?

(*b*) To which of the categories given in the table would the following transactions belong?

(i) A British tourist in Spain pays for his/her hotel bill

(ii) The sale of Jaguar motor cars in the USA.

(iii) The flow of interest, profits and dividends into the UK from UK investments overseas.

(*c*) Describe the changes in balance of payments between 1980 and 1985.

(*d*) How might the government allocate the £927 billion surplus on the balance for official financing in 1985?

(*e*) Assume that an economy makes a large balance of payments deficit.

(i) Give three possible causes of this deficit.

(ii) What measures can the government of that country take to reduce the size of the deficit?

Answers

(*a*) (i) This visible balance in 1980 was £1,178 billion. This can be calculated from knowing that visible balance+invisible balance = current account balance, i.e. 1,178+2,028 = £3,206
(ii) Current balance = The invisible balance surplus minus the visible balance deficit, i.e. 5,020−2,068 = £2,952 bn

(*b*) (i) An invisible import
(ii) A visible export
(iii) An invisible export

(*c*) 1980 . . . a visible surplus of £1,178 billion plus an invisible surplus of £2,028 billion resulted in a current account surplus of £3,206 billion. However, the balance for official financing was a deficit of £1,372 billion. This implies a large outflow abroad of investment funds on investment and other capital flows.

1985 . . . a visible deficit of £2,068 billion plus an invisible surplus of £5,020 billion resulted in a current account surplus of £2,952. However, the balance for official financing was a surplus of £927 billion which implies a significant inflow of funds on investment and other capital flows.

(*d*) The surplus can be allocated in two ways:
– add to reserves of gold and foreign currency reserves.
– repay loans made from the International Monetary Fund (IMF) and also from other monetary authorities received in previous years.

(*e*) Answer for (i) Three possible causes of a balance of payments deficit:
– high prices of domestically produced goods (inflation).
– the exchange rate may be too high meaning that exports are expensive and imports are cheap.
– low quality of domestically produced goods.
Answer for (ii) Higher interest rates to attract investment to the company:
– deflationary policies to reduce inflation.
– lower exchange rate to increase exports and reduce imports.
– protectionist measures e.g. tariffs and quotas.

Answers to multiple choice questions

MC1	A	MC8	C
MC2	D	MC9	D
MC3	B	MC10	D
MC4	D	MC11	B
MC5	D	MC12	C
MC6	E	MC13	E
MC7	A		

MONEY AND BANKING

CONTENTS

The important subjects of money and banking in all their aspects are favourite topics with examination boards. This chapter studies the following:

1 Money – qualities of a good monetary medium, the functions of money, stages in the development of money, the cheque, Giro and clearing house systems.

2 Joint stock banks – the functions of commercial joint stock banks and how banks create credit.

3 The Bank of England – the functions of the Bank of England including control of monetary policy.

4 The National Savings Bank – Girobank plc – the money services provided through the Post Office.

5 Other major financial institutions – building societies, the discount houses, merchant banks (accepting houses) and issuing houses.

MONEY

Qualities of a good monetary medium

If something is to be acceptable as a good monetary medium it should possess the following qualities:

Portability: easily carried from place to place;

Durability: a long life, will not perish or wither away or be easily defaced;

Divisibility: easily divided into smaller amounts of money for small purchases;

Acceptability: accepted by people in the economy as having some value;

Scarcity: it should be limited in supply.

THE FUNCTIONS OF MONEY

It should perform the following four functions:

1 A medium of exchange

Money acts as **the medium** between any exchange. For instance workers will accept money for the labours they have performed and will use it to purchase their requirements of a variety of commodities and services. In a modern economy, money allows specialisation to take place since the workers know that they can use the money in order to satisfy their wants.

2 A measure of value

Money overcomes the disadvantages of amounts encountered in barter. How many of X should be exchanged for how many of Y? This problem is overcome since all goods and services are given a value in terms of money which can serve as a standard for comparing the values of different commodities, etc.

3 A store of value

When a commodity such as gold, silver, copper, etc. is acceptable as a form of money it can be stored. It is very convenient to hold wealth in this way. However, money may well lose its value if stored over a period of time, perhaps because of inflation (rising prices). This means that the monetary exchange value declines in terms of the goods and services which can be purchased.

4 A means of deferred payments

Money should be both acceptable and durable. This being so the buyer may be able to defer payment for a short period of time. The seller will accept this arrangement because of confidence in the fact that money will still have value when payment is eventually made. This often applies in modern business negotiations when say a three-month period is granted before payment need be made (see the section on Bills of Exchange on page 201). Of course inflation or rising prices may limit confidence in money as a means of deferred payment.

STAGES IN THE DEVELOPMENT OF MONEY

Money has not always had the form which we know today. It could be anything which a society wishes to give value and accept as money. Some forms have not always conformed to the qualities mentioned previously.

Barter The exchange of goods for other goods. This is used in relatively primitive societies. The disadvantages are that to work it depends on the 'double coincidence of wants' (when the two people exchanging goods both want the other item being offered). There is however the problem of amounts. How many of product X is worth how many of product Y?

In a modern economy barter would not be the usual form of exchange although it does occur from time to time, e.g. Nigeria recently bartered oil for Brazilian machinery.

One commodity used as money There have been many occasions when a particular commodity has been accepted as money. This normally occurs in undeveloped countries (for instance seashells have been used in the South Pacific Islands). It can also occur in moments of economic collapse in advanced economies, e.g. the use of cigarettes in Germany in the late 1920s and 1940s, thus there are obvious drawbacks in using commodities as money.

Coins As units of account they have been a good form of money. Originally they had value in themselves since they were made from the previous metals of gold or silver. However, in Britain's modern economy the coins in use are made from alloys of copper, nickel and bronze and as such have no real value in themselves.

Legal tender This refers to the fact that notes and coins of the Bank of England must be accepted in settlement of a debt in Britain. It also limits the amounts of coin which can be paid at any one time. (Notes issued by the Scottish Banks are legal tender only in that country but nevertheless usually accepted throughout Britain at their full face value.)

Bank notes Bank notes have their origins in the receipts for deposits of valuables issued by goldsmiths in the seventeenth century. These receipts were used as a means of exchange and were acceptable as a method of payment. Before 1914 most Bank of England notes were convertible in that they could be converted into gold. There is still written on these notes the words 'I promise to pay the bearer on demand the sum of (five) pounds,' referring to the fact that the bearer is entitled to gold. In today's economy however this is a worthless statement because notes are inconvertible and cannot therefore be converted into gold. These notes and coins are often referred to as 'token money' because they have no real commodity value but are still accepted as having *money* value.

Bank deposits subject to withdrawal by cheque In recent times Britain has increasingly become a 'cashless society' in that most payments, especially business transactions, are made in the form of a cheque. It is important to note that a cheque itself is not money but a representation of it. The money is the bank deposit whilst the cheque is merely a transfer order authorising the transfer of money from one bank account to another. A cheque however is not legal tender and cannot be enforced in payment of a debt in the same way as bank notes or coin.

Credit cards A recent innovation and becoming increasingly popular particularly in the field of personal financial affairs. Credit cards have the following characteristics:

1 A customer can make monthly purchases up to his/her credit limit – a figure agreed between the customer and the bank – thus saving on the use of cheques and possibly on bank charges as well.

2 Credit card details are printed on to a receipt/voucher issued by the retailer and signed by the customer.

(*a*) The top copy is kept by the customer as a receipt and record for checking with his or her statement.

(*b*) One copy is kept by the retailer as a record of the sale.

(*c*) One copy goes to computer headquarters of the issuing organisation. Details of the purchase are recorded and added to the retailer's and customer's accounts.

3 Once a month the computer centre sends the customer details of purchases and amount owing.

4 The customer is obliged to pay a minimum proportion of the debt within the next month and payment is recorded by computer.

5 If the customer pays all of the debt within the month his or her accounts is then clear and no interest is charged.

6 If the customer pays none or part of the debt, the computer calculates how much interest is to be charged and this is added on to the next month's account.

7 The monthly interest rate (about 2 per cent) is thus calculated twelve times a year and the actual annual rate would be quite high. It is therefore an expensive way to borrow money.

MC1. Some commercial bank credit cards allow the holders to

A buy goods on credit in certain shops
B cash a cheque in a post office
C draw an unlimited amount of money from any bank
D obtain special discounts
E obtain unlimited credit

MC2 Of all methods of payment the only recognised legal tender is

A cheques
B bank notes/coins
C cheques and bank notes
D Bills of Exchange
E bank notes and Bills of Exchange

MC3. Token coins are

A not legal tender
B valueless
C worth less than the value of the metal they contain
D worth more than the value of the metal they contain
E none of these

Consider the following question:

1 ▶ What are the main forms of money? What would be the effect on trade if the government doubled the supply of notes and coin?

CHEQUES AND THE CLEARING HOUSE SYSTEM

Cheques

As we have noted, a cheque is not considered as money. In this connection money is the bank deposit and the cheque is only an order to transfer money from the payer's account to the payee's account.

1 Crossed cheques and open cheques A crossed cheque is one which has two parallel lines drawn across its face. This means that unlike an 'open' cheque (where the person presenting the cheque to the branch bank on which it is drawn can obtain cash immediately) it must be 'cleared' through a bank account. It is therefore a safeguard against a thief or forger since cash will not be handed over straightaway and the cheque can be traced through the bank account. Most banks issue cheque books which are already crossed as an extra precaution for the customers.

2 A general crossing This is the two parallel lines we have mentioned already. Sometimes the words 'and Co.' will be written between the two lines but this has no legal significance.

3 A special crossing Consists of the name of the payee's bank written across the face of the cheque with or without the two parallel lines. Thus if 'Bank of Scotland' is written across the cheque its payment is restricted to that particular bank. Sometimes as an additional precaution a certain branch is added thus restricting payment to that bank *and* branch, e.g. 'Bank of Scotland, Lothian Road, Edinburgh'.

4 'Not negotiable' is sometimes written in the crossing as an extra safeguard. It does *not* mean that the cheque cannot be negotiated – passed from one person to another in settlement of a debt – but if the cheque has been stolen it enables the rightful owner to recover his or her debt. Thus the receiver should be on guard to ensure that the person passing (negotiating) the cheque really does own it. In the absence of the words 'not negotiable' the right to claim the value may belong to the person holding the cheque *even though it had been stolen*.

5 Endorsing a cheque If a cheque is endorsed it means that the payee signs his or her name on the back. Thus a cheque could be transferred to a new payee. For instance a cheque is written payable to B. Smith. Smith can transfer the cheque to a new payee R. Pearce by writing on the back of the cheque 'Pay R. Pearce' and signing his or her name, Pearce will also have to sign the cheque and the value of that cheque will be paid into his or her account.

6 Bearer cheques These are not a safe type of cheque and are actively discouraged since anyone who presents such a cheque at the bank and branch where the account is kept (the bearer) receives payment.

7 Order cheques These are worded 'Pay . . . or order' and in normal circumstances only paid by the bank to the person named after the word 'pay'. It is in fact 'a command' by the drawer to the bank to pay a specified person or firm (the payee) the stated amount.

8 A/c Payee This can be written between the two parallel lines which places a restriction of transfer on the payee. The cheque should normally be cleared into the account of the named payee. If however the payee wishes to pass the cheque on to another person the bank must make enquiries before paying into that new person's account.

9 Dishonoured cheques A dishonoured unpaid cheque is one where the drawer may not have sufficient funds to cover the amount of the cheque, and in this case it would be returned marked 'Refer to Drawer'. Other instances where cheques would be returned by the bank would be where the date is incorrect, the words and figures differ, the cheque is incorrectly endorsed, or it has not been signed. The bank will not honour the cheque but will return it to the payee advising the reason for non-payment.

MC4. When dealing with a cheque, the bank's duty is to carry out the instructions of the

A payee
B drawee
C manager
D Bank of England
E drawer

MC5. I receive a cheque in payment of a debt. As it is an open cheque, I draw two parallel lines across the face, write my name on the back and send it to another person to whom I owe money. In doing so, I

A have acted wrongly, since I had no right to cross the cheque
B have acted correctly, and my creditor may pay it into his bank
C need not have endorsed it
D have prevented my creditor from passing it on to one of his creditors
E should first advise my bank

MC6. I receive a crossed cheque from a customer, Mr Smith. Later the cheque disappears from my office, and cannot be found. I should

A inform my bank to stop payment of the cheque
B ask Mr Smith to inform his bank to stop payment of the cheque
C wait until the cheque is found, otherwise lose the money

D do nothing about it, since the cheque must eventually find its way into my bank account.
E make out a duplicate myself

MC7. Which of the following best defines a cheque?
A an order by a drawer requiring a banker to pay the payee
B a promise by a banker to pay the payee
C a promise by a drawer to pay the drawee
D an order by a bank requiring another bank to pay the payee
E a demand by the payee to the bank for payment

MC8. A cheque I have paid in to my account is returned to me by my bank marked 'Refer to drawer'. This means that:
A the cheque was incorrectly drawn, e.g. the date is missing or the words do not agree with the figures
B I neglected to endorse it before paying it in
C the drawer did not have sufficient money in his account to meet it, and has made no overdraft arrangements with his bank
D the drawer wishes to see me before the debt is settled
E my bank requires another cheque to be drawn

You should be able to answer the following essay questions:

2 ▶ What are the advantages of making payments by cheque? How do cheques differ from
(*a*) bank notes
(*b*) postal orders
(*c*) credit cards?

You can answer the first part of this question from this chapter. Refer to page 201 for a discussion on Bills of Exchange and page 197 for postal orders.

3 ▶ State what is meant by 'crossing a cheque' and give examples of crossings. Explain the two terms 'not negotiable' and 'account payee only'.

4 ▶ On 1 June 1986 Miss S. R. Thomas wrote an order cheque to Miss G. Gregory for £50 drawn on Barminster Bank, Wolverhampton.
(*a*) Name the drawer, the payee and the drawee.
(*b*) The cheque is crossed 'Account payee' and 'not negotiable'. Explain the effects of these crossings.

5 ▶ (*a*) Why have cheques largely replaced currency as a means of settling debts?
(*b*) Mention any restrictions in the use of cheques to settle transactions.

In answering 5 (*a*) you should make the following points:

1 Cheques are more convenient than bundles of notes and bulky coins.
2 They can be crossed to make it impossible for a thief to obtain the cash.
3 They can be made out for any amount at any time and place and eliminate the need for cash.
4 They are more convenient for sending through the post.
5 They are only of value after being signed by the drawer.

Part (*b*) can be answered by reference to crossed cheques on page 183.

THE CLEARING HOUSE SYSTEM

When a cheque is made payable and given to someone the cheque itself has to pass through the banking system to be **cleared** – that is the account of the drawer (or payer), the person who writes the cheque, must be debited by the amount of that cheque. Likewise the bank account of the payee (the person who receives the cheque) must be credited.

When both payer and payee have accounts at the same branch in the same town the procedure is quite simple:
Brown of Lloyds Bank, Worcester, pays Smith of Lloyds Bank, Worcester, £100 by cheque. Smith pays the cheque into his bank account at Lloyds, Worcester. Smith's account is credited with £100 and Brown's account is debited with £100 on the same day.

When both payer and payee have accounts with the same bank but in different towns then:
Brown of Lloyds Bank, Worcester, pays Jones of Lloyds Bank, Portsmouth, £100 by cheque. Jones pays the cheque into Lloyds Bank, Portsmouth, for the immediate credit of his account. The cheque is sent to Lloyds' Head Office in Lombard Street, London. Head Office then send the cheque to Lloyds, Worcester, where Brown's account will be debited by the amount of the cheque. As in the previous example no actual money in the form of notes or coin has been moved.

When payer and payee belong to different banks in the same or different towns then:
Brown of Lloyds Bank, Worcester, pays Edwards of Midland Bank, Birmingham, £100 by cheque. Edwards pays the cheque into his account at Midland Bank, Birmingham, and his account is immediately credited with this amount. This bank then sends the cheque to their Head Office in London who take it to the Bankers Clearing House, also in London. At the clearing house, representatives of all member banks meet in order to exchange cheques drawn on each other. The cheque is passed by the Midland Bank Clearing House representative to the Lloyds Bank representative. It is taken to the

Lloyds Bank Head Office and the following day is received at Lloyds Bank, Worcester, where Brown's account will be debited.

At the end of a day's clearing at the Clearing House, settlement between banks is made and balances will be transferred out of deposits held at the Bank of England. This will be because customers of some banks may have written more cheques than they have received, leaving one bank in debt to other banks.

Consider the following essay question:

6 ▶ Explain briefly the cheque clearing house procedure necessary for payment by cheque.

COMMERCIAL BANKS

Commercial banks may also be called joint stock banks (because they issue shares), clearing banks (because they clear cheques) or high street banks (because they are situated mostly in the main or high street of towns). In essay questions commercial banks may be called by any of these alternative names.

The four principal commercial banks in Britain at the present time are Barclays, Lloyds, Midland and National Westminster. However, there are other important commercial banks including the Royal Bank of Scotland, Clydesdale Bank, TSB Group, Bank of Scotland, Standard Chartered and the Co-operative Bank, which have numerous branches throughout Britain.

The origins of the commercial banks are to be found in the goldsmiths of the seventeenth century who accepted deposits of valuables and in return issued receipts which were the beginnings of bank notes (see also page 181). The goldsmiths developed into private banks (usually partnerships) and in turn developed into joint stock banks. Amalgamations have taken place over time and today there are only a few large commercial banks remaining.

THE FUNCTIONS OF COMMERCIAL BANKS

Acceptance of deposits

When an individual opens an account with a bank this, from the bank's viewpoint, is regarded as a liability since that money is owed by the bank to the depositor (hence the customer is a **creditor**). There are four types of account which can be opened:

1 Current Accounts The advantages of a current account are that: money is secure; is repayable on demand; a cheque book is given and the holder therefore enjoys the advantages of being able to issue cheques (see page 183); the holder may use most of the services offered by the bank.

The disadvantage is that no interest is payable on money in the account – thus the customer should endeavour to keep the minimum balance in the account so as not to incur charges and the maximum realistically possible in interest-bearing accounts.

2 Deposit accounts The advantages are that they receive a rate of interest on deposit balance (subject to tax deducted at source) and the holder can deposit surplus funds at any time.

Depositors should whenever possible constantly review their balances in order to obtain the most effective rate of interest. Other possibilities include building society term deposits, local authority loans, unit trusts, national savings, etc. A great deal of course will depend upon the depositor's personal choice of accessibility of funds and his or her tax position.

The disadvantages are: no cheque book; the depositor will have to wait for a period of time (usually seven days) before withdrawing money; there is a restriction on use of the bank's other services; the rate of interest is often below the amount that may be obtained elsewhere.

3 Savings accounts These earn a low rate of interest and are intended for the small saver who is saving for a particular purpose. Small sums can be withdrawn on demand.

4 Budget accounts These accounts cover such regular demands as rates, electricity and gas bills, insurance premiums. The depositor calculates how much there is to be paid every month and transfers this amount from the current account into a budget account. He or she can make payments by standing order when the bills fall due, adjusting the account accordingly at the end of the year.

MAKING LOANS

The making of loans is a highly profitable part of a bank's business. They are made in a variety of ways:

Creating a loan account Here the customer has an agreed amount credited to his or her account. At the same time a loan account is debited with that same amount. The loan is repaid by regular instalments out of monthly salary, etc. Interest is usually calculated on *the initial amount* borrowed and is included in the repayments. It is therefore an expensive way of borrowing and not as cheap as the overdraft.

Granting an overdraft An overdraft allows a customer to overspend, or withdraw, on his or her current account up to an agreed sum and for a given time. A rate of interest is charged on *the daily amount* borrowed and is therefore more economical than a loan account.

Interest payments on loans The rates of interest charged by the commercial banks is based upon a **base rate**, the size of the margin above that rate depending upon the nature of the loan and the status of the customer. A change in the base rate normally signifies a change in the (London) market rates, thus the base rate is widely used as an indicator of market trends.

ISSUING CREDIT CARDS

The credit card system is mainly organised by the commercial banks (see page 182).

It is worth noting that the government often dislikes this aspect of banks' activity since they have the power to create money which may cause inflation. We discuss how banks do this and what the government does to restrict their ability to do so on page 194.

ACTING AS AGENT FOR PAYMENT

There are two principal ways by which banks are involved in this process:

1 Making payments to creditors at home:

Cheques (see page 183). This method is used when the creditor knows or trusts the drawer and is willing to accept his or her cheque. It may also be used when paying on an irregular basis.

Banker's order (or standing order) A banker's order is used when a regular amount can be paid by the bank on authorisation from the customer. Thus the bank saves the customer time and trouble in remembering to pay these regular bills and in addition saves the customer postage and correspondence. It is also a useful method of payment when sums such as insurance premiums have to be made at regular intervals.

Direct debits These are similar to banker's orders (above) but are authorisations by the customer for the bank to accept any amount from named persons or organisations for the debit of his or her account.

Bank Giro (or credit transfer) Where a business has a number of creditors to pay monthly, it can avoid the cost and inconveniences of writing several cheques by using the Bank Giro.

The firm can make out one cheque covering the total of all payments plus a list of creditors with details of account numbers and bank branches. Private customers can also use this service to pay their bills, such as gas, water, telephone, electricity, etc.

Banker's drafts A cheque may not be acceptable to a creditor especially if the drawer is not known. A banker's draft is in reality a bank cheque, signed by the bank's officials drawn on itself and made payable to the payee. The drawer will at the same time write a cheque, drawn by him or herself, in favour of the bank. The creditor will therefore accept the banker's draft as being safe and secure. The method of payment is frequently used when the creditor will not accept the personal cheque and needs more security, as in the case of a house sale.

2 Making payments to creditors abroad

Banker's drafts These are widely used in international trade. They may be drawn in any currency and are payable through the bank or its agents abroad.

Accepting bills of exchange An ordinary bill of exchange (see page 201) may not be acceptable to an overseas creditor who may have no knowledge of the purchaser of the goods. In such a case the bank, for a commission, will agree to accept (or guarantee) the bill. By such an acceptance the bill of exchange becomes more negotiable since the name of the bank is known worldwide.

Bank credits These are used when the bank accepts bills of exchange drawn on a British importer either for a single transaction or a year's trading. A credit amount or limit is agreed and the bank guarantees the payment of the bill to a foreign merchant. The bank therefore becomes responsible for the payment of the bill – this system is used when many bills of exchange will need to be accepted.

Documentary Credit Here the bank agrees to accept bills of exchange on behalf of the customer who is importing the goods. Thus the foreign exporter can more readily offer the bill for discount at his or her bank abroad. The British importer is responsible for paying the bill when due but the bank has the right to the goods if the bill is not paid. Documentary credits are used if the foreign exporter wishes to have payment and cash in the short term.

Consider this question:

7 ▶ Commercial banks specialise in the making of payments to creditors both at home and overseas.
(*a*) What methods are available?
(*b*) Under what circumstances would each be used?

Other services provided by banks include:

1 Purchase and sale of foreign exchange and travellers' cheques.
2 Investments – the bank may employ a firm of stockbrokers to buy or sell stocks and shares on behalf of its customers – it will also keep the securities safely and collect dividends for its customers.
3 Custody of valuables such as deeds, silver, jewellery, etc.
4 Night safes – businesspeople can deposit cash after the bank has closed.

5 Cheque cards, credit cards, status enquiries, cash dispensers, company registration and overseas reports.

6 Executor and trustee business – the administration of a dead person's estate may be taken on by a bank if so requested. In addition specialist departments may undertake a private individual's tax returns and give advice on tax matters.

7 Factoring – the bank may agree to factor the debts of its client. It purchases, collects the debts and in return has some responsibility in the running of the firm.

The functions of commercial banks are an extremely important topic in the syllabus and you should be prepared to answer questions similar to the following:

8 ▶ (*a*) Explain the different types of bank accounts which can be opened.
(*b*) What are the advantages to the trader of having a current account at a commercial bank?

9 ▶ Distinguish between a bank deposit account and a bank current account. Explain from the point of view of a trader why a current account is necessary and when a deposit account can be useful.

10 ▶ (*a*) Discuss instances where both individuals and firms are able to borrow from commercial banks.
(*b*) Briefly describe a situation in which loan facilities would be:
(i) agreed
(ii) refused by the bank.

MC9. My standing order at the bank means
A I can receive cash from my account without presenting cheques
B the bank will refer to me before paying cheques I have drawn
C I can overdraw my account up to an agreed figure
D the bank will pay on my behalf an agreed amount at agreed intervals until I cancel the order
E none of these

MC10. Suppose you have overdraft arrangements and your bank statement shows an overdraft of £1,000; this definitely means you
A may not draw any more cheques until repayment is made in full
B are owed £1,000 by the bank
C may not use any of the services
D owe the bank £1,000 only
E will have to repay over £1,000

MC11. When opening a current account at a bank, you will be asked for

A birth certificate
B specimen photograph
C driving licence
D passport
E specimen signature

MC12. I can overdraw on my current account at the bank provided that
A I inform the bank and am willing to pay interest
B I have a deposit account at the same bank
C I have the written to the bank and can provide security
D I have the bank's permission and am willing to pay extra bank charges
E all branches are advised

MC13. The holder of a bank current account is entitled to
A a share in the bank's profits
B ask the bank for an overdraft
C receive interest on the balance of the account
D vote at the bank's annual general meeting
E receive preferential treatment on all services

THE BANK OF ENGLAND

The Bank of England is often called by examiners 'the Central Bank', this is because it is at the centre of the British banking system. The Bank of England originated in 1694 when William III wanted to raise money to fight the French. It developed into the most important private bank. In the Bank Charter Act, 1844 its pre-eminence was established and Bank of England notes were to be the most important bank notes issued. In 1946 it was nationalised and at the present time keeps the principal government accounts and is therefore the government's bank.

THE FUNCTIONS OF THE BANK OF ENGLAND

1 Notes issue

The Bank Charter Act, 1844 ensured that the Bank of England was to become the main note-issuing bank of the country. Today the Bank of England has a monopoly in this apart from a few Scottish and Northern Irish banks.

2 The bankers' bank

The commercial banks use the Bank of England in a similar manner to private customers using a commercial bank. The banks keep reserves at the Bank of England which as we have seen are used, among other things, to make payments after a day's clearing of cheques.

3 External responsibilities

The Bank of England has close contact with the central banks of other countries. It provides services for other central banks, e.g. holding their reserves of sterling. International organisations such as the International Monetary Fund and International Bank for Reconstruction and Development also keep some reserves with the Bank of England.

4 Open market operations

Since 1981 this has been an important aspect of monetary policy. The emphasis is now on open market operations in commercial bills. The Bank aims to keep short-term rates of interest within an unpublished band which it may change from time to time. Discount houses, when they are short of funds, must now offer to sell acceptable bills to the Bank of England which the Bank will agree to take in exchange for cash only if the discount terms are within the unquoted band of interest rate. Hence the reluctance of financial institutions to borrow from the Bank of England unless absolutely necessary, i.e. the Bank is **'a lender of the last resort'**.

5 The government's bank

This is a most important function of the Bank of England and includes:

Protection of gold and dollar reserves – it determines the lending rate (see page 195), administers government regulations as regards control of foreign exchange and arranges loans to improve Britain's reserves.

Management of Exchange Equalisation Account – if the pound is in danger of dropping in value in terms of foreign currencies and the government does not wish this to occur, the Exchange Equalisation Account will purchase pounds, with foreign currency, on the exchange markets. If the pound is rising in value however, the government may require the Exchange Equalisation Account to sell pounds to keep its value down. Thus the value of the pound is kept more stable over a short period of time so assisting importers and exporters and promoting confidence in the economy.

Management of the Exchequer Account – the Bank of England receives tax revenues into this account and administers government spending.

Management of the National Debt – the National Debt is the amount owed by the government to individuals and organisations both at home and abroad. Foreign governments may also hold some of the debt as their reserves. The debt consists of Government securities, both long- and short-term, issued by the Bank of England to help to finance Government spending. An important type of security is the **Treasury Bill** which is a short-term loan to the government (three months) paying interest at the current rate. In addition the Bank of England organises payment of interest on the National Debt.

Operation of the government's monetary policy This is such an important function we shall examine it in great detail in the next section.

HOW COMMERCIAL BANKS CREATE CREDIT, THE BANK OF ENGLAND AND MONETARY POLICY

You should follow this analysis closely, especially as it is quite difficult to understand.

The money supply consists of notes and coins in circulation, and bank deposits. Of course the government can create money itself by issuing more notes and coins. However, banks themselves can create money (or credit in this context) since they can create bank deposits. For the purpose of example we may assume that a bank makes a loan to a customer of £1,000. If the customer pays this to his or her creditor who is a customer of the same bank, the following situation has arisen:

Bank's liabilities	Bank's assets
Deposits £1,000 (from customer)	Loans £1,000 (to customer)

The bank has therefore created credit.

Of course not every customer of the bank requires a loan – many keep their accounts in credit without having the need to overdraw and large sums are kept on deposit. At an early stage in their development banks realised that depositors would not require all their money back at once. All that the bank was required to do was to keep back some of the deposits in reserve asset form to meet demands of depositors. The bank was therefore in a position to lend out the rest at interest.

As an example assume there is a 10 per cent reserve asset ratio (i.e. 10 per cent of deposits have to be kept back in the form of liquid reserve assets).

In its most sophisticated form an initial deposit of £1,000 can support the creation of £9,000 of additional deposits.

Bank's liabilities		Bank's assets	
Initial deposit	£1,000	Reserve assets	£1,000
Created deposits	£9,000	Loans	£9,000
	£10,000		£10,000

In other words the bank has treated all the initial deposits as reserve assets enabling it to create loans of £9,000. Reserve assets at £1,000 are 10 per cent of total deposits standing at £10,000. Thus the bank is confident it can meet any demands on it by depositors.

Limits to this process of credit creation

The Bank of England and the government may sometimes wish to restrict the banks' ability to create credit because it is considered inflationary since it will increase consumer demand.

In addition to the balances held at the Bank of England, the clearing banks are required to keep a further proportion of their deposits in short-term easily redeemed assets. Thus they must satisfy the Bank of England that **adequate liquidity is available.**

Government monetary policy

A restrictionist monetary policy is created when the government, through its agent, the Bank of England, attempts to reduce money supply. The instruments of a restrictionist monetary policy include:

1 **Open market operations** – the Bank of England sells securities (government stocks and shares) on the open market. These are purchased by investors who write cheques out to the Bank of England. The commercial banks' deposits at the Bank of England are reduced accordingly. This reduces the minimum reserve assets and the power of the banks to create credit.

2 **Special deposits** – the Bank of England may call in special deposits from the commercial banks. This again reduces the power of the commercial banks to create credit.

3 **Government directives** – the government may issue directives through the Bank of England to stop creating credit. This may be to one particular sector of the economy or to the economy in general.

4 **Funding** the Bank of England will sell long-term government securities e.g. Treasury Stock, Exchequer Stock, etc. through the Stock Exchange. It is similar to open market operations but extends over a longer period since the stock may not be repaid for many years.

5 **The Bank's lending rate** The Bank of England conducts its operations so as to keep short-term interest rates within an unpublished band. All other interest rates tend to follow its lead, making credit more expensive and therefore less attractive.

These are the weapons of monetary policy. As we have seen a restrictionist monetary policy is introduced in an attempt to reduce inflation. On the other hand an expansionist monetary policy (where the monetary weapons are used in the opposite way, e.g. a decrease in the Bank's lending rate) will be introduced in an attempt to increase employment and stimulate economic growth and output.

The Bank of England, its functions and its management of monetary policy is an important area of work. You should be able to answer the following essay questions:

11 ▶ Compare and contrast the principal functions of the Bank of England with those of the commercial banks.

12 ▶ It is sometimes said that 'banks can create money and credit'. Is this a true statement?

13 ▶ 'The Bank of England is a Central Bank.' What is meant by this statement?

14 ▶ Commercial banks are said to 'create credit'. Explain how this is done and state how the government may limit this process.

To answer this last question you need to explain how commercial banks can increase the money supply or create credit (as on page 194). This government may impose restrictions on their ability to do so and this is outlined on page 195.

15 ▶ (*a*) What differences are there between a credit account at a store and a deposit account at a bank?
(*b*) Describe fully four banking services which are offered to businessmen other than the operation of their accounts.

MC14. The Central Bank in Britain is called
A Lombard Banking
B The Midland Bank
C The Bank of England
D The National Bank
E Royal Bank of Scotland

MC15. Inflation means that money
A rises in value
B falls in value
C is decimalised
D becomes scarce
E becomes larger in denomination

MC16. English bank notes are printed by order of the
A Bank of England
B Royal Mint
C Stationery Office
D Treasury
E Prime Minister

FINANCIAL FACILITIES OFFERED BY THE POST OFFICE

THE POST OFFICE

The following are facilities for payment offered by the Post Office in Britain:

Postage stamps Rarely used and only for very small payments by post. In certain situations the Post Office will repurchase stamps in exchange for cash.

Postal orders Issued by the Post Office for varying sums of up to £20. The value of the order can be increased by fixing postage stamps in the space provided. The Post Office makes a charge called **poundage** depending on the amount of the order.

Postal orders are issued blank and the sender is recommended to fill in the name of the payee and the office of payment. They are marked 'not negotiable' (see page 183) thus protecting the payee in the event of theft. They can be crossed like a cheque especially if the postal order is to be paid into a bank account.

A counterfoil is attached to the order and should be kept by the sender as a reference in case of loss. Compared to cheques postal orders suffer disadvantages:

1 the time and inconvenience spent in purchasing postal orders and filling them in;
2 most traders have bank accounts thus cheques are more easily issued;
3 uncrossed postal orders are easily misappropriated without detection;
4 for large amounts they are more expensive than cheques (for small amounts the postal order would probably be cheaper).
5 There is no poundage tax on cheques.

Postal orders are popular topics in examination questions. You may be required to compare postal orders and cheques as in the following questions:

16 ▶ Explain the circumstances under which postal orders would be used to settle an account rather than cheques. How can one increase the security of these items when transmitting via the postal system?

Overseas money orders Available up to £50 to certain countries abroad. The sender is required to fill in a form stating the amount of the order, the name of the payee, where payable and whether an open or crossed order. The form is handed together with the money to the Post Office clerk and the order is sent to the payee abroad. Alternatively a telegraphic money order which is speedier may be sent to the payee. The payee abroad is required to produce evidence of identity after which he or she will be paid out in the local currency.

THE NATIONAL GIROBANK

The National Girobank (Girobank plc) offers full banking facilities through the Post Office network as follows:

Private accounts for personal use – these include current, deposit, budget and loan accounts as follows:

(a) Current accounts may be opened at any Post Office. Cheque books are issued in the normal way to account holders and up to £50 cash may be withdrawn if required at nominated Post Offices. Facilities also exist for salary or wages to be credited by employers, standing orders to be debited, transfers between account holders and cheque guarantee cards issued to approved customers. In addition small overdrafts are allowed for short periods and statements sent out after every credit entry or ten debits.

(b) Deposit accounts can be opened by current account holders. Interest is paid half yearly and withdrawals may be made without notice by transfer to current account. A bonus interest is also paid on certain minimum balances held.

(c) Budget accounts are available to current account holders over the age of eighteen. This type of account is used to pay regular bills of varying amounts such as gas, electricity, telephone, etc, when due. An agreed fixed amount is transferred monthly from current account to cover the total amount due. A customer may overdraw up to four times the monthly transfer but repayment has to be completed by the end of the year.

(d) Personal loans are also available to current account customers over eighteen who may borrow certain minimum and maximum sums from one to three years. In certain cases (such as home improvements) loans may be extended up to five years.

Business accounts for all types of firms from sole traders to nationalised industries. Special facilities are offered including the collection of deposits through specialised accounts. Statements are sent at regular intervals or after every transaction according to the customer's requirements.

The National Girobank also offers the following facilities:

1 transfers from one account to another;
2 deposit into accounts by both the account holder or non-account holder;
3 payments in cash up to £100 at a nominated Post Office;
4 a cheque guarantee card for use in shops, restaurants, garages, etc;
5 other facilities including links with the International Giro network;

Consider the following question:

17 ▶ Compare a Girobank account with a current account at a commercial bank in relation to the following:

(*a*) deposits
(*b*) withdrawals
(*c*) methods of making payments
(*d*) other services

Refer to page 187 for a discussion on current accounts at the commercial banks.

CASH ON DELIVERY SERVICES

The sender completes a form stating the value of the goods – the trade charge, which is to be collected from the recipient. The receiver must pay the trade charge to gain possession of the goods when delivered. If payment is refused the goods are returned to the Post Office and ultimately to the sender. A charge is made by the Post Office proportionate to the trade charge.

NATIONAL SAVINGS BANK

A national system for depositing and withdrawing savings from any Post Office. A limit is placed on how much any one investor can save. There are two types of account:

(*a*) the **ordinary account** on which interest is paid and withdrawals can take place on demand at any Post Office on presentation of the deposit book

(*b*) the **investment account** which receives a higher rate of interest but notice has to be given before withdrawals take place.

The funds of the National Savings Bank can be used to purchase government stock and thereby make loans to the government.

Consider the following questions:

18 ▶ Explain how you would make payment of the following amounts from a London office:

(*a*) £0.67 to a firm in Woking
(*b*) £52 to a firm in Leeds
(*c*) £100 to an employee who is working away and has no banking account

Explain in each case the advantages of the method you suggest over other methods.

19 ▶ Describe each of the following services offered by the commercial banks and give an example of the use of each service by a trader during the conduct of his business:

(*a*) standing order
(*b*) bank overdraft
(*c*) direct debit
(*d*) night safe

MC17. Crossed postal and overseas money orders
A can be cashed at the Post Office
B can be paid into a bank account
C cannot be refused by a creditor
D can be 'uncrossed' by a payee
E none of these

BUILDING SOCIETIES

In Britain at the present time there are about 160 separate societies dominated by a small number of large organisations including the Halifax, Abbey National, Leeds Permanent, Woolwich Equitable, etc. Many of the smaller units tend to be local in character but taking the building society movement as a whole it forms an important part of the money market.

The purpose of building societies is to borrow funds from people willing to invest their surplus funds in return for a safe investment and tax-free interest to the standard rate of tax payer. The total amount due to depositors is over £104,000 million. A high proportion of this amount is lent to owner-occupiers of private dwelling houses. Repayments are made out of current income over any period but usually between twenty and twenty-five years. The amount lent to borrowers is about £90,000 million at the present time.

Since the societies are lending depositors' money, certain safeguards have to be met before a loan is agreed. These include:

(*a*) The society must not over-lend since a large amount of the deposits are repayable on demand.

(*b*) Title deeds of the mortgaged property are held by the society until the loan is completely repaid with interest.

(*c*) Full insurance cover must be taken out by the property owner.

(*d*) The society will lend up to about 90 per cent of the property value, as valued by a qualified surveyor.

(*e*) The society has to be satisfied that the borrower will be able to repay the loan over the stipulated period. The maximum loan therefore is usually 2½-3 times the annual salary of the borrower(s).

DISCOUNT HOUSES, ACCEPTING HOUSES AND ISSUING HOUSES

DISCOUNT HOUSES

The London Discount Market consists of ten discount houses. Their main function is to 'discount' a variety of bills, securities or 'promises to pay' issued by the government, Local Authorities, banks and industrial firms. Discounting is the process of buying a security for less than its face value and holding the security until it matures. The Discount Houses fulfil a very useful function, providing short-term funds which are always in great demand by both government and industry. They deal amongst other things in Bills of Exchange (see page 201) and Treasury bills. Discount Houses also act as underwriters (i.e. they will purchase any surplus not taken up by the members of the money market) to the Treasury bill issue.

Discount Houses need a great deal of capital to finance their activities. They receive money from deposits by the public, foreign sources, borrowings from the commercial banks and the Bank of England. The loans from the commercial banks are considered by the commercial banks to be part of their easily redeemed assets and are termed 'money at call' (see page 188).

For an analysis of how the Bank of England acts as 'lender of the last resort' to the Discount Houses refer back to page 193.

ACCEPTING HOUSES (OR MERCHANT BANKS)

Examples include Barings, Lazards and Rothschilds. The traditional business of Accepting Houses is the accepting of **Bills of Exchange**, which are widely used in the settlement of international debts. They are unconditional orders made by importers accepting liability for the payment of money to exporters at an agreed future date. This means that for a commission, the Accepting House will guarantee that a bill will be paid on maturity. Thus, the bill will be more easily discounted on the discount market. By endorsing the bill therefore, the Accepting House guarantees payment of the bill should the drawer default. This is an important role since it allows trade to take place between two firms (perhaps in different countries) who are not known to each other. The name of the Accepting House however will be known worldwide. (This aspect of their business is in decline due largely to the reduced role of the commercial Bill of Exchange and competition from commercial banks in the business of overseas credit).

They fulfil a wider role in that they control unit trusts (see page 215), and give financial advice to firms on investment management, on insurance and on sponsoring new capital issues. They also provide an expertise which is in great demand by foreign and British firms alike.

ISSUING HOUSES

These specialise in the issue of new securities. Examples are Rothschilds and Morgan Grenfell. Many Issuing Houses also act as Accepting Houses. They arrange the public issue of stocks and shares on behalf of governments and firms. You should refer to page 205 for an analysis of the new issue market. Issuing Houses will underwrite a new share issue to ensure that all shares are taken up. The offer loans to companies and also offer advice on new issues as regards price of issues and numbers of shares to be sold.

Consider the following questions:

Explain the role played by Issuing Houses in the London new issue market.

To answer this question refer also to page 211 on the new issue of shares.

Describe the work of the London Accepting Houses (and other financial institutions) in the financing of foreign trade through Bills of Exchange.

What part is played by the Discount Houses in the British financial system? Do you feel that their continued existence is justified? Give your reasons.

CASE STUDY

John has recently received £5,000 in redundancy money from his previous employer and with his wife Jane they have a further £3,000 in savings in a building society. They are considering the purchase of an existing business in a busy thoroughfare for £33,000. This is to be paid for by using their savings and redundancy money and borrowing the remainder from a local bank.

The following is a summary of their anticipated expenses and takings for the year:

Payments	£	Receipts	£
Salaries (John and Jane)	12,000	Sales	42,000
Annual interest (fixed) on loan	5,000		
Cost of materials	14,000		
Sundry costs	1,000		

(*a*) Advise John and Jane on two types of legal ownership they should consider.

(*b*) What accounts should they have at the bank
(i) as individuals
(ii) for the business?

(*c*) Calculate the rate of interest to be paid on the loan.

(*d*) What security would be required by the bank?

(*e*) Give two reasons why the bank manager may refuse the loan.

Answers to multiple choice questions

MC1	A	MC10	E
MC2	B	MC11	E
MC3	D	MC12	D
MC4	E	MC13	B
MC5	B	MC14	C
MC6	B	MC15	B
MC7	A	MC16	A
MC8	C	MC17	B
MC9	D		

THE STOCK EXCHANGE

CONTENTS

In this chapter the following topics will be discussed:

1 The **meaning of the Stock Exchange**, including what is the Stock Exchange? Examples of stock exchanges, why investors buy securities, and the management of the Stock Exchange.
2 **How the Stock Exchange works**, including stockbrokers and market makers, how shares are bought and sold, types of shares traded, speculation, factors which may cause share prices to change, the Official List.
3 What are the **advantages and disadvantages** of the Stock Exchange?
4 **Unit trusts and investment trusts.**

THE MEANING OF THE STOCK EXCHANGE

What is the Stock Exchange? The Stock Exchange is a type of market where dealings in government stocks, public company shares and similar types of **securities** take place. It provides the means whereby buyers and sellers of stocks and shares, etc, can carry out their necessary exchanges. In other words, it is largely a market for securities that have already been issued. It is important for you to note that not all stocks and shares of public companies are sold on the Stock Exchange. When stocks and shares are first issued they may be sold in one of the following ways:

1 by Issuing Houses (see page 201) to the general public acting as agents for the company;
2 entirely to Issuing Houses who will later sell them to the general public or large institutions such as insurance companies;
3 placed with particular shareholders;
4 offered to existing shareholders and the general public.

As a result, when the person or institution that first bought the securities wishes to sell them at a later date they will be sold on the Stock Exchange.

EXAMPLES OF STOCK EXCHANGES

The London Stock Exchange is the most important exchange in Britain and forms part of a network which includes a number of exchanges in other cities in Britain, such as Bristol, Manchester and Glasgow.

The Stock Exchange in London

Dealings in stocks and shares began in Britain in the second half of the seventeenth century with the growth of joint stock limited companies (see page 92). The buying and selling of shares took place in numerous London coffee houses. Eventually Old Jonathan's Coffee House and then the New Jonathan's Coffee House became the centre of dealings and the first real Stock Exchange. Today the Stock Exchange is housed in a twenty-six storey building in London which was opened in 1973.

The stock exchanges in other British cities

Stock exchanges in Britain are divided into units but closely linked in almost every respect to the London Exchange. For example, the Scottish unit in Glasgow links with the one in London. Dealers in these stock exchanges have detailed knowledge about local company shares and are also members of the London Stock Exchange.

The importance of the London Exchange can be seen in its dealings with securities from all over the world. It is in close contact, by means of telephone, telex and cable with all major stock exchanges abroad, including Paris, New York, Hong Kong and Tokyo.

WHY DO INVESTORS BUY SECURITIES?

You should be aware that securities are bought for two reasons:

1 The security will earn a dividend

Perhaps even more important is the **yield** which the share may pay. For example, if a share bought for £1 earns a 10 per cent dividend (i.e. 10 pence) the dividend, or yield, received by the investor is also 10 per cent. If a £1 share is bought for £2, however (assuming its market price has increased), it will still earn a 10 per cent dividend (i.e. 10 pence) but its yield will be only 5 per cent. In other words,

$$\text{yield} = \frac{\text{Nominal value (original price) of share} \times \text{dividend}}{\text{Market value of share}}$$

2 The security may increase in value

Shares bought today may be sold at a higher market price in the future. In the above example the £ shares have been sold for £2 because there is a demand for them from other investors. As the number of shares issued by the company in question is fixed, the price of each share will increase. On the other hand the £1 share above may fall in value to, say 50p – particularly if the company has not made any profits or its prospects are poor.

It is most important for you to know that it is not only private individuals who buy shares. Most securities are bought by institutional investors such as insurance companies, pension schemes, trade unions, commercial banks (see page 96).

THE MANAGEMENT OF THE STOCK EXCHANGE

Management is carried out by:

1 the **Stock Exchange Council** – forty-six unpaid members responsible for the overall control of the Exchange;

2 the **administrative units** responsible for maintaining an efficient Exchange – they are responsible for discipline and conduct amongst members;

3 **committees** which are appointed to assist and advise each administrative unit.

MC1. A stock exchange is

A a central market for buying and selling all kinds of goods

B a place where any business can borrow money from the members

C a place where a register is kept of all public and private limited companies

D a central market for buying and selling all kinds of securities

E none of these

MC2. A shareholder receives a dividend of 10 per cent on the shares which were purchased for £300. The nominal value of the shares is £200. The amount of dividend is

A £10

B £20

C £30

D £50

E £60

MC3. When some shares in a limited company have a face value of £100 and a market value of £95

A the company has made a trading loss

B the shares are said to be at a premium

C the stockbroker and shareholder between them lose the £5 difference when the shares are sold

D the capital of the company remains the same despite a fall in the value of the shares

E the shares are said to be at a discount

HOW THE STOCK EXCHANGE WORKS

BROKER – DEALERS

From 1986 the members of the Stock Exchange have been divided into two groups as follows:

Stockbrokers Their activities can be summarised as follows:

1 They act as agents for people who wish to buy or sell shares; buy

them from or sell them to a market-maker and always act in their clients' interests.

2 They arrange for transfer for shares, the registration of the change of ownership of shares and obtain the share certificates for the client.

3 Advise clients on future trends, send circulars, price lists and prospectuses.

4 They advise companies at which price to set their new issues.

5 They charge a commission for services based upon the total value of share business transacted.

Market-makers These are 'wholesalers of shares' and deal only with the brokers above. They:

1 Act not only as stockbrokers but also as dealers in a specialised section of the market such as shares in oil, or property companies, etc.

2 Quote 'two-way' prices for buyers and sellers of shares – buying at the lower price and selling at the higher – the difference being their profit.

You should know the difference between stockbrokers and market-makers; it is a very important distinction and forms the basis of many questions.

Consider the following questions:

1 ▶ The Stock Exchange is often described as a 'perfect market'. Give a sufficient description of its work to justify this claim and point out how the division of its members may be considered to help towards the attaining of this perfection.

2 ▶ Describe the principal functions of the Stock Exchange. What are the differences between brokers and market makers on the London Stock Exchange?

To answer this question you need to refer to the section on the functions of the Stock Exchange on page 205.

HOW SHARES ARE BOUGHT AND SOLD

You should be prepared for questions on this section, it is a favourite topic of examiners.

For the purpose of expediency, suppose an investor wishes to *buy* some shares from a well-known company.

1 The investor contacts a stockbroker (his or her bank manager may arrange this) giving precise details of how many shares are to be purchased and what type of share, e.g. preference, ordinary, etc.

2 The broker contacts a dealer about the shares which the investor wishes to purchase, not revealing whether it is a buying or selling transaction.

3 The dealer gives two prices. The low price is the one at which 'he' is prepared to buy. The high price is the price at which 'he' is prepared

to sell. If the broker is not satisfied he will go to another dealer for a further quotation.

4 When both broker and dealer agree, they both make a note of the purchase and the bargain is checked next day. Each party will always honour the bargain, hence the motto of the Stock Exchange 'My Word is My Bond'.

5 The broker sends the client a **contract note** showing the purchase price of the share, the broker's commission, the amount of contract stamp duty (a duty or tax to the government), the amount of the transfer stamp (again a government duty).

6 Until the settlement day arrives, the client does not pay any money. Settlements take place on specified days and not at any other time. There are twenty-four settlement days in the year, mostly two weeks apart. An investor may therefore receive up to fourteen days' credit before he or she pays if the previous settlement day has just passed.

7 Settlement of deals is largely completed by a computer network known as *Talisman* and is concerned with the recording and movement of shares between buyers and sellers. (Should an investor wish to sell shares on the Exchange, the broker will sell the shares to the dealer at an agreed price and eventually pay the investor the amount due.)

You may expect to be set essay questions on how shares are purchased (or sold) on the Stock Exchange. The following are some examples which you should consider:

3 ▶ Describe the process by which you would purchase through the Stock Exchange 100 Ordinary Shares in a British industrial company whose shares are quoted on the Stock Exchange.

4 ▶ You are a shareholder in a public limited company. You wish to sell part of your holding. How can this be done? Would your answer be different if your holding was in a private company?

5 ▶ Explain in detail the way in which a sale of preference is made through the London Stock Exchange.

The answer to this question is adequately dealt with in the previous section and you should refer to it for the answer.

TYPES OF SHARES TRADED ON THE STOCK EXCHANGE

You should know that it is not only the shares of public companies which are bought and sold on the Stock Exchange. There are other types of securities such as:

Government stock or bonds The government issues stocks and bonds to finance its expenditure. They pay a fixed rate of interest and repayment is guaranteed. They are considered to be safe because they are backed by the government and given the name 'gilt edged securities'. Bonds in the first instance are usually issued in units of £100 at a fixed rate of interest and repayable or redeemed by the government on a particular date, e.g. 8 per cent Savings Bonds repayable 31 December 1999. Since it is a type of loan it can for subsequent transactions be divided into any quantity, e.g. £438.21 of stock could be bought.

Local government stock or bonds These are issed by local authorities to help finance long-term spending on local rather than national projects, the benefits of which will be felt for many years, e.g. building a new civic centre or swimming pool. Again such investments are very safe, carrying a fixed rate of interest and guaranteed repayment.

Shares There are many types of shares. A detailed account can be found on page 95 in the chapter on private enterprise. A knowledge of the different types of shares is essential to the answering of many questions.

Debentures These are similar to bonds but are only issued by joint stock companies (see page 97).

Share holding in Britain

Age group	% shareholders	% adult population
over 65	25	18
55–64	18	15
45–54	19	14
35–44	18	16
25–34	13	17
15–24	7	20
	100	100

SPECULATION ON THE STOCK EXCHANGE

Many of the transactions on the Exchange are for investment purposes. However, some investors are speculators and they purchase and sell shares with the view of making quick profits. There are three types of speculators known as **bulls**, **bears** and **stags**, and you should know the meaning of each of these terms. Be prepared to answer questions on speculation.

Bulls A bull will buy shares in the hope that they will *rise in price* before the next settlement day. He or she could make a profit in the following way:

1 Shares are purchased at an agreed price and the usual contract note is made out. No money is due before next settlement day.
2 In the meantime the shares have risen in value – the bull therefore

immediately sells them at the new 'higher' price but receives no money before next settlement day.

3 When settlement day arrives, the bull receives the money from the sale of shares and pays for those bought. After paying the broker's commision, the remainder is profit.

Bears A bear will sell shares in anticipation that they will *fall in price* before next settlement day. He or she could make a profit in the following way:

1 The bear sells shares 'he does not have' but receives no money before the next settlement day.

2 Before next settlement day the price of the shares falls when he or she will buy at the new lower price.

3 On settlement day the shares now in his or her possession are sold at the previously agreed higher price. After paying the broker the commission what is left is profit for the bear.

Stags When **new issues** of shares take place, the public may be invited to apply for them. Very often these are oversubscribed (i.e. more people want the shares than there are shares available) and the market price of the share will rise.

A stag will anticipate such an oversubscription and will buy as many of the shares as quickly as possible with a view to selling them at a higher price later.

Speculators are often criticised for bringing about the price movement they want by acting together. For instance bulls may act together and start buying shares in a particular company. This will cause prices to rise and they will then sell these shares (making a profit); the price will subsequently fall and they will buy them back again.

Factors which may cause share prices to change

Like any other cost, the price of shares is determined by the supply of and demand for that share. If there is little demand for the share then its price is likely to fall. On the other hand if the demand increases then the price of the share will rise. Demand and supply could be influenced by:

The annual results of the company Particular attention will be paid to the balance sheet to see how much profit the company has made and how much of this profit is distributed in dividends to shareholders.

Rumours and newspaper articles about the company in particular or the market in general.

Other factors Share prices tend to go up or down reflecting the general economic and political situation. For instance, if Britain's unemployment is rising, inflation is at a high level and there is a great deal of industrial unrest, the share prices will probably fall until a more stable situation exists. In other words, outside factors such as a war in a certain 'sensitive' part of the world would cause share prices to fall rapidly because of the lack of confidence in the national or world economic situation.

The Official List

Each unit (or section) of the Stock Exchange publishes a daily Official List containing the names of securities in which they deal as well as the latest prices. The **Stock Exchange Daily Official List** is published in London and contains the names and prices of nearly 10,000 quoted securities; an abridged version of the Official List appears in the leading financial papers (especially the *Financial Times*).

Cross section of page from *Financial Times*

Example

(a)	(b)	(c)		(d)	(e)	(f)	(g)
289	198	Amersham paints		208	+3	23	11.05
78	30	Woking bricks	6% Pref	78	+8	6	7.69

(*a*) This year's highest price
(*b*) This year's lowest price
(*c*) The name of the security in alphabetical order
(*d*) The closing price (yesterday) of the share
(*e*) The increase or decrease on the previous day's price (usually in pence)
(*f*) The percentage dividend, based on the nominal value of the shares, e.g. if the share's nominal value is 25 pence and dividend is 23 per cent of this – each share receives a dividend of 5.75 pence
(*g*) This shows the yield (see page 206) or the percentage dividend to the shareholder based upon the market price of the share.

MC4. Gilt edged stock is
A government stock
B stock in gold mines
C stock which has risen in value
D foreign stock
E stock which is worthless

MC5. Blue chips are
A government securities
B first-class ordinary shares
C founders' shares
D debentures
E first class preference shares

MC6. Which of the following would not be sold on the Stock Exchange?

A shares in public companies
B local government bonds
C stocks in nationalised industries
D foreign stocks
E shares in private companies

MC7. A 'bull' is a speculator who

A buys shares at lower prices hoping to sell at higher prices
B sells shares now and hopes to buy at lower prices in the future
C buys new issues
D buys gilt-edge securities
E only buys blue chips

WHAT ARE THE ADVANTAGES AND DISADVANTAGES OF THE STOCK EXCHANGE?

Disadvantages

It is often said that the Stock Exchange is nothing more than a casino where speculators can force the price of shares up or down to satisfy their own desires for profits. There have been periods in the history of stock exchanges when shares have risen because of speculation only to suffer disastrous declines later e.g. the Wall Street (New York's Stock Exchange) crash in 1929.

Advantages

There is no doubt that speculation does take place on the Stock Exchange, but the financial institutions and most private investors look on their holdings more as long-term investments than as a way of making a fortune overnight. The Stock Exchange performs a number of useful **functions:**

1 It provides a market for shares buyers and sellers and enables companies and governments to raise funds.
2 It encourages people to invest in stocks and shares because they know they will be able to sell these securities when they wish; their money will not be locked away for ever.
3 It enables people who wish to invest in companies to spread their money around. This way they avoid the risk of putting all their money into a company which ceases to trade and goes into liquidation.
4 Some of the speculation may be useful because brokers and dealers are experts on share movements. If share prices are falling too low, the market makers may buy them up and stabilise the price.
5 It advertises share prices allowing the public to follow their investments and change them as necessary.
6 It protects the public against fraud. If a share appears on the Official

List it is almost a guarantee of honesty since the firm will have been investigated by the Stock Exchange Council.

7 It is a 'barometer' of the health and well-being of the economy. If prices fall sharply on the Stock Exchange this probably reflects a general lack of confidence by investors and is soon noted by all other sectors of the economy.

MC8. Which of the following is not put forward as an advantage of the Stock Exchange?

A it is a place where the government can raise capital
B it encourages the purchase of more shares
C it encourages speculation in share buying
D it is a barometer of the economy
E it is closely associated with the international stock exchanges

You can expect essays to be set on the functions of the Stock Exchange and you should be able to answer the following:

6 ▶ Describe the work of the Stock Exchange and discuss its importance to industry and the individual.

7 ▶ The function of the Stock Exchange is to act as a market for both home and overseas securities.
(*a*) Why is this important?
(*b*) Briefly indicate the main types of securities referred to in the above statement.
(*c*) Explain how the purchase and sale of securities takes place on the London Stock Exchange.

The following essay requires an analysis of speculation on the Stock Exchange as well as the functions of the Exchange.

8 ▶ What are the functions of the Stock Exchange? Describe the role of
(*a*) bulls
(*b*) bears
(*c*) stags.

This question consists of two parts and you should be able to write about both parts to the question. The functions of the Stock Exchange are well documented on page 205 and you should refer to them. In describing the part played by 'bulls', bears' and 'stags' refer to page 210.

The Unlisted Securities Market

A market for both small and medium sized companies not wishing to have a full quotation on the Stock Exchange but nevertheless want to obtain capital for expansion by selling a small proportion of their shares to the general public. Thus the owners of the company are able to keep their original control and voting rights on policy decisions.

The FT-SE 100 Share Index

A statistical analysis showing market trends based upon 100 quoted companies on the London Stock Exchange and using December 1983 as the base level figure of 1,000.

UNIT TRUSTS AND INVESTMENT TRUSTS

You should be able to distinguish between **unit trusts** and **investment trusts**, both of which are organisations which purchase shares on the Stock Exchange.

UNIT TRUSTS

A unit trust uses its funds to make investments during the period of the trust which may be over many years. It is possible for an investor to purchase sub-units in the trust thus allowing people of limited means to enjoy membership. A variety of securities are purchased and divided into units worth say £2,000. This money is then subdivided into sub-units of say £1 each, which are offered to the public. Thus the investor is in the same position as if he or she had bought a small holding in each of the securities which constitute the trust unit. The main advantage is that they provide the unit holders with a wide range of investments and thus risks are minimised.

INVESTMENT TRUSTS

These are joint stock companies with limited liability (see page 92). Investors buy shares in the Trust which then purchases securities in other companies. Profits made through buying and selling of these securities and dividends are divided amongst shareholders according to how many units they own.

CASE STUDY

As **managing director** of a **private limited company** you consider there is a need for more capital and that the Board of Directors should consider the possibility of a **public quotation.** Some members however think that the **Unlisted Securities Market** would justify the immediate needs with consideration of a full **Stock Exchange quotation** at a later stage.

(*a*) What are the duties of the managing director?
(*b*) Why should the company want to become public?
(*c*) Explain the purpose of the Unlisted Securities Market.
(*d*) What is meant by a full Stock Exchange quotation?

Answers to multiple choice questions

MC1	D	MC5	B
MC2	B	MC6	E
MC3	D	MC7	A
MC4	A	MC8	C

INSURANCE

CONTENTS

Insurance is one of the central facets of commerce. Consequently it is a likely topic in commerce examination questions and you should revise the subject well. The chapter will be subdivided into the following sections:

1 The nature and purpose of insurance – the pooling of risks, insurable and non-insurable risks.

2 The principles of insurance – insurable interest, utmost good faith, indemnity, contribution, subrogation, the doctrine of proximate cause.

3 The contract of insurance – the proposal form, cover note, insurance policy, premiums and the insurance claim.

4 Types of insurance – life insurance (assurance), fire insurance, accident insurance, marine insurance.

5 Insurance companies and Lloyd's of London – brokers, underwriters and documents used.

THE NATURE AND PURPOSE OF INSURANCE

The pooling or risks

Risks are apparent in any field of human acitivity. In industry the risks may involve anticipating demand or transporting goods. Demand for products may fall leaving the manufacturer, wholesaler or retailer with surplus commodities. On the other hand, demand may rise resulting in shortages. Also when the commodity is transported it may be damaged, stolen or lost.

On a more personal level we are all aware of risks involved in everyday life. Accidents occur in the home and on the roads, at work and at play. The purpose of insurance is to provide compensation in cases where accident or damage does occur. Thus by 'pooling risks' people pay certain sums of money (known as the **insurance premiums**) to insurance companies at regular intervals so that in the event of accident or damage the unfortunate person suffering loss is paid compensation. Of course if everybody required compensation at the same time there would not be sufficient money to settle all claims. However, experience shows that only part of the pool held by an insurance company will be required at any one time. The remainder is invested by the insurance company in stocks and shares to earn profits, thus adding to the size of the pool.

Insurable and non-insurable risks

It is usually only possible to insure against a certain risk taking place if its probability is calculable from past experience or events. For instance the probability of an aeroplane or car crash can be calculated, as can the probability of house fires. Statistics will exist for these occurrences which enable insurance companies to calculate the size of the premiums: the greater the probability of a risk becoming reality the higher will be the premium. Thus the life insurance premium of a coal miner is likely to be much greater than that of a schoolteacher.

Actuaries are the people who fix premiums for insurance companies, and their calculations are based on the law of averages.

It should be understood, however, that not all risks are insurable. If there are no statistics available on a particular risk it may be quite impossible to fix a premium. It is not possible for instance for a businessman to insure against being unable to sell commodities because of a change in consumer taste or to cover losses due to bad management. Other non-insurable risks include those where the person requiring insurance has no insurable interest and therefore cannot suffer loss, e.g. a person would not be able to insure the Houses of Parliament or Edinburgh Castle.

MC1. Which of the following are non-insurable?

A loss of profits
B non payment of debts by customers
C losses due to thefts by employees
D an accident to an authorised visitor
E stock unsold because of change in fashion

THE PRINCIPLES OF INSURANCE

All forms of insurance are subject to certain basic principles which must be followed. These are:

1 Insurable interest

Only the person who will directly suffer loss or liability if a risk occurs is allowed to insure against that risk occurring. Thus only those having an **insurable interest** in something can insure against its loss. A person can insure his or her own life, car or house but cannot insure the life or possessions of another if there is no insurable interest.

2 Utmost good faith

All contracts of insurance depend on the details stated on the proposal form being correct. Any failure to conform with this may result in the policy becoming void, and in the event of the risk taking place, a person may lose not only all his premiums but have to stand any loss himself. It is assumed that the insured shows **utmost good faith** when completing the proposal form. For instance if a person insures him or herself for a large sum payable at death and states his or her age as twenty-one years but is in fact eighty-one this would clearly be a breach of utmost good faith and the contract would be void.

3 Indemnity

The principle of **indemnity** is to restore the person suffering loss to his or her former position and status as far as this is possible. It is important to note that the insured should not make a profit, if the risk insured against actually occurs. For instance if a person's house burns down, when its market value is £24,000 and it is insured for this amount, he or she can only claim £24,000 and no more. If, however, the property is badly damaged and repair would cost £12,000 then he or she would only receive £12,000 compensation and not £24,000. Likewise if a person has insured property for £24,000 (which is reflected in the size of the premium) but in fact at the time of its destruction it was worth £34,000 he or she can still only claim a maximum of £24,000.

It is worth noting that life insurance does not conform with the principle of indemnity. If someone dies or is killed in an accident, it is obviously an impossibility to restore them to their previous situation. However, a 'benefit payment' can be made to the person's next of kin as a form of compensation.

4 The average clause

Most insurance companies include this in their policies. A house for example insured for £24,000 (the purchase price of two years ago) could attract a maximum claim of £24,000 today despite its new value of say £30,000. In order to claim the higher amount it would have been necessary to have increased the insurance to the current value (and no more) and paid the higher premium.

5 Contribution

If a person has insured against the same risks with several insurance companies at the same time, the amount of loss is shared between the companies. Thus if a person insures his or her £24,000 house with two companies and it is burned down, the owner does not receive two amounts of £24,000. Instead he or she will receive compensation proportionate to the terms of the policies up to a maximum of £24,000. If he or she was paying exactly the same premium and under the same terms to both companies they will both pay £12,000.

6 Subrogation

Once the insured accepts a sum as compensation from the insurance company he or she does not have any futher rights over the thing insured. Thus if a person insures the home contents for £10,000 and they are destroyed in a fire and £10,000 is received in compensation, he or she cannot then sell the badly singed carpet or three-piece suite to other people. If the owner did so this would go against the principle of indemnity since he or she would then be making a profit. The insurance company can of course sue any other person responsible for the risk occuring.

7 The doctrine of proximate cause

If the property which is insured is damaged or destroyed because of some risk occurring against which one is not insured then no compensation can be claimed. Thus if a person insures the house against fire and storm the policy would not cover a rotten tree in the garden. If in the midst of a storm the tree falls down on to the house causing £3,000 worth of damage no claim can be made on the policy and the householder would have to suffer the loss.

1 ▶ 'The insured is not allowed to make a profit out of insurance, yet the insurance company may do so.' Explain this statement.

2 ▶ (*a*) Explain with examples the statement: 'The essential ingredients of a valid contract of insurance are – utmost good faith, indemnity and insurable interest.'
(*b*) Why are some business risks insurable and others not?

3 ▶ (*a*) What do you understand by the term 'insurable interest'?
(*b*) 'A cannot insure B's premises against the risk of fire but that does not mean that B's premises are uninsurable.' Explain this statement.
(*c*) B insures his house against the risk of fire for £40,000. The house however is only worth £30,000. State, with your reasons, how much B will receive in the event of a total loss.

In order to answer (*a*) discuss the fact that only risks that have a direct interest for the insured can be covered. Part (*b*) requires a discussion on 'insurable interest'. It appears that A has no interest in B's premises. If A has lent money to B however and taken the premises as security then he *would* have an interest and could insure the property accordingly. However, in more general iterms the statement implies that there is nothing to stop B from insuring the property himself (or herself). Part (*c*) requires a statement on the average clause and indemnity. Clearly B should not make a profit out of insurance and he cannot claim £40,000 if the property is worth less. He may only claim maximum of £30,000 in the case of total loss or a proportion of this amount depending upon the extent of damage incurred.

THE CONTRACT OF INSURANCE

The proposal form

Everyone wishing to insure must first complete a **proposal form** supplied by the insurance company. The form includes a number of questions which must be answered in utmost good faith. In the case of property the form would require its present value, situation, ownership, use, etc. The proposal form is signed by the proposer who confirms that the answers are correct. If the proposal form is accepted by the insurance company it becomes the basis of the contract.

Cover note

Whilst inquiries are made by the insurance company and the policy is prepared, a **cover note** is issued giving temporary cover against risks after the first premium has been paid.

The contract and insurance policy

When insurance is arranged between the insured and the company there is a legal contract. The **terms of the contract** are to be found in the insurance policy which gives a full account of what has been agreed.

Premium

These are the periodic payments made by the insured to an insurance company. The size of the premium will depend on how many other persons have insured against the same risk. If many people have insured against the risk then the premium is likely to be low. The size of the premium will also depend on the amount of risk involved. Basically the greater the risk the larger the premium. For instance a healthy twenty-one-year old bank clerk will pay a lower life insurance premium than someone about to retire at sixty-five years of age.

Consider why the car insurance premiums paid by two people living in the same area and owning similar cars are different even though they both have 'clean' licences.

The claim

When the risk insured against actually takes place a claim form is completed by the insured for consideration by the insurance company. The amount of compensation will depend on the principles of insurance already discussed. **Assessors** are those persons who decide how much the insurance company will pay in compensation.

MC2. A trader insures his plate-glass windows against damage. If he receives £400 from the insurer to make good some damage, this payment is his

A indemnity
B insurable interest
C premium
D capital gains
E average clause

MC3. The principle of indemnity in insurance means

A the insurance company will not pay out in claims more than the insured has paid in premiums
B the insured will get some of his money back if he makes no claims
C the insured must himself pay some of the losses he suffers
D the insured is to be compensated only for actual loss suffered
E the insured receives new goods in lieu

TYPES OF INSURANCE

Life insurance (or assurance)

The distinction between insurance and assurance is important. Insurance is concerned with the possibility that an event may happen, whereas assurance is concerned with the the fact that the event will happen (e.g. either the policy will mature or the policyholder will die). There are different types of life assurance:

1 Whole life assurance This refers to the policy that is paid only on the death of the assured.

2 Endowment assurance In this case the policy is for a fixed period of years and payable at that time or on the death of the assured if this were to be sooner.

3 Term assurance The policy holder insures his or her life for a particular period after which the insured receives nothing. Mortgage guarantee policies are of this type giving life insurance cover during the period of the mortgage. If death of the policyholder occurs during this time the mortgage is settled in full by the insurance company.

4 With profits In addition to the value of the policy the assured is entitled to a share in the company's profits. These bonuses are usually paid when the policy has matured. Many endowment policies are of this type.

5 Mortgage protection In the event of the premature death of the assured who has a mortgage (loan) on his/her house the insurance company pays off the mortgage of the assured. (See term assurance above.)

6 Unit linked policies These are issued by insurance companies in association with investment trusts (see page 215). Units are bought in the trust and the amount paid out on the policy will depend on the value of units bought at the maturity date.

7 Family income policies If the insured dies after taking out this policy the dependants will be paid an agreed amount at regular intervals up to a specified date. This type of insurance is particularly appropriate to a man or woman with a young family.

Whole life or endowment policies, over two years old, have a **surrender** value based upon the value of the policy and the amount of premiums paid. Thus an insurance policy can be used as security for a bank loan if the assured temporarily hands over the rights to the policy to the bank.

Normally before granting life cover the insurance company will require details of the proposer's state of health and other details. Thus a medical examination may be required and in some cases insurance cover may be refused.

Fire insurance

Householders and business people take out fire insurance to cover risks to both property and its contents. Fire insurance covers not only the risks of fire but also damage caused by storms, floods, burst pipes, riots, accidental damage, etc. In addition this branch of insurance covers claims made by the public whilst on the insured person's premises. The following points should be noted:

1 Insurance premiums may be reduced if the premises have special precautions against fire damage such as a sprinkler system.
2 Some insurance policies include a **new for old** clause for an extra premium. If this is not specified the policyholder will receive only replacement value.
3 If a particularly valuable item is to be insured an **all risks** policy may be necessary.
4 Property and contents should as far as possible be insured to present market values. Many companies offer **index-linked** insurance to keep in line with price rises caused by inflation. If this is not done the **average clause** may apply (see page 221).
5 The business person should also consider the possibility that if the workplace is destroyed it may be some time before a start can be made again. The insurance should therefore cover the possibility of loss of profits – a risk covered by **consequential loss**.

For what reason would two different householders (or business persons) pay different amounts of premiums for fire insurance?

4 ▶ A friend has asked for your advice on the insurance of her house valued at £30,000 and contents worth £1,000. She is considering insurance of the house at £20,000 since it is unlikely to be completely destroyed by fire, and the contents for £2,000 in case they are stolen.
(*a*) What advice would you give to your friend, bearing in mind the principles of insurance?
(*b*) How would the situation of the property affect the premium?

Explain the principles of insurance relating to the particular example – utmost good faith, insurable interest, indemnity, contribution, subrogation and the proximation clause. The 'average clause' should be especially mentioned if the friend is going to under-insure. The friend needs to consider more than just fire insurance – most companies include further cover against a wide range of risks. A cross-section of other risks should be included in your answer mentioning the 'index-linked' and 'new for old' possibilities.

As far as the situation is concerned the premium is calculated on the overall risk. A property situated next to a petrol filling station for example would have a higher premium than one in a country lane.

Accident insurance

The main type of accident insurance is **insurance of liability.** This occurs when the insured protects himself or herself against any claims made by another party. A good example of this is car insurance. In insurance there are two main parties involved in the contract. The first party and second party refers (*a*) to the insured and (*b*) the insurance company. Another part to be considered is the third party – any other persons likely to be affected by the contract.

1 Third party car insurance The motorist insures himself or herself against liability for the death, injury or damage to the property of *another* person.

2 Comprehensive insurance In this type of insurance not only will the third party receive compensation but so will the insured. Comprehensive insurance is thus more expensive. The size of premium will depend on such things as age of the insured, the type of car, previous accident record and where he or she lives. **No claims discount** are often allowed by insurance companies when no claims have been made for a number of years.

Accident insurance may also include insurance against risks to property not covered by household insurance or other insurance such as fire insurance. The risk of vandals damaging a shop front is an example.

Personal accident insurance is another category of accident insurance. These are policies which can be taken out to insure against death or disability in a special case. For instance persons going on holiday or travelling by aeroplane may take out personal accident insurance.

Insurance of interest is the final category of accident insurance. This covers the possibility of claims against the insured arising from the wrongful actions of employees. Some employers take out a **fidelity guarantee insurance** against the possibility of employees misappropriating the firm's money.

Pluvius policies insure the organisers of outside activities such as rallies, fetes, etc. against losses in revenue caused by bad weather.

Marine insurance

This is insurance of both ships and commodities against the perils of the sea. The main world market for this type of insurance is Lloyd's of London (see page 228).

Hull insurance covers against damage to both the hull and ship's machinery.

Cargo insurance covers the cargo being carried. This type of insurance policy is important, the policy usually being attached to the bill of lading (see page 172) and handed to the purchaser of the cargo.

Freight insurance covers the possibility that the shipper may not receive the freight charges if the cargo is lost. In this event, the shipper may be sued for the return of the money paid for carriage.

The shipowner should insure against various liabilities. These may include death or injury to passengers or crew, also accidental damage or pollution caused by the ship.

Aviation insurance

This is also usually arranged through Lloyd's. The aircraft itself is covered under the hull insurance sections whilst liability to passengers, freight, etc is included under the heading of accident insurance.

MC4. 'An insurance policy which provides a sum of money after an agreed number of years or at death if this occurs before the policy matures.' This describes

A marine insurance
B motor insurance
C fire insurance
D endowment insurance
E term insurance

MC5. What type of insurance would be appropriate to a large firm that employed persons who have to handle large sums of money?

A fidelity guarantee
B third party
C consequential loss
D accident
E burglary

MC6. If I receive £5,000 compensation from an insurance company after my business has been destroyed by fire:

A I can spend this money in any way I please
B I must agree to spend all of it on replacing assets lost
C I must agree to spend part of it on replacements
D I must agree not to put myself in a better position than I was in before the fire, by spending more than £5,000 on replacements
E I will lose my no claim bonus for that year

MC7. Which is the insurance that settles a claim only on the death of the life assured?

A Endowment
B Term
C Whole life
D With profits
E All risks

Insurance for the business person

A person who owns his or her own business should carry cover for most of the following:

1 Fire insurance covering: property and contents; burglary and theft; consequential loss; and liability to the public.

2 Accident insurance covering: motor vehicles; liability for accidents and damage not covered by fire insurance; fidelity guarantee; and risks of non-payment by customers.

3 Death of partner (if any).

4 Adequate **life assurance** for self in order to safeguard family interests.

THE INSURANCE MARKET

There are two groups of insurers with whom an individual or business persons can take out a policy:

1 Insurance companies

Many of these are national organisations with offices throughout Britain and who belong to the British Insurance Association. A person seeking insurance may approach a branch office or arrange for an agent of the company to call at his or her home. Alternatively a person may deal with an insurance broker who represents the person seeking insurance independent of any company and who seeks the best possible insurance and terms for the insured.

2 Lloyd's of London

The origin of this market can be traced to the seventeenth-century London coffee houses where customers interested in shipping gathered to exchange information. In 1897 Lloyd's was incorporated by a special Act of Parliament. It is still best known for its original handling of marine insurance but it now deals with many other types such as aviation, motor and general insurance. It does not deal with life assurance. Members of Lloyd's are either brokers or underwriters. Brokers are agents for those wishing to have risks covered. The broker enters details of the client's needs on a **slip.** He will go to the various firms of underwriters in order to find the most advantageous premium. The underwriter agreeing to accept liability makes a note on the slip how much of the risk will be covered and at what charge.

Thus the broker has secured a lead and he contacts other underwriters until all the risk is covered. The policy is completed by inserting details on a standard form and sending it to the client.

Brokers:

1 charge commission on contracts;
2 charge commission on money due on claims;
3 deal directly with the public.

Underwriters:

1 assume the risks of insurance;
2 bear unlimited liability;
3 deposit a minimum capital sum into a central fund to cover underwriters who may default on claims.

In view of world-wide insurance interest and increasing business involving many millions of pounds, underwriters have formed themselves into syndicates in order to give themselves more protection.

You can expect examiners to set specific questions on Lloyd's.

Consider this question for instance.

5 ▶ (*a*) What do you understand by the term 'Lloyd's of London'?
(*b*) What is the function of
(i) Lloyd's underwriters;
(ii) Lloyd's brokers?
(You need not give great detail on the way in which they conduct their business.)
(*c*) What resemblance is there between the Corporation of Lloyd's and the Stock Exchange?

6 ▶ (*a*) Explain fully why it is possible to insure against loss of profits due to a fire but not against loss of profits due to changes in fashion.
(*b*) If you wished to insure against fire, how could an insurance broker help you?
(*c*) If a fire should occur what actions would have to be taken before you could receive compensation for your losses?

Data response question

The following advertisement appeared recently in the Press

> Are you adequately INSURED?
> All types of insurance available
> including Endowment and Mortgage Protection
> No medical examination if under 55
> Annual bonus
>
> CONTACT A1 INSURANCE BROKERS

(*a*) What is meant by
(i) Endowment Insurance and
(ii) Mortgage Protection?
(*b*) Why is there no medical examination required if under fifty-five?
(*c*) Explain the meaning of annual bonus.
(*d*) What is an insurance broker?

Answers to multiple choice questions

MC1	E	**MC5**	A
MC2	A	**MC6**	A
MC3	D	**MC7**	C
MC4	D		

BUSINESS ACCOUNTS

CONTENTS

This chapter is subdivided into the following topics:

1 The balance sheet
2 Types of capital
3 Is the business profitable?
4 Analysing profits
5 The rate of turnover (sales)
6 Mark-up and margin
7 The return on capital invested
8 The relationship between costs, revenues and output
9 Personal budgeting and finance planning

THE BALANCE SHEET

This is a statement as to the financial standing of a business at a given time – usually at the end of the financial year – prepared by an accountant showing the assets and liabilities. Its purpose is to be informative so that the owners of the business – whether sole trader or company – may compare and contrast the present with the past balance sheets and make decisions accordingly.

There are at the present time various methods of presentation, especially since Britain's entry to the Common Market. For the purpose of this chapter the 'Common Market type' will be explained, especially as it is becoming increasingly used and accepted in business.

In financial terms a business has either assets or liabilities. The former are items that are **owned** and belong to it. These may be divided into two groups representing items that are owned and kept for a long time such as premises, and one group representing those for only a short while such as stock. Thus the two sections are known as:

1 Fixed assets which includes the value in money terms of items such as premises, fixtures and fittings, machinery, vehicles, etc.

2 Current assets which includes the value of items that are constantly changing, being used up and replenished. These are stocks of unsold goods in the storeroom or shop, debtors (money due to the firm from sales to customers), cash in the bank, and cash in the till, etc.

On the other hand the liabilities represent items in money terms that are **owed** by the business to others. Again they are usually divided into two groups – long-term liabilities and the short-term. These are:

1 The capital which the business owes to its owner who may be a sole trader, partner or shareholder. Ultimately the business will cease trading and when it does it will have to repay the then owner(s) the amount invested in the enterprise. Hence the capital invested by the owners is *from the firm's point of view* a liability.

2 Current liabilities includes the value of items that are constantly changing such as creditors (money due to be paid by the firm for purchases from its supplies) and money owed to the bank for loans or overdrafts, etc.

All the above are listed in a statement called a balance sheet as follows:

Balance Sheet A. Smith as at 31 December 19.2

Fixed assets	£	£		£
Premises	20,000		*CAPITAL*	45,000
Fixtures, etc.	5,000			
Machinery	10,000	35,000		
Current assets			*Current liabilities*	
Stock	7,000		Creditors	1,500
Debtors	1,800			
Bank	2,200			
Cash	500	11,500		
		46,500		46,500

The balance sheet quotes the balances on the named accounts of the business at the close of trading on a certain day each year – in this instance on 31 December 19.2. These figures will be compared with those quoted on 31 December 19.1 and 19.0 in order to ascertain 'trends' and other information necessary for a successful enterprise. These include an analysis on the following lines:

TYPES OF CAPITAL

(*a*) **The owner's capital** represents the amount owing to the proprietor at the date of the balance sheet. It includes the previous year's balance plus this year's profit less the proprietor's drawings (living expenses) – £45,000. Should the business be sold for exactly the figures quoted above, this amount would be left for the proprietor.

(*b*) **Fixed capital** is defined as the assets that to all intents is permanent – the fixed assets in fact £35,000. In reality these *depreciate* (fall in value) with time and this represents an expense to the business. Occasionally as in the case of premises, however, they may increase in value – a business will periodically adjust these balances so as to show up-to-date figures and have no hidden profits or losses.

(*c*) **Circulating capital** is also known as the **current assets** – £11,500. These balances represent assets that are constantly circulating through the business – selling stock for cash, selling on credit terms (to debtors), paying money into and out of the bank and till every day.

(*d*) **Working capital** is a term that refers to a firm's ability to pay its way – the amount available for the day-to-day operation of a business. It is calculated by subtracting the amount owed for short-term (current) liabilities from the short-term (current) assets. In the above balance sheet the working capital is £11,500 – £1,500 = £10,000 – a healthy situation from the firm's point of view in this instance, showing a substantial surplus should the current liabilities demand immediate payment.

(*e*) **Capital employed** is the total assets £46,500 less the debtors £1,800 = £44,700. The reason for deducting debtors from available funds is that the business by allowing credit to customers is in fact using part of its capital outside the firm.

IS THE BUSINESS PROFITABLE?

It is the work of an accountant to analyse and interpret information so as to ascertain profitability. However the proprietor would be advised to study ways by which business may be improved using the following types of criteria:

1 Gross profit in comparison with sales

Since the gross profit is the difference between sale price and buying price it is important that this should be sufficient to cover all expenses. This may depend upon the type of business – the gross profit being larger in luxury sales – it is usual for the figure to be expressed as a percentage.

If during the year goods were purchased for £70,000 and every item sold for £100,000 the gross profit would be £30,000.

Expressed as a percentage, this would be $\frac{30,000}{100,000} \times 100 = 30\%$

2 Net profit in comparision with sales

The net profit is the actual profit of a business at the end of a trading period, i.e. gross profit less the expenses (salaries, rent, rates, etc.) of running the business.

Suppose in the above example the expenses had been £20,000, the net profit would be £10,000.

Expressed as a percentage to sales, this would be

$$\frac{10{,}000}{100{,}000} \times 100 = 10\%$$

3 Running expenses in comparison with sales

It is always important to contain expenses within a firm especially as these have a direct effect on profit.

Expressed as a percentage to sales, this would be

$$\frac{20{,}000}{100{,}000} \times 100 = 20\%$$

It is apparent therefore that a comparison of yearly sales and annual expenses, etc. figures is not sufficient to obtain a clear picture of a firm's prospects. The use of percentages makes the figures more meaningful and acceptable to owners, investors and other organisations including banks and finance houses which may have lent money.

MC1. The amount which represents the excess of current assets over current liabilities is called

A circulating capital
B capital owned
C working capital
D capital employed
E owner's capital

MC2. Which of the following is a current asset?

A premises
B stock
C fittings
D capital
E investments

MC3. Which of the following is an example of fixed capital?

A owner's capital
B raw materials
C cash
D debtors
E office equipment

MC4. Working capital is calculated by

A adding together bank, cash and debtors
B taking the total assets less debtors
C the fixed assets plus current assets
D the current assets minus current liabilities
E the fixed assets minus current assets

MC5. Which of the following is a fixed liability?

A capital
B creditors
C fixtures and fittings
D bank loan
E premises

1 ▶ (*a*) What is a balance sheet?
(*b*) How do the fixed liability items in a sole proprietor's balance sheet differ from those in a plc? Give reasons for these differences.
(*c*) Why do sole proprietors not have to file their accounts annually with the registrar of companies, whereas limited companies do?

In order to answer (*a*) you need to identify the key features of the balance sheet: Liabilities and Assets, Fixed and Current Liabilities, Fixed and Current Assets. Explain these terms, what they represent and how the figures quoted represent money valuations on the date of the balance sheet.

For part (*b*) it is important not to confuse this with the fixed assets. The fixed liability of a company will be the amount of shares issued which may be of differing types and denominations. A sole proprietor's liabilities will be the amount of capital that he or she has put into the business plus any profit less any drawings. Thus the figure for a company's liability is likely to be unchanged from year to year unless of course it issues further shares, whereas the capital for the sole proprietor will change by the addition of annual profit, etc.

In part (*c*) a detailed discussion of company registration is not required. The answer merely refers to the protection afforded to prospective shareholders, traders, bankers, etc, so that they may refer to a central source owned by government prior to their dealings with the company. It would be impractical for dealings with sole proprietors to be subject to this type of control, especially as it is possible for most people to set themselves up in business at any time.

2 ▶ A company publishes the following figures (in thousands):

	£
(i) Authorised capital	5,000
(ii) Issued capital	2,400
(iii) Fixed assets	1,800
(iv) Current (floating) assets	800
(v) Current liabilities	200

(*a*) Explain all five items.
(*b*) Show how you would calculate the working capital of the company.
(*c*) State two other methods by which capital might be obtained.

3 ▶ (*a*) Explain the following terms:
(i) fixed capital;

(ii) issued capital;
(iii) authorised capital.

(*b*) Adequate working capital is essential for a successful business. Describe the sources of working capital and the factors which determine the amount required.

ANALYSING PROFITS

The business person when comparing the percentage profits may find that the current year is lower than last year's figure. This may be for any of the following reasons:

1. The purchase price of goods to be sold may have increased without any corresponding increase in sale price.
2. A great deal of stock may be left unsold at the end of a season due to over-buying or change of fashion.
3. More stock may have been stolen, pilfered or damaged during the year.
4. Higher expense payments for rent, rates, wages without any appreciable increase in sales.
5. Greater competition from similar businesses in the immediate locality or from larger organisations such as hypermarkets, etc.
6. Loss of business due to problems connected with the business but largely outside the control of the proprietor.

MC6. The net profit of a business is obtained by
A adding trade expenses to sales
B deducting trade expenses from gross profit
C deducting gross profit from sales
D adding sales to gross profit
E dividing the gross profit by sales

MC7. If the gross profit of a firm was £10,000 and the cost of the goods sold was £5,000, then the sales figures for that year was
A £5,000
B £10,000
C £15,000
D £20,000
E cannot be calculated from this information

MC8. A trader who expresses gross profit as a percentage of sales will obtain
A a time comparison of gross profit of one year with another
B a realistic figure for the net profit
C a comparison of this year's net profit with gross profit
D the working expenses as a percentage of sales
E the sales as a percentage of gross profit

MC9. If a firm's sales for the year total £40,000 and the cost of the goods sold was £20,000, expenses being £10,000 then the percentage of net profit to sales is

A 40%
B 70%
C 30%
D 25%
E 50%

THE RATE OF TURNOVER (SALES)

It is important for a business person to know the **rate** of turnover for a given period. This is necessary in order to review the sale of 'slow-moving' items since those which are unsold for a long time represent capital not being put to its best possible use.

To calculate the rate the following formula is used:

$$\text{Rate of turnover} = \frac{\text{cost of goods sold}}{\text{cost of average stock}}$$

The **cost** of goods sold is the cost price of actual sales. Suppose sales were £48,000 for the year and an average profit of 25 per cent is maintained, then the cost of goods sold would be $\frac{100}{125}$ of 48,000 = £38,400.

(Check this answer by adding 25 per cent to cost price to obtain sale price.)

Ideally a business person would check stock at regular intervals, but for the purpose of this exercise to find the average stock held, the value at the beginning of the financial year will suffice together with its value at the end, divided by two.

Suppose stock was valued at the beginning of the year at £4,000, and the stocktake at the end of the year was £3,680, then the average stock held over the year amounted to: £4,000+£3,680 (7,680)÷2 = £3,840.

$$\text{The rate of turnover therefore} = \frac{38{,}400}{3{,}840} = 10$$

In other words the goods are in stock for an average of five weeks before sale (52 weeks÷10). Obviously the higher is this rapidity of turnover the larger the volume of goods sold and possibly a greater profit is made.

MC10. In order to obtain the rate of turnover the formula to be used is

A sales divided by average stock
B average stock divided by sales at cost
C sales divided by stock at cost

D stock at cost divided by average sales
E sales at cost divided by average stock

MARK-UP AND MARGIN

Whilst ratios, turnover, gross profit and net profit are an important part of business the retailer is very much concerned with percentages. Thus the retailer on buying a product for re-sale will add a certain percentage to the cost price in order to obtain the selling price. This is termed the **mark-up** and is calculated as follows:

$$\text{Mark-up} = \frac{\text{sale price} - \text{cost price} \times 100}{\text{cost price}}$$

It is standard practice therefore to relate sale price to cost price, marking up the latter according to the type of business, what the market will bear and the need for competitiveness.

Nevertheless there are some retailers who prefer to express their profit to sales rather than to the purchases, using the following formula.

$$\text{Margin} = \frac{\text{sale price} - \text{cost price} \times 100}{\text{sale price}}$$

Suppose therefore that the cost price of an article was £50 and it was sold for £200, calculate (*a*) the percentage mark-up price and (*b*) the margin. Which of the two figures do you consider gives the retailer the information required? (Answer: This depends on the practice of the business – both are equally important. The main thing is to compare the current year with previous years keeping to one formula throughout.)

THE RETURN ON CAPITAL INVESTED

A business person will want to compare the profit figure with the capital invested in the business, i.e. the percentage that net profit bears to capital. Suppose the capital balance is £30,000 and at the end of the financial year a net profit of £6,000 is made, then the return will be

$$\frac{\text{net profit}}{\text{capital}} \times 100 = \frac{6{,}000}{30{,}000} \times 100 = 20\%$$

It will now be necessary to compare this with returns obtainable from possible alternative investments such as bank deposit accounts, building societies, Post Office investment accounts, stocks and shares, etc. There are no hard and fast 'rules' in this connection since many factors may influence the business person's or investor's choice as to whether or not to continue in business. These include future business and personal prospects, provision of employment for self or family, ease of obtaining capital, economic trends, personal tax situations, etc.

4 ▶ The following relates to the trading of a business in two successive years:

	Year 1	Year 2
Sales	104,000	120,000
Cost price of sales	78,000	91,200
Expenses	14,560	15,000
Average stock in hand during the year at cost price	10,400	11,400

(*a*) Calculate for each year:
(i) the gross profit and net profit, and express each as a percentage of turnover;
(ii) the rate of stock turn.

(*b*) When you have completed the calculations of (*a*), comment on all the data available.

5 ▶ The financial records of a firm for two successive years, Year 1 and Year 2 contain the following information:

	Year 1	Year 2
Average stock on hand at cost price	£28,560	£28,560
Rate of stock turn	5	6
Gross profit as a percentage of selling price	32	28
Expenses	£32,560	£32,000

(*a*) Give the turnover and gross and net profits for each year.

(*b*) Comment on your findings as a result of your calculations and the information in the financial records given above.

The answer will be as follows:

(*a*) **Year 1**

In order to calculate the turnover it is necessary to find the cost price of sales. Using the formula shown on page 239.

$$\text{Rate of turnover} = \frac{\text{cost of goods sold}}{\text{cost of average stock}}$$

$$5 = \frac{\text{cost of goods sold}}{\pounds 28{,}560}$$

$$\text{Cost of goods sold} = 5 \times 28{,}560 = \pounds 142{,}800$$

Now given that gross profit as a percentage of selling price (turnover) is 32 per cent then the cost of stock sold must be 68 per cent of turnover. Consequently

$$\text{turnover} = \frac{142{,}800 \times 100}{68} = 210{,}000$$

Thus turnover = cost of goods sold + gross profit
210,000 = 142,800 + gross profit
Therefore gross profit = £67,200
Finally net profit = gross profit – expenses
= 67,200 – 32,560
= £34,640

(*b*) **Year 2**
Using the same method now calculate the answers for this year. (Turnover £250,000, gross profit £70,000, net profit £38,000).

Note the increase rate of stock turn – give possible reasons – together with continuing stock policy but reduced percentage of gross profit. Also slight reduction in expenses which leads to exactly the same net profit on increased turnover. Give reasons why this should be so.

6 ▶ (*a*) What is meant by the phrase 'capital of a business'?
(*b*) Explain the difference between fixed capital and working capital.
(*c*) If a business has a turnover of £100,000 in a year, a gross profit of £30,000 and other expenses of £10,000, calculate its net profit as a percentage of turnover.
(*d*) What is meant by rate of turnover? Why should firms attempt to have a high rate of turnover?

THE RELATIONSHIP BETWEEN COSTS, REVENUES AND OUTPUT

COSTS

The costs of production are the money expenditures on the use of factors of production by the firm. There are broadly two main types of costs: **fixed costs** and **variable costs**.

Fixed costs These are sometimes referred to as overheads and do not change with output and include interest, repayments, rents, rates and salaries. As output increases therefore fixed costs remain the same.

Variable costs These are sometimes called direct costs and vary with output and include wages and raw material costs. Thus as output increases variable costs also will increase.

When a firm's fixed costs and variable costs are added together therefore the total is known as **total costs**. If these are divided by output this gives the **average total costs per unit of output** which may be compared (*a*) between factories and (*b*) between products.

RELATING COSTS TO REVENUE: THE CONCEPT OF BREAK EVEN

Revenue is the income the firm receives for selling its products. The total revenue is thus calculated by sales × price, e.g. if a firm sells 100 units for £5 each then total revenue would be £500. Break even occurs at that level of output where total revenue is equal to total costs. Consider the following graph.

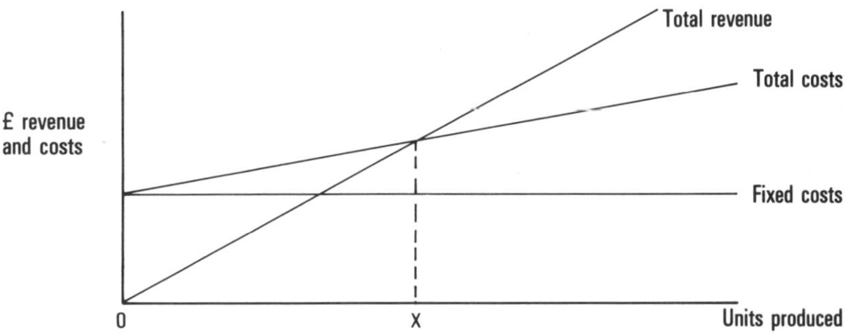

The break even output is OX. At levels of output less than OX there is a projected loss. At levels of output above OX a profit is projected. At this break even level of output total revenue is equal to total costs.

At output OX if the firm wishes to make a profit it will either have to increase sales (if it can) beyond OX, increase the selling price (and therefore total revenue) and/or reduce the level of total costs.

SOCIAL COSTS AND COST BENEFIT ANALYSIS

Social costs are the costs to the community as a whole of producing certain products. It is an attempt to measure it in terms of the effect on the community, population and environmental damage. For instance, the mining of coal may lead to spoil heaps and deaths of miners whilst heavy lorries may cause damage to property, noise, traffic jams and accidents. Both the production and consumption of commodities may involve social costs and benefits (called externalities). These social costs and benefits are usually ignored by private entrepreneurs who are concerned only with money costs and benefits. However, increasingly, in both public and private enterprise a technique known as **cost–benefit analysis** is being used to measure social costs and benefits. A main problem, however, is the measurement of social costs and benefits to the family and to the community.

PERSONAL BUDGETING AND FINANCIAL PLANNING

An essential part of modern life is the need to understand the importance of careful budgeting for present and future needs, to plan spending so that in the long term, weekly/monthly expenditure does not exceed weekly/monthly income. We have already seen in Chapter 1 that necessities such as food, shelter and clothing are needs that have to be satisfied first of all. Surplus income (if any) can be applied to other important but not quite so essential demands – perhaps involving the use of credit (buying now – paying later). There are many pitfalls for the unwary as far as credit is concerned and hence the need for Consumer Protection (page 79). Legislation however can never be the complete answer to unscrupulous dealers and it really is important that the individual buys wisely. A legal term – *caveat emptour* (let the buyer beware) – adequately sums up the need for caution.

Compare and contrast the two following cases of financial management: Smith and Brown are both employed at the same firm and each earns £10,000 per annum. They are both married, each have two small children and no other income. The Smith family are buying their house through a building society whilst the Browns are in rented accommodation.

The following is a summary of their respective expenditure for last year:

	Smith	Brown
Income tax and national insurance, etc	1,800	2,000
Mortgage interest and repayments	3,800	–
Food and clothing	1,700	1,900
Rates, repairs and insurance of property	500	100
Rent	–	3,600
HP payments and licences, etc	400	750
Travel expenses and holidays	600	1,000
Sundry expenses	850	1,150
	£9,650	£10,500

Which of the two do you consider the best able to manage the family's financial affairs?

Possible areas for consideration include:

(*a*) Brown pays nearly as much rent as Smith pays in mortgage repayments, etc. Smith has the benefit (and the upkeep) of a house which is gradually being paid for and is likely to appreciate in value. What has Brown to show for the payments?

(*b*) Has Smith taken out a mortgage protection insurance to cover the mortgage should he die prematurely?

(*c*) Are Brown's HP commitments excessive at £14 per week? What happens if he is made redundant?

(*d*) Smith has been able to put aside a modest sum out of income to save for future needs or emergencies. Is this sum invested wisely, earning interest?

(*e*) Brown has spent more than the available income. Has there been the need to borrow? If so who from and at what rate?

Can you suggest ways in which Brown can keep within the annual income?

Answers to multiple choice questions

MC1	C	**MC6**	B
MC2	B	**MC7**	C
MC3	E	**MC8**	A
MC4	D	**MC9**	D
MD5	A	**MC10**	E

PEOPLE IN BUSINESS

CONTENTS

WAGES AND SALARIES

There are at the present time about 23 million people gainfully employed in this country, earning a living and receiving a wage. In other words, they are selling their expertise by producing goods in a factory or farm, working in an office or directly providing a service for the benefit of others. In return for this effort money is received which can be used to satisfy some of their needs. In broad terms therefore a person receives a wage or salary according to the scarcity value of his or her expertise. Someone who has qualified after several years of expensive training, for example, would expect to receive a higher wage than a person whose training was minimal. Thus the economic principle of demand and supply is as much a fact of life when dealing with labour as it is with everything else in our society.

The majority of people earn their living by working for another person or organisation. Taking the Civil Service, Social Services and nationalised industries as a whole it can be readily appreciated that the government is the largest employer in terms of employees on the payroll and is consequently able to control wages and salaries to a greater extent than is commonly realised. Whether one is a public or private employee however is immaterial in that those working for a living will receive their wages or salary based upon one or more of the following:

Time rates

This is the most usual form of payment whereby the employer agrees to pay the employee a certain amount of money based on a period of time. Depending upon the type of employment, whether full-time or part-time, permanent or temporary, the employee will receive a remuneration based upon a weekly, monthly, quarterly or annual wage or salary structure.

Example 1

An office worker is employed on a part-time basis working mornings only, 9 a.m. – 1 p.m., Monday – Friday. In a particular week the employee worked on four days only because Monday was a public holiday. Calculate the amount of weekly wage if the agreed rate is £4 per hour.

Daily wage = 4 hours × £4 = £16

For 4 working days wage = £16 × 4 = £64

Example 2

An employee earns £8400 annum based on the employer's published scale and payable monthly. Calculate the gross amount received each month by the employee.

$$\text{Monthly gross amount received} = \frac{£8400}{12} = £700$$

(Note that in the above example no deductions are made for holidays. Deductions may be made however for any absence through sickness over a certain number of days – the employee claiming loss of earnings from the National Insurance.)

Piece rates

As the name suggests, this is a method of payment based upon the output of the individual. Thus a person producing or assembling 100 articles will receive half the amount of a person assembling 200 articles even though the same amount of time was taken. This method of payment is frequently found in the industries connected with light assembly work, ready-made clothing and the building industries where output can be easily measured. There are many critics of the system however which is frequently associated with 'sweated labour'.

Overtime

Occasionally because of the pressure of work it may be necessary for an employee to work more than the agreed hours. When this occurs it is usual for employees below management level to be paid at a rate higher than the norm (1½ – 2 times) or to be given time off in lieu.

Bonus payments and profit sharing schemes

In addition to the above an employer may give employees a bonus at the year end depending upon profits. When this occurs it is often paid as a percentage of basic salary and according to the length of service.

Other payments

There are many and various incentives that a good employer may consider. These include commission payable to the sales force, payment of all pension contributions, provision of catering and sporting facilities, membership of private medical schemes, discount on items purchased, use of car, etc. All of these need to be taken into account when wage/salary bargaining is introduced and equally important when comparing payments made to the workforce in Company A and Company B.

Take-home pay

The examples given so far relate to the gross wage or salary rather than the actual sum received. A person earning £700 each month for example (see above), would not receive this amount since the employer is bound by law to make certain deductions such as income tax and employee national insurance contributions. These deductions are made according to **tax 'codes'** supplied by the Inland Revenue (basically the more you earn the more tax you pay) and contribution scales supplied by the Department of Health and Social Security (DHSS). Further deductions may be made by the employer with the approval of the employee. These may include subscriptions to a union fund, deductions for private pension schemes (superannuation), savings schemes, mortgage repayments, holiday funds, etc. Each employee therefore when receiving his or her payment will receive a 'pay-slip' giving details of the gross and net amounts together with a list of the deductions made. Whilst there is no standard format, the following is a typical example of those in current use.

APC (UK) LTD	ADDITIONS	DEDUCTIONS	DETAILS OF EMPLOYE TO DATE
DATE TAX MONTH	BASIC PAY	INC TAX	GROSS PAYS
N. INS NO PAYROLL NO	OVERTIME	NAT.INS.	TAXABLE
EMPLOYEE'S NAME	BONUS	SUPERANN.	SUPERANN.
	TAX REFUND	UNION SUS	INC. TAX
		HOLIDAY FD.	NAT. INS.
TOTAL GROSS PAYMENT			
TOTAL DEDUCTIONS			METHOD OF PAYMENT
NET PAY	TOTAL ADDITIONS	TOTAL DEDUCTIONS	BANK CODE

This employee at the end of May will be paid £700 gross from which certain deductions have been made – both statutory and voluntary. A net sum therefore, say of £445, would be credited to the employee's bank account by the credit transfer system (see page 189).

INTERNAL ORGANISATION OF BUSINESS

The many and variable types of business units highlight the need for good management. Even the sole trader needs to organise resources in such a way as to obtain the best results if he or she is to stay in business. Similarly the other more complex organisations including partnerships, cooperatives and limited companies need a structure that covers legal, personnel, financial and economic matters that may be broadly grouped as follows:

Planning

The entrepreneur must have clear ideas of the aims of the business, realistic targets to be reached and markets to secure. In other words, foresight, good judgement and anticipation as well as knowledge of products, etc, are essential ingredients for the successful entrepreneur.

Control

Work is organised in such a way that the chain of command is clear, responsibilities are known and enthusiasm permeates throughout the entire workforce. This involves communication and discussion at all levels from boardroom to shop floor and, where appropriate, members of trade unions or their representatives.

No two organisations are exactly alike but a typical company structure is as follows:

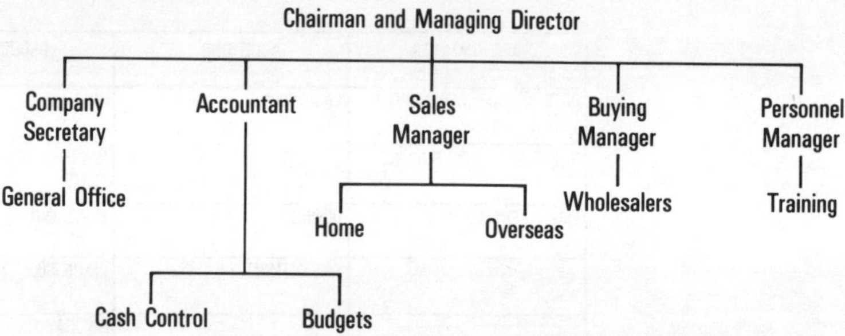

Decisions on policy therefore are made at Director level acting on behalf of the shareholders and communicated to Managers having special responsibility for given areas. Routine matters therefore are dealt with within departments which are expected to work in close cooperation with each other.

SELECTION AND RECRUITMENT

An important consideration for all employees (or potential employees) of any organisation is its future prospects. Is it a go-ahead national/international business, is it a family-run business, how many employees are there and what facilities are provided for training and promotion? These and many more questions need to be answered in a satisfactory manner if employer and employee are to value each other's commitment.

Perhaps in business one of the greatest mistakes made by employees is to have the firm belief that qualifications once achieved are the be all and end all of sustained effort, that promotion to a higher grade will be automatic and salary increments naturally follow. In reality of course nothing is further from the truth. A person with exceptionally high qualifications could be quite useless in the business world – the most important asset by far is a person's **personality** followed by his or her dealings with customers and colleagues – particularly the former since they are paying the wages. Nevertheless it is important that staff should obtain some *relevant* qualifications and keep up to date with current trends. It is also advisable to be aware of new technology wherever possible especially when this is introduced by competitors.

INDUSTRIAL RELATIONS

This subject in very broad terms relates to the partnership that exists between and within management and the workforce. It is an area in which people often have strong views and in which the British Press and television 'make' news – more so than in any other country. Because of this it is often regarded as a constant battlefield between the warring factions. Few would deny the right of managers to sensible management or the need for proper working conditions being made available to the workforce. In a properly ordered society or firm therefore industrial relations largely relate to both of these to the benefit of each. The principle organisations dealing with this are:

The Trade Unions

A trade union is an organised association of workpeople having its own independent legal status formed for the maintenance and promotion of common interests. Unions vary in size from a few hundred to over 2 million members, half the labour force of 23 million being members. Their aims include:

(*a*) the review of wages paid, hours of work, conditions of work;
(*b*) the provision of educational facilities for members;
(*c*) establishment and control of welfare funds for members in need through sickness, etc;
(*d*) the need for full employment.

There are four types of trade union:

Craft Union which relates to members of a specific craft but also includes many of the unskilled workers.

Industrial Union which includes members in most of the present day industries such as steel, railways, electricity, etc.

General Union is as the name implies non-specific and relates to most factory workers, dockers, clerks, etc.

Technical Unions representing more of the 'white collar' employees, often relating to the newer industries such as scientific staff, computer operators, etc.

Employer Organisations

These are institutions representing a group of employers in a particular trade or business that look after the interest of its members. Examples include the British Bankers Association, Newspaper Publishers Association, Engineering Employers' Federation, etc. Their work is both complex and varied since some are very much concerned with industrial relations in a particular trade, conditions of service, rates of pay, etc whilst others show a greater interest in acting as 'watchdog' against government interference. In all cases however specialist advice is given on legal matters and occasionally they act as arbitrators between employers and unions.

CONTRACTS OF EMPLOYMENT

Everyone in paid employment is in law legally contracted to work for that employer according to agreed terms and conditions of service. These must be provided in writing to the employee working more than sixteen hours a week within thirteen weeks of the commencement of employment and include such things as rates of pay, hours of work, holiday entitlement, length of notice, grievance procedures, etc.

The Advisory Conciliation and Arbitration Service (ACAS)

ACAS is an independent conciliatory service set up by the government to give free and impartial advice in situations of unresolved disputes between employer and employee. The parties may seek the assistance of members to help in settling the dispute or mediate on their behalf without any obligation to accept findings. Alternatively the parties to the dispute may agree to accept the decision of independent members of the service and thus settle any differences.

REDUNDANCY

This occurs when an employer is unable to sustain the present numbers of the workforce and has therefore either to close the business down completely or partially. In both cases this involves the loss of jobs through no fault of the employee. The employee has a number of rights when faced with this situation:

(*a*) A statutory payment where at least two years unbroken service has been given. The amount payable is dependent upon age of employee and length of service.

(*b*) The right to consultation by the employer.

(*c*) Time off work at the employer's expense to seek alternative employment.

CASE STUDY

Kayvee plc is a manufacturing company with a workforce of 250 and having **national and international interests** in drilling equipment. In order to extend and develop potential markets the company will require **additional finance** of about £1 million. **Government assistance** is being sought with a view to the export potential and discussions are taking place at board level with **the Unions** regarding additional staff and **conditions of employment.**

(*a*) Explain the meaning attached to 'national and international interests'.
(*b*) How can the additional finance be acquired?
(*c*) In what way could the government assist with these proposals?
(*d*) Why should the unions be concerned with this project?
(*e*) What is meant by 'conditions of employment'?

EXAMINATION TECHNIQUE

CONTENTS

REVISION

Good revision ensures a good examination result – make sure that your revision covers the whole syllabus. This is necessary because the multiple choice questions may be set on all aspects of the syllabus and essays will cover a wide variety of topics.

You should, if possible, make a thorough study of previous examination papers to make sure that you can answer past questions. In your revision work practise answering questions and noting down important points, setting yourself a target in a given number of minutes.

Short answer questions

These may be the multiple choice type of question or the open response short answer question perhaps requiring one or two sentences (or even words) in response to the question. Examples of the open response short answer question:

1 Name two internal economies of scale.
2 What is franchising?
3 (i) Define a public corporation.
(ii) Give two examples of public corporations.

Examiners should have indicated the number of marks being allocated to each question. You will normally be required to answer *all* questions so don't miss any out. These questions test your recall and knowledge. Read the question carefully and give a relevant and clear answer in response.

Multiple choice questions

1 Read the instructions closely. If you are required to answer all the questions then it is important that this is done. Make sure that you fill in details of your name, candidate number and centre number correctly. You will not usually lose marks if you get the answer wrong but you must ensure that you answer in the correct way. For instance, you may be required to draw a pencil mark vertically or horizontally through the correct alternative letter. Make sure you know what is required.

2 Read the question thoroughly and closely There is normally quite a lot of information to consider in any one question and mistakes can easily be made. For instance the word *not* in any question can dramatically change your response.

3 When approaching an individual question and after reading the information thoroughly, it is normally best to identify the responses it *could not* possibly be. This will leave you with the possible correct answers and you obviously have to make a choice of what you consider to be correct.

4 If you have no real idea of what the correct answer is, it is advisable at least to make an attempt.

5 Be careful not to spend too much time on certain questions. If you are having problems with a question leave it and return to it later. Bear in mind that you have a definite time limit which is strictly adhered to by the invigilator.

6 It is important to check over your answers making sure you have answered every question.
Above all *read* the questions properly and follow the answering instructions.

ESSAY QUESTIONS OR EXTENDED WRITING QUESTIONS

1 Read the question paper thoroughly (including the rubric) and decide what questions, and in which order, you are going to answer.

2 Follow the instructions carefully Make sure you answer the correct number of questions. On no account should you answer more or less than the required number of questions. Examiners will ignore any questions above the required number. If you do not answer enough questions you will obviously limit the marks it is possible for you to obtain. Make sure you know which questions are compulsory and which questions involve an element of choice.

3 You must be careful not to spend too much time on any particular question even if you feel that you could spend more. If you do, it means you have less time to spend on the others and you are likely to lose marks by not explaining the details adequately.

4 Always plan your response briefly for a minute or so before answering. This will give your answers an organisation and structure and will ensure you do not forget to include some points.

5 Attempt those questions you know best at the outset whilst you are fresh. Again remember not to spend too much time on the questions you know best.

6 Make sure you answer the question set. The information in the essay must be relevant to the particular question. You will not get any marks for information which is not relevant, no matter how correct or well-written the information is. Avoid all irrelevant detail. It is sometimes a good idea to include a sketch or drawing within the framework of your answer to emphasise a particular point.

7 Where you have to make calculations always show the working and detail. Thus you will receive some marks even if you get the final answer wrong.

8 Always read over what you have written. Make any necessary corrections and omit anything which does not make sense.

9 Pay attention to details of style of English. It is important that your essay is well organised with paragraphs. Spelling and punctuation should be of a good standard. Above all, make sure you answer the correct number of questions and answer the question which is set.

10 Extended writing questions will be structured and some are data based. By 'structured' is meant that there are many parts to the questions (a, b, c, d) possibly increasing in level of difficulty. Each part should have allocated to it a number of marks. You must take these marks into account when answering the question – you will need to write in more detail for a part which gives more marks. For instance if part (a) gives 2 marks and part (d) 10 marks you will need to include more detail in response to part (d).

By 'data based' is meant that the extended writing question is perhaps based on statistics or a prose passage. These are very similar to data response questions.

11 Once you have decided what information is relevant to the question, you need to decide how the examiner wishes you to deal with it (i.e. in great detail or perhaps just one or two lines of definition). Here are some words often used in questions by examiners with a brief indication on how you should approach such questions.

Outline – this implies brevity and you should just give the important details.

Describe – just a straightforward account or description is needed.

Define – state exactly the meaning of a word, phrase or concept.

Explain or account for – detailed and coherent coverage giving reasons to explain your response.

Analyse – again implies a detailed response and explanation of relationships between variables.

Assess – you need to evaluate the value of a statement or other variable. This may involve arguments for and against.

Discuss or examine – detailed investigation needed with arguments for and against.

Illustrate – here you need to explain something with the use of examples.

Compare or distinguish – an instruction to show the similarities and differences between variables.

State or list – a command to do something which will be self-explanatory from the question.

12 Within the structured extended writing questions there will be a relationship between those structured parts of the question: giving more marks with possibly words such as 'explain', 'account for', 'analyse', 'assess', 'discuss' or 'examine', somewhere in the question.

Also those structured parts of the questions giving relatively few marks may have words such as 'define', 'outline' somewhere in the question.

DATA RESPONSE QUESTIONS

1 In this type of question you will be presented with data in some form and you will be asked to interpret it and use it as a basis for analysis.

2 The aim of data response questions is to test your understanding of principles and theory and your ability to apply this to specific questions. The objective is to make relevant your study of commerce to the real world with relevant questions.

3 A data response question may be presented in one of five main forms.

A statistical tables
B graphs
C pie charts
D photographs
E prose passage – from a book or newspaper

4 Read the data carefully several times. Make a list of relevant points. When presented with a statistical table or graph, always look for patterns in the date.

5 As far as possible do not describe when you should analyse the data (refer back to the meanings of these terms).

6 Much of the advice on how to answer extended writing questions applies here. To repeat the advice – be relevant at all times and do not include detail which is not required. Also allocate your time sensibly not only between questions (i.e. do not spend too much time on one question) but also within questions. By this is meant that many of the data response questions are structured, and the techniques discussed in point **10** on extended writing questions need to be read again.

Preparing for the examination

It has already been mentioned that revision is vital to ensure a good examination result. Some weeks before the examination you should plan a revision timetable to make sure that you have enough time to revise all the required topics. Your notes should be of good quality which will be of great help when revising. Read through these slowly and thoroughly and understand the important ideas. You should have copies of past papers to help you in revision. Practise doing the different types of question.

Remember that a good result does not depend on luck, it depends on hard work and good planning.

INDEX